Also by CommerceNet Press

Opening Digital Markets: Battle Plans and Business Strategies for Internet Commerce by Walid Mougayar

Understanding Digital Signatures: Establishing Trust Over the Internet and Other Networks by Gail Grant

Building Database-Driven Web Catalogs by Sherif Danis and Patrick Gannon

The Search for Digital Excellence by James P. Ware et al.

The CommerceNet Guide to IMarket by Arthur D. Little

Understanding SET: Visa International's Official Guide to Secure Electronic Transactions by Gail Grant

How to Invest in E-Commerce Stocks by Bill Burnham and Piper Jaffray

Make Your Website Work for You by Jeff Cannon

The Future of Work by Charles Grantham

Buying a Home on the Internet by Robert Irwin

Buying a Car on the Internet by Jeremy Lieb

Buying Travel Services on the Internet by Durant Imboden

Online Auctions by Luanne O'Loughlin and Mary Millhollon, edited by Jaclyn Easton

CommerceNet is a nonprofit industry consortium for companies promoting and building electronic commerce solutions on the Internet. Launched in April 1994 in Silicon Valley, CA, its membership has grown to more than 500 companies and organizations worldwide. They include the leading banks, telecommunications companies, VANs, ISPs, online services, software and service companies, as well as end-users, who together are transforming the Internet into a global electronic marketplace. For membership information, please contact CommerceNet at Tel: 408-446-1260; Fax: 408-446-1268; URL: http://www.commerce.net. For information regarding CommerceNet Press, contact Loël McPhee at loel@commerce.net.

StrikingItRich.com

Profiles of 23 Incredibly Successful Websites
You've Probably Never Heard Of

Jaclyn Easton

CommerceNet Press

McGraw-Hill

New York   San Francisco   Washington, D.C.   Auckland   Bogotá
Caracas   Lisbon   London   Madrid   Mexico City   Milan
Montreal   New Delhi   San Juan   Singapore
Sydney   Tokyo   Toronto

McGraw-Hill

A Division of The **McGraw·Hill** Companies

First McGraw-Hill paperback edition, 2000

1   2   3   4   5   6   7   8   9   0   AGM/AGM   0   9   8   7   6   5   4   3   2   1   0

ISBN 0-07-135579-0

The sponsoring editors for this book were Susan Barry and Kurt Nelson, the editing supervisor was Fred Dahl, and the production supervisor was Elizabeth J. Strange. It was set in Fairfield by Inkwell Publishing Services.

Printed and bound by Quebecor/Martinsburg.

McGraw-Hill books are available at special quantity discounts to use as premiums and sales promotions, or for use in corporate training programs. For more information, please write to the Director of Special Sales, Professional Publishing, McGraw-Hill, Two Penn Plaza, New York, NY 10121-2298. Or contact your local bookstore.

 This book is printed on recycled, acid-free paper containing a minimum of 50% recycled, de-inked fiber.

This book is dedicated to my father,

Jac Holzman

for teaching me about

striking it rich

in business...and in life

CONTENTS

Foreword   *ix*

Acknowledgments   *xi*

Introduction   *xiii*

Sites by Category   *xxi*

Common Internet Terms   *xxv*

Profile 1: Ask The Builder   *1*

Profile 2: Cassette House   *13*

Profile 3: Coastal Tool and Supply   *23*

Profile 4: Discount Games   *35*

Profile 5: The Expert Marketplace   *45*

Profile 6: FragranceNet   *55*

Profile 7: Gamesville™   *65*

Profile 8: HorseNet   *77*

Profile 9: International Golf Outlet   *89*

Profile 10: iPrint   *103*

Profile 11: Ken Crane's Laserdiscs   *111*

Profile 12: The Knot   *121*

Profile 13: KoreaLink   *133*

Profile 14: Long Island Hot Tubs   *143*

Profile 15: Motorcycle Online   *153*

Profile 16: The Mountain Zone   *165*

Profile 17: Practical Online Weightloss Clinic   *177*

Profile 18: DogToys.com   *187*

Profile 19: Reel.com   *197*

Profile 20: Ridout Plastics   *207*

Profile 21: Tradeshop   *215*

Profile 22: U.S. Wings   *225*

Profile 23: Weirton Steel   *235*

Index   *243*

FOREWORD

These stories of 23 successful Websites introduce many of the success secrets of e-commerce pioneers. Each, in his own way, validating the Internet's unlimited and unique potential.

While I know of no single formula to guarantee prosperity in Internet retailing, I can share with you the rules we've applied at Amazon.com that have contributed enormously to our efforts.

- Obsess over your customers.
- Remember that the Web is an infant.
- If you make one customer unhappy, he won't tell five friends— he'll tell 5,000 on newsgroups, listservs, and so on.

At Amazon.com we work hard to keep these principles in mind. At their heart is a single question that can help you predict the success of any Net-based enterprise: Does the Website harness the unique characteristics of the Internet to create a strong value proposition for customers, one that could not be easily duplicated in the physical world? If the answer is "yes," the Website may do well. If not, it will almost certainly turn out to be a hobby.

We try to answer "yes" by assembling a package of three things, none of which would be practical offline, and all of which provide genuine value to customers: (1) vast selection, (2) extreme convenience, and (3) low prices. Here's how we apply this value proposition.

Starting with number one, vast selection, we offer more than 2.5 million book titles. There are more than three million books in print at any time worldwide, but the largest physical book superstores can only carry about 175,000 of them. Keep in mind that these are huge stores, often converted from movie theaters and bowling alleys. Even in the largest metropolitan areas, it's just not economically practical to build larger bookstores. Likewise, selling via a traditional paper catalog could never work for us. If we were to print the Amazon.com catalog, it would be the size of more than 40 New York City phone books—not something we'd want to mail out several times a year!

Because we exist exclusively in cyberspace, we offer a convenience factor that physical stores and catalogs cannot. Amazon.com doesn't require you to get in a car, find parking, or search in multiple stores.

This inherent convenience of the Web also means Amazon.com isn't encumbered by expenses compulsory to maintaining a physical presence, like rent, construction costs, and building maintenance. This is why we can offer such extreme discounts. We can give money back to our customers, which we do by offering savings up to 40%.

Assembling a strong customer value proposition is important in any business, but it's especially important online. Since the Web is an infant technology, there are many innate inconveniences associated with it. Modem lines disconnect; call waiting interferes; browsers crash. This means you must create overwhelming value in order to compensate for the inconveniences your visitors will suffer at the hands of this wonderful but immature technology.

Perhaps the most important reason to build an unusually strong value proposition is the wondrous "word of mouth" factor that is amplified on the Net. Every customer can be his or her own ombudsman. Disappoint customers and any one of them can tell thousands of people. This shifts the balance of power away from the business and toward the customer. In my opinion, that's a great thing for both the customer and the merchant. But only if the merchant recognizes it. If you create real value for customers, they will become evangelists, using the Internet as their megaphone.

If you've found something you believe people really want and the Web can deliver this product or service better than any other medium, then you probably have a winner. And with that I wish for you profound success.

JEFF BEZOS
Founder and CEO, Amazon.com., Inc.
Seattle, Washington

ACKNOWLEDGMENTS

Dad: See dedication at the front of this book.

Robert Casady: Since there isn't one word that begins to capture your wonderfulness I'll settle on these for now: With all my heart I thank you for your patience, support, attentiveness and relentless devotion. You are a prince.

To my team at the William Morris Agency: My brilliant, lead agent John Mass. (John, you are not only one of the most honorable agents I know, but also one of the kindest. Thank you for always treating me like one of your most important clients); attorney extraordinaire Eric Zohn for his pursuit of the perfect contract; Marcy Posner for lending her "big potato status" to what started as a boutique project; Larry Kramer for his boundless enthusiasm and attention to my television career (I am so lucky to get to work with you!); and Tracy Fisher for her panache handling of foreign matters.

My McGraw-Hill editors: Scott Grillo for his golden ".com" title concept; and Michelle Reed for the "rescue."

Jeff Bezos: I clearly remember after our first phone conversation the week you opened Amazon.com and thinking you were a genius. My opinion stands. Thank you for lending your name to a book for the first time. I am honored.

LATimes.com executives Leah Gentry and Carol Perruso. You are complete joys to work with. Thank you for being so supportive of all of my initiatives. Additional thanks to Elaine Zinngrabe and Patricia Marroquin.

All the folks at CBS News, Los Angeles, especially my producers, floor director Tony Henkins and especially anchors Paul Dandridge and Tritia Toyota for being so receptive to my Internet segments.

I remain forever indebted to the restorative powers of Patrick Butcher, Feline G. Butcher, Kate O'Sullivan, Vique Mora, and Amrit Nam Curtis.

Extra special thanks to Maria T. Abreu, M.D., Philip Hassard, M.D., and Kostas Papadakis, M.D., for your attention and extraordinary expertise.

Rob Frankel (www.robfrankel.com) who is the best branding expert on the planet. Thank you for titling this book and for being an incredible friend.

Jeannine Parker—whom I refer to as "The Lifeguard of Silicon Beach." JP, your unique perspectives have taught me to challenge every assumption. You are not only one of the warmest humans I know, but also one of the smartest and most creative.

Roger Reitzel: Without you Log On USA would never be the success it is. I remain forever indebted.

My two oldest friends Carrie Carlisi and Jack Chipman, I adore you both and don't know what I'd do without you.

My brothers Marin Sander-Holzman, Adam Holzman, sister-in-law Jane Getter and nephew Russell Getter Holzman.

My stepfather, Kirk Lamb. I cherish everything about you.

Fredric Lehrman for teaching what success really is and providing a context to make it mine.

Extra special thanks to the following friends and business associates for their constant support: Jeff Cannon, Tony Cook, Ellen Cooper, Kay Dangaard, Renee Edelman, Adora English, Ramey Warren Black, David Avalos, Susan Goldberg, Bob Levitan, Steve Marmel, Glenn Meehan, Bobbie Rose, Marc Schiller, Mike Switzer, and Joseph Vaughn-Perling and Bill Van Vliet.

David Bohnett, Alan M. Webber, Angela Kapp, Rick Boyce, Eric Pulier, Scott Kurnit, and Vic Sussman. Thank you for your supportive statements and for setting such exemplary examples for the business community.

A deep bow to CommerceNet Press/CommerceNet Consortium: Loël McPhee for her care and creative feeding and Stacey Bressler for her bull's-eye marketing perspectives. Additional thanks to Randy Whiting.

... and finally to the 23 groups of people behind these "incredibly successful Websites" for trusting me to tell their stories.

INTRODUCTION

I wrote this book for two reasons: First, to assure business people that there is indeed wealth in the Web. Despite statistics, plenty of modest-sized online retailers and information providers are profiting from the online world. Some, but not all, are millionaires, and many of those who aren't are living extremely well—doing exactly what they love. Isn't this the American dream?

Second, I wanted to teach by example. I have been on the e-commerce beat since 1994, when there were so few Website launches you only had to check the NCSA listings of new sites *once a week* to completely catch up. I know exactly what works and what doesn't. But I am not a Web retailer. I am not an information provider. I felt it was imperative that someone give a voice to those who could speak not from theory, but from experience.

HOW THIS BOOK CAME TO BE

In 1995 I was frustrated. Every article I read said that no one was making money on the Internet. Pundits were even calling the Web a fad. I knew differently.

I just finished writing my first book, *Shopping on the Internet and Beyond*—the first ever written on the topic and published long before its time. In fact it was released in the summer of 1995, as Amazon.com was just launching.

To give added depth to some of the shopping site reviews, I conducted phone interviews with many of the store owners. Off the record, I always asked about sales volume. Most weren't seeing six-digit profits yet, but they were making money. "This really is going to change the face of commerce," I thought. "Those who are in it now are going to make millions."

Cut to 1997, two years later. Derogatory comments describing the Web as "an e-commerce wasteland" continue, but these out-of-synch analysts were willing to acknowledge a few notable successes, mostly computer-related entities, like Dell and Cisco. At least the fad issue was fading.

At this point I had begun clipping articles about every successful site I read about. I knew that my hunch was correct. With the exception of search engines and the "brand name" Websites such as Disney's Daily Blast and CNN, small businesses were doing as well as the big guys, both as retailers (referred to as *transaction sites*) and as information providers (called *content sites*). The big difference is that they were doing it with fewer resources. As you will read, often the creativity required to compensate for a lack of money borders on genius.

It took months of intense research to find just the right mix of sites. (See the Site Breakdown List on page xxi.) But, for me to profile a site it had to be doing more than well. It had to be doing better than anyone else, and it had to have faced greater challenges. This is one of the primary reasons I did not profile sites that sell computer hardware or software or that offer computer-related information. This is a prequalified crowd, making their launches much too easy. Selling $150 hard drives on the Net is a snap compared to a $975 panel saw (see Coastal Tool and Supply, Profile 3).

The same applies to adult content. The unspoken truth about Internet commerce is that the true trailblazers are the sex site proprietors. Anyone doing business on the Net owes a lot to them. They were the first to offer real-time credit card approvals, use streaming video and audio on demand, find foolproof subscription systems, and eliminate credit card fraud for the proprietor. Despite their value to us as business people, they don't qualify for profiling. Their subject matter has been in demand since the world began, making their product an easy sell in any environment and hence not applicable to mainstream business.

What is the reason for 23 sites? CommerceNet Press, my editors at McGraw-Hill, and I felt this was the greatest number of profiles we could feature in detail without overloading you with too much information.

DEFINING "INCREDIBLY SUCCESSFUL"

To qualify for profiling, a site had to be "incredibly successful." Such success is usually defined monetarily and profit was certainly my first qualifier. Sites had to be showing significant revenues or profits to even be considered. But "significant" varies from site to site. For example, Ask The Builder is a single-person content site with minimal expenses. Obviously his six-figure revenues have far more meaning than a ten-person enterprise earning the same money. Although his revenues may be lower, the return on his investment of time and money is remarkable.

Other distinguishing success characteristics included growth rates, estimates of future earnings, and the degree to which they "own their category."

Owning a category is extremely important. For long-term profits, mind share is crucial. Ask skiers for their favorite Web destination and they will probably answer The Mountain Zone. Being thought of as the leader goes far beyond branding. These Websites are so far ahead of their competition that it will take years or extraordinary sums of money for their competition to catch up. Given how young the Web is, I consider this "category owning" criterion the most important, because it's indicative not only of their success today, but of their future success as well.

THE PROFILE PROCESS

I can only describe the profiling process from the selected site's perspective as a digital bootcamp. After a prequalifying voice interview, the site owner(s) had to complete a 121-item questionnaire. The questions were not multiple choice, but detailed queries about everything from a budget breakdown of their launch costs to a specific listing of all their advertising buys, including their return on each one. This took most of them about a month to complete. Though completing the questionnaire was arduous, most of my profiles admitted that they had a much clearer vision of their businesses. The process forced them to think about aspects of their business that they otherwise had not considered.

After I reviewed their responses, they were e-mailed a set of follow-up questions, usually about 30. After reconciling these answers with the original responses, we moved to the telephone, where I conducted a two-hour voice interview. Transcribed, these inquisitions ran about 20 pages long.

Swimming in data, I distilled the most important points to about 3,000 words, which is about two to three times the length of the average magazine article. Then there was another follow-up interview for clarification. Finally sites were e-mailed their profiles to approve for accuracy.

People ask me how I knew that my profiles were telling me the truth. Since I did not require audited financial statements, an element of trust was definitely in play. On the other hand, I have a technique that I feel does not make them necessary.

In the prequalifying voice interview, long before they even received the questionnaire, I asked a series of rapid-fire questions about their numbers and Website statistics. Since this was my first interaction with them, they had no way of knowing what questions I was going to ask. And since I asked the questions so quickly, they could not instantly calculate a "right" answer unless they were mathematical geniuses. Admittedly, a few sites were not invited to join this project because their numbers did not reconcile.

Naturally this leads to the question, "Why would site owners divulge this data?" The reasons vary. The most common response related to their success. They don't mind revealing their numbers because they are doing so well so fast. The numbers have no meaning to them. They are only benchmarks of their success at a certain point in time. Sharing them does not give any of their competitors much of an advantage. (Be sure to visit this book's Website for updates at http://www.StrikingItRich.com.)

A QUANTITATIVE LOOK AT THE PROFILES

Guess what? Not everyone making money online is under 30. While my hand-picked selections are far from scientific, I think it's interesting to note that the ages of the site owners range from 25 (Jason Apfel, FragranceNet) to 63 (David Humble, Practical Online Weightloss Clinic). More than 43% of the profiles are over 40. The average age is also 40.

Thirteen states are represented, with California as the leader with six (26%).

The oldest Website profiled is Motorcycle Online, which launched in August 1994, followed by Long Island Hot Tub and Pool Supply in November 1994. Nine of the profiled sites started in 1995, with ten in 1996 and two in 1997.

What is the best fact of all? Every one of these Web entities is consistently showing triple-digit annual growth.

HOW TO READ THIS BOOK

You can read the profiles in any order. They are organized alphabetically, not by type (transaction, content, subscription) because I found that each genuinely relayed useful information applicable to everyone. For example, HorseNet, a content site dedicated to equestrian themes, relays search engine tips that are helpful to any type of Web enterprise.

However, I also realize the benefits of a breakdown by category. So we have included a diagram on page xxi.

Second, don't be put off by the nature of the business. Sites in businesses that were of no interest to me yielded as much fantastic information as those whose focus I inherently found appealing. Motorcycles (Motorcycle Online) and steel (Weirton Steel) held little appeal for me, but I soon realized that the product or service is a minor point. It's how the business is run—as well as its strategies and history—that is so engaging. I am certain you will have the same experience.

THE IMPORTANCE OF AMERICA ONLINE

You will notice that most of the profiles include detailed references to America Online (AOL), from the number of visitors they shuttle to the site to the percentage of customers who are members. The reason is simple. America Online is not only a propriety online service, it is also the world's largest Internet service provider. When AOL is having problems it can dramatically affect the revenues of retail sites, the amount of visitor traffic to content sites, and even the relationships between site and visitor. As you will read in the iPrint profile, when AOL was having intermittent technical issues, some of iPrint's customers actually blamed iPrint.

Personally I curse AOL because I feel it gives people a lousy perception of the Internet. Its original browser—which a large percentage of their members continue to use—does not support basic Web functionality including some order forms, vital to a retail site.

AOL service can be incredibly slow, with page load times in the minutes rather than seconds during peak periods. And in an effort to try to speed up their service, they sometimes cache pages on their systems. When a member types in the Web address of a popular destination, instead of fetching the latest pages from the requested site, AOL serves up an earlier copy. Often the latest version and the stored copies are different.

Despite my animosity, I am thankful to AOL for getting people online. It may constantly rank at the bottom in surveys of technical performance, but it was the first to create a truly easy online experience. Devout Internet/online users know that they can hand their grandmother an AOL disk (of which they have boxfuls) and never need to answer a support question. For that I am grateful.

America Online is also responsible for up to 50% of the traffic on some of these profiles, and I know that without the service some of them would not have achieved their success so quickly.

WHAT'S COMMON AMONG THESE SUCCESS STORIES?

One quality these Webpreneurs share is that they trusted their instincts. This is true for both types of Website owners I profile: (1) Those who combined the Net with an existing interest or entity and, almost like a by-product, started making a lot of money. (2) Folks who saw the Web as a new channel and, applying their business savvy, scouted opportunities and selected the one they thought had the best fit.

Both adventures depended on intuition. Some voices were soft and subtle, others so loud the site owners didn't sleep for weeks as their brain perpetually processed the possibilities.

Whether they began as accidents or considered business decisions, today all these site owners adore what they do. As you will read, many have been offered millions of dollars to sell their enterprises. All but one have, and the one who did took over a Web venture similar to the one sold.

You will also note that most of these profiles took advantage of the Web without getting caught up in the novelty. These sites rarely if ever use Java, Shockwave, frames—anything that clutters the interface or requires extra speed.

Furthermore another commonality shatters a long-held belief: Success on the Internet does *not* depend on interactivity. These stories prove 23 times over that moving information or selling goods on the Web is about one thing: relationships. When you think about it, this makes sense. As my friend Kit Galloway points out, interactivity is overhyped, "even vending machines are interactive."

CONCLUSION

I encourage you to visit the StrikingItRich.com Website, which not surprisingly, you can find at **www.StrikingItRich.com.** This is your source for updates on all the profiles as well as additional success tips.

Please feel free to contact me directly, especially if you are an "incredibly successful Website" that you think I should know about. I can be reached at **easton@easton.com.**

Finally, keep one important point in mind. While the Internet is growing at an astronomical rate and it seems as though everyone is already online, there are plenty of opportunities. Despite the world's awareness of the Web, this is still a communications mechanism in its infancy.

To that end, let this book demonstrate to you that no matter what your goals are in the webbed world, you *can* be one of the ones striking it rich.

JACLYN EASTON

SITES BY CATEGORY

MOST SITES ARE LISTED IN AT LEAST TWO CATEGORIES.

CONTENT SITES

Ask The Builder
Gamesville
HorseNet
KoreaLink
Motorcycle Online
Mountain Zone
The Knot

Advertising as Prime Revenue Source

Ask The Builder
Gamesville
KoreaLink
Motorcycle Online

Advertising and Transaction

HorseNet
Mountain Zone
The Knot

PAID SUBSCRIPTION SITES

Expert Marketplace
KoreaLink
Practical Online Weightloss Clinic

TRANSACTION SITES

Cassette House
Coastal Tool and Supply
Discount Games
DogToys.com
Expert Marketplace
FragranceNet
International Golf Outlet
iPrint
Ken Crane's Laserdiscs
Long Island Hot Tubs
Practical Online Weightloss Clinic
Reel.com
Ridout Plastics
Tradeshop
U.S. Wings
Weirton Steel

Business-to-Business Sales

iPrint
Ridout Plastics
Weirton Steel

Consumer Retail

Cassette House
Coastal Tool and Supply
Discount Games
DogToys.com
FragranceNet
International Golf Outlet
iPrint
Ken Crane's Laserdiscs
Long Island Hot Tubs
Practical Online Weightloss Clinic
Reel.com
Tradeshop
U.S. Wings

International Clientele

Cassette House
Coastal Tool and Supply
Discount Games
DogToys.com
FragranceNet
International Golf Outlet
iPrint
KoreaLink
Long Island Hot Tubs
Tradeshop
U.S. Wings

Web-Only Presence

FragranceNet
iPrint
Practical Online Weightloss Clinic
Tradeshop
U.S. Wings

With Offline Catalog

Coastal Tool and Supply
International Golf Outlet
Long Island Hot Tubs

With Offline Store

Coastal Tool and Supply
Discount Games
Ken Crane's Laserdiscs
Long Island Hot Tubs
Reel.com

COMMON INTERNET TERMS

Animated banner: Banner ads that have movement, often like a cartoon or a movie, complete with several frames.

Auditing: Verifying the number of visitors to a Website or Webpage through a third-party auditor such as ABC Interactive or BPA.

Autoresponder: Automatically sends out an e-mail response when e-mail comes in. Used to instantly send out information without human intervention. Excellent for acknowledging receipt of a message.

Bandwidth: The speed at which data is transfered; how much information can be moved efficiently. Low bandwidth is a 28.8/33.6K modem. High bandwidth is a T1 or T3 line.

Banner ad (or ad banner, online ad): A graphic image that is hot-linked to an advertiser's Website. The industry has agreed on nine standard sizes, the most common being 468 pixels wide by 60 pixels tall. A pixel is one screen dot.

Banner ad exchange programs: Trading/barter of banner ads among smaller sites. The Link Exchange Network is the most famous.

Cache: In the context of the online world, the space on your hard disk that stores Web-related page information. Effectively shortens the load time of frequently visited sites because the browser retrieves the desired page from your hard drive cache first, before seeking to retrieve it across the Internet.

This glossary was written by Jaclyn Easton and Rick Boyce. Rick Boyce is a Board Member of the Internet Advertising Bureau, SVP of Advertising and Commerce at Wired Digital and the inventor of the banner ad.

CASIE (Coalition for Advertising Supported Information and Entertainment): An industry organization founded by advertisers and advertising agencies that promotes awareness of, and solutions for, advertiser issues surrounding the Internet (http://www.casie.com).

Click rate (or ad click rate or click-through rate): The percentage of times an ad is clicked divided by the number of times it's served. If an ad is served 200 times and 10 visitors actually click on the ad, the banner has a click rate of 5% (10 divided by 200).

Click-throughs (or ad clicks or transfers): Occurs when a visitor actually clicks on an ad banner and is transported to the site of the banner's advertiser.

Content: Information on a site. Some consider it as everything but the ads and the navigation bars. Includes text, audio, video, and any functionality like a database.

CPM: Cost per thousand, the "M" referring to the Roman numeral for 1,000. Literally translated, the cost of 1,000 ad impressions. Average CPMs on the Web vary greatly depending on the overall quality of the publisher and demand for available ad inventory. Generally, the more targeted a site's content, the higher its CPM. Run-of-site inventory on a general interest Website ranges from $5 to $35. Banners on an upscale niched interest, such as a financial services site, can go as high as $70–100 or more.

Directory: A technique, made popular by Yahoo, for organizing Websites by topic from general to specific for ease of navigation.

Frames: Division of your browser window into several parts so that only part of a page needs to be loaded when a link is clicked. A way to conserve load times and to aid navigation. A typical frames-based page maintains persistent navigation on a narrow left-hand frame while the content fills the frame on the right. Can often be distracting and pointless if not designed well.

Hits: *See* "Hits Are Not People" (page xxx).

HTML: Hypertext mark-up language (a geeky term you don't need to know). The base language that Webpages are written in.

HTML e-mail: E-mail read through a sophisticated e-mail program like Eudora or with a browser. Looks like a Webpage, right down to clickable links.

Hyperlink: Synonym for link.

Impression (or adviews or exposures): Occurs when an ad banner is served to a visitor. If one page has three ads, that counts as three impressions.

Internet Advertising Bureau (IAB): An industry organization founded by Web publishers that works to advocate, increase acceptance of, and standardize Internet advertising (http://www.iab.net).

Keywords: Typically used in the context of search engines, words or phrases that are input as a search request and that trigger a results page, which (hopefully) contains the information you are looking for.

Link: Any banner, button, or text that, when clicked, transports visitors somewhere else. Banner ads are by definition links.

Meta tags: Part of an HTML document that stores keywords describing the site. These keywords are determined by the designer. Some, but not all, search engines use this to categorize sites.

Page impression: A successful page request that displays the desired content in a user's browser.

Page request: Data submitted to a server asking for specific content when a user clicks a link. Not all page requests are page impressions due to Internet latency or users activating the stop button, which could prevent a page impression from being generated.

Pageviews (or page impression or impression): When a Webpage is presented to a Website visitor. Homepages generally get many more pageviews than subpages.

Pay-per-click (or cost-per-click): A performance-based pricing model where the advertiser pays the publisher for actual click-throughs and not for impressions served. While less common than CPM pricing, this method is preferred by performance-driven direct marketers.

Pay-per-lead (or cost-per-lead): Another performance-based pricing model but, unlike cost-per-click, a Web publisher is paid only when someone clicks on a banner ad and becomes a qualified lead by completing an order or request form.

Reciprocal links: When two sites exchange hyperlinked "mentions" on each other's site. Standard practice on the Web, especially among noncommercial sites, like hobby and fan pages.

Rich media banners: Banner ads that make use of a programming language like Java or HTML or a plug-in like Shockwave or Real Audio to increase ad impact and heighten users' experience and ability to interact with the banner.

Run-of-site (ROS): A general Web banner buy in which an advertiser's banners are scheduled to appear randomly across a site rather than being focused within specific content areas. Derives its name from newspapers where the practice was invented. Typically, ROS buys offer broad reach at relatively low CPMs because specific content has not been requested.

Search engines: Websites whose purpose is to get you to what you are looking for. Think of them like the index of a book. Most are automated and use "spiders" or "robots" to crawl the Web and index Websites by topic. The most popular are Alta Vista, Infoseek, Excite, Hotbot, and Lycos. *Also see* Yahoo.

Secure server: A system used for e-commerce to process credit card and other sensitive information with the least likelihood of outside penetration. On most Web browsers an icon in the lower left-hand corner (often a key or padlock) tells you when your browser is connected to a secure server, indicating that it is safe to exchange confidential information such as a credit card number.

Session: Synonym for visitor.

Spam (or junk e-mail or unsolicited commercial e-mail [UCE]): Unsolicited e-mail that tries to sell you something or get you to visit a Website.

Sticky or stickiness: A Web publisher's ability to attract visitors back to the site more frequently. Personal homepages, customizable interfaces, and Web-based e-mail services are all examples of sticky services.

Unique session: Synonym for unique visitor.

Unique visitors: The net, unduplicated reach of a Website, usually looked at over a day, week, or month. An important metric for measuring Website traffic, particularly in combination with pageviews. For example, total pageviews per month divided by unique visitors per month equals pageviews per unique visitor per month, an important indicator of site "stickiness." *See* Stickiness.

URL: Uniform Resource Locator. Think of it as a synonym for a Web address.

Visitor: The total number of people who access a Website over a day, week, or month. Unlike "unique visitors," which is a net number, "visitor" is a gross number, meaning that two "sessions" by a single user would count as two visitors.

Yahoo: Technically a directory, not a search engine. Yahoo should be thought of as a table of contents of the Web. All indexing is done by humans in a hierarchical system; hence far from all Websites are listed. Also, the most popular Website in the world.

Hits Are Not People!

Perhaps the most misunderstood concept in online computing is the phrase "hits." You hear the term in reference to Websites and the figures are trumpeted in press releases daily: "Our New Website gets over 1,000,000 hits in 1 month!" What does this mean?

The natural assumption is that a hit is a person. One million hits is really one million people, and the term "hit" functions as a sort of verb/noun. Actually, hits has nothing to do with people and in fact it's nearly impossible to make a direct correlation between the two. Let me explain.

Here's what happens after you type in a Web address. I want to go to *The Los Angeles Times* homepage. After typing in www.latimes.com in my browser, it goes out to the Web and knocks on the door of www.latimes.com and in computer language says, "Hi. Jaclyn would like to see your homepage. Please send over the files needed to do that."

Now, think of a browser as a word processor. It receives files, then brings them up in the software, and formats them to look a certain way, as determined by what the files tell it.

As I am writing this, I went to *The Los Angeles Times* homepage and found 11 graphics plus text. This means a total of 12 files are required to put this page together at my end: 11 for the graphics and one for all the text. Guess what? That is a total of 12 hits for the one page. In other words, 12 "requests," also known as hits, were made of that machine to complete the page at my end.

If a site has more graphics, it generates more hits. Some days *The Los Angeles Times* homepage may have 16 graphics and text, thus racking up 17 hits per visit to that one page alone. Some pages have one graphic and text, thus chalking up only two hits. Keep in mind too that each page you visit on a site generates more hits. If you look at five pages on *The Los Angeles Times* site, you could be accounting for 50–75 hits.

The logical question you are asking yourself, then, is why do we even bother to count "hits" if the term has nothing to do with people? In the "old days" of the Internet (a relative term meaning 1993 through 1995 or thereabout), this was (and to a degree still is) the most accurate accounting of machine usage. New technology has come into play that lets a site more accurately calculate visitors. If you go to a page that says, "You are visitor 1,388" they mean people, not hits.

The question I wish I could answer is why the press continues to use the term "hits" when it's such an inaccurate and misleading moniker. Many believe it's because they simply don't know better.

After reading this and understanding the true meaning of a "hit" you are going to cringe every time a news agency inappropriately uses the term. In fact, the misuse is so widespread and misleading you are probably going to think, "Hey, all these people can't be wrong. These are some of the most prestigious news organizations in the world. Jaclyn must be nuts."

If I am wrong, you can "hit" me!

—Jaclyn

StrikingItRich.com

ASK THE BUILDER HOMEPAGE

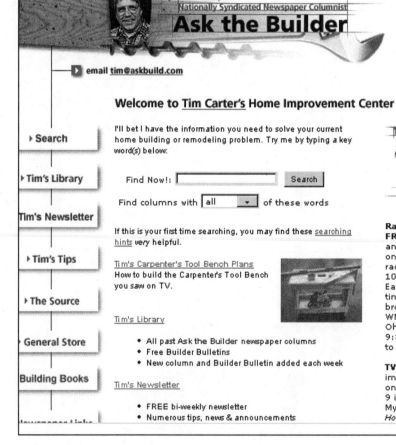

by Tim Carter
Nationally Syndicated Newspaper Columnist
Ask the Builder

Chicago Tribune
Read the Ask The Builder Column
Ask The Builder

email **tim@askbuild.com**

Welcome to Tim Carter's Home Improvement Center

I'll bet I have the information you need to solve your current home building or remodeling problem. Try me by typing a key word(s) below:

Find Now!: [   ]   [Search]

Find columns with [all ▾] of these words

If this is your first time searching, you may find these searching hints very helpful.

Tim's Carpenter's Tool Bench Plans
How to build the Carpenter's Tool Bench you saw on TV.

Tim's Library

- All past Ask the Builder newspaper columns
- Free Builder Bulletins
- New column and Builder Bulletin added each week

Tim's Newsletter

- FREE bi-weekly newsletter
- Numerous tips, news & announcements

- ▸ Search
- ▸ Tim's Library
- Tim's Newsletter
- ▸ Tim's Tips
- ▸ The Source
- ▸ General Store
- Building Books

This Week's Column

 Go

Radio & TV

Radio: Call me **TOLL FREE / 888-737-1450** any Saturday morning on my *Ask the Builder* radio show that airs 10:00 a.m. to Noon Eastern Time. At this time it is only broadcast on 1450 AM WMOH in Cincinnati, Ohio. Call between 9:30 and 10:00 a.m. to get through.

TV: I am the home improvement expert on WCPO-TV Channel 9 in Cincinnati, Ohio. My 2 minute *Around the House* segments air

TIM CARTER

ASK THE BUILDER

www.askthebuilder.com

Imagine this. You decide to launch an advertiser-supported content site. You make several cold calls to companies that manufacture products related to your enterprise with the hope that they will advertise. On the fourth call you sell a banner ad for $12,000, get paid instantly—and you haven't even launched your site. Now consider that it's December 1995, a time when the Web is being referred to as the CB radio of the 1990s—an overhyped toy, not a basis for e-commerce.

Professional builder and remodeler Tim Carter, 45, lived this fantasy, which turned out to be an auspicious beginning for Ask The Builder, a Website that is fulfilling his dreams while sparing his visitors home improvement nightmares. Simply put, Ask The Builder is an information mecca that supplies professional advice, tips, and resources related to every aspect of home improvement.

Unfortunately, Carter's smooth-as-glass beginning disintegrated in only a few short months. While his first sale was a breeze, securing a second sale was as difficult as the first one was easy.

Carter would later find out that luck played a big part in his first sale. The company was Pella, a high-end window manufacturer that already had a Website and understood the benefits of the Net long before its competitors and other home improvement companies.

Despite their Web smarts, neither Carter nor Pella had any idea of a fair price for this new form of advertising. "Neither of us knew the value of a banner ad," Carter remarks. "My original offer was $15,000 for six months. Pella countered with $12,000 paid upfront. That sounded good to both of us."

Though they didn't know it, selling for a time period instead of a predetermined number of visitors who would see the ad was not the norm, even in late 1995, during the dawn of Web advertising. Because the technology of the Web makes it ex-

1

tremely accountable, banner ads are generally sold on "views" or "impressions" rather than for a specific time period. The views accountability is regarded as the most risk-neutral deal for advertisers because they know that eventually a predetermined number of eyeballs will see their marketing missive.

Although Carter may have been inexperienced with respect to the financial terms related to Web advertising, he approached his sales scientifically. He began by sifting through three months of trade journals, taking notes on which types of companies were buying the most ads. "I noticed that window, plumbing, and roofing companies marketed the most heavily," he says. "I knew that I would not have to educate them on the value of advertising. This was very important to me."

After his first instant sale he never imagined that he would have to make 200 more calls over two months, followed by another four months of active pitching before he would sell another. "I hit a brick wall. There was a huge resistance on the price. Furthermore, everyone was asking, 'What is the Web?'"

This resistance forced Carter to reexamine his prices, ultimately reducing his banner ad rate from $30,000 per year to $12,000. This went nowhere and he slashed his prices again to $6,000 a year ($500/month, paid upfront) for his second sale to Heartland Building Products, a deal that closed about six months after his first sale to Pella. (With this deep price cut, Carter did extend Pella's run to reflect his new pricing.)

Apparently his new $6,000/year rate turned out to be the magic number for Ask The Builder and remains the banner ad rate for Carter's package deal of banner ads and category exclusivity.

What Carter learned from his foray in ad sales is that he should hire a pro to handle selling. Filling the position in 1997 put him on track to increase Ask The Builder's revenues for 1998 to a total of $400,000 (on which he pays a 15% commission). This is almost pure profit for this one-man enterprise with negligible expenses.

Of course, now that Ask The Builder is established, Carter is approached at least twice a week by companies hoping that they can advertise on the site. "I have learned that patience is everything," says Carter. "It has taken manufacturers three years to catch up to what I saw in 1995."

Despite advertising inquiries from complementary companies, the bulk of proactive sales still come from old-fashioned cold calling and gleaning names and numbers from *Remodeling* magazine's index. He follows up with a brochure he produces on his color ink jet printer.

Now that most sales are handled by a professional, Carter feels he can concentrate on his true vocation. Tim Carter is one of the country's most respected home improvement advisors. In 1993 *Remodeling* magazine named him one of the Top 50 Remodelers of the Year. Carter seized this honor and parlayed it by self-syndicating an Ask The Builder newspaper column, a move that would provide heaps of content for the site he would launch two years later.

As of April 1998, the Ask The Builder newspaper column was running in more than 50 newspapers, including the *Chicago Tribune*, the *Detroit News*, and the *Boston Herald*. Carter then parlayed the success of his newspaper columns into a weekly radio show that airs Saturday mornings on WMOH-AM in Cincinnati, Ohio. (In time, Carter plans to also broadcast his shows off his site.)

Despite his mass media accomplishments, Carter knew the Web was his destiny from the minute he saw it.

"I launched my site only a month after I saw the Web for the first time," he reminisces. "I knew exactly what it would be used for: the delivery of accurate information quickly. I had the info and I knew the newspapers that ran my column would include my URL for free." To date, these URL mentions are Ask The Builder's primary publicity, though the quality of the site now generates enough of a buzz that he estimates he gets an editorial mention somewhere about every 60 days.

What struck Carter most when he first saw the Web was that he had the critical ingredient for a successful Website: content. Even before his launch he had accumulated a two-year archive of his newspaper columns, and these, along with his Builder Bulletins (detailed follow-ups to published columns), are the basis of the Ask The Builder library. Carter considers this area the heart and soul of his site. By being able to search for documents by keyword or by topic, visitors instantly have access to hundreds of documents that relate his personal advice on every aspect of home improvement. (The content grows every seven days, as Carter uploads a new column about eight weeks after its initial print run in his syndicated newspapers.)

To put Carter's Web success in perspective, one cannot overemphasize the importance of content. But what Carter intuitively understood and exemplifies is not just content, but the *right content* in the *right context*. The winning combination is the editorial breadth of the information and how he gets people to that information. At Ask The Builder, visitors can browse by category or search by keyword, instantly moving to the information they are looking for.

Also important is that not all of his content is original. Some is just plain useful. For example, in addition to his archived columns, Ask The Builder offers a massive listing of manufacturers' 800-numbers grouped by category.

Ironically, while this listing is cherished content to his visitors, attempts at selling links to the manufacturers' Websites listed in the area have been a total flop. "For $500 a year, only $1.37 a day, I offered manufacturers a hotlink from this directory listing to their site. I sent out 1,000 mailers and have yet to sell one link."

In fact, the only nonpaid links you'll find on Ask The Builder are in the "What's New" section where appropriate sites get acknowledged for seven days. Since Ask The Builder is a business proposition, not an avocation, Carter is not big on reciprocal linking and has only requested links from 10 of the 300 sites that link to his, a percentage that is indicative of his growing legion of Web fans.

Despite Carter's weekly appearances on radio, in print, and on TV (he has a weekly five-minute segment on local Cincinnati news), Ask The Builder's traffic reports show that his biggest fans are not necessarily related to his high profile. The peak visiting times at Ask The Builder consistently occur on Mondays from 11:00 A.M. to 1:00 P.M. Eastern and Fridays from 1:00 P.M. to 4:00 P.M. Eastern, days away from his weekend print, TV, and radio profile. Furthermore, about 7% of his visitors originate from non-U.S. locales such as Australia, South Korea, and Malta.

Even though Ask The Builder gets over 12,000 visitors a month and mid-six-figure annual revenues, Carter equates his site's success to people, not numbers. "Not a day goes by that I don't receive a thank-you from a homeowner," he says. "That is my favorite measure of success."

This personalized attention is also his biggest challenge. Carter answers virtually all the site's e-mail himself—a considerable task since he gets over 50 messages a day, most of which are sent via the "mail to" option on his Website.

Although many sites have to deal with a deluge of hundreds of e-mails, 50 does not seem all that time-consuming until you consider the nature of his topic. These are not simple queries asking which brand of paint he likes best or if it's better to decorate with new brick or old brick. These are highly detailed communications that require equally detailed responses. A typical example:

> My wife and I own a duplex in Florida that was built in 1947. We are at a critical juncture because the flat roof needs replacing and we have thought of going with a pitched roof. But we have a problem. The corner of our slab is cracked and sagging about an inch and a half, like many of the houses located as close to the ocean as ours. I don't think the foundation will sink anymore, but don't know what it would take to bring it up ($$$). If we get a pitched roof, I would like to annex the second unit and bring the bedroom where the crack is located out about 6 feet. Any tips?

Generous answers are the norm for Tim Carter, whose generous response to this e-mail covered everything from selecting a residential structural engineer to the benefits of a sloped roof.

Unlike the example, one of Carter's biggest frustrations is that 35% of the questions he is e-mailed can be answered via one of his Ask The Builder columns and Builder Bulletins in the Ask The Builder library.

Since the columns and bulletins are advertiser-supported, the only intellectual property for sale on the site are Carter's 30 different Bid Sheets. These standardized forms for construction bids, written by Tim Carter, ask "a minimum of 20 detailed questions" that most people would never think to ask and serve to weed out the nonprofessionals who would be scared by such an inquisition. The bid sheets sell for between $5 and $25 depending on complexity and length.

At one point Ask The Builder sold subscriptions to an area called Tim's Tips, a collection of "1,200 unique and helpful solutions with over 50 new questions and answers added each week." For $3 a month and a six-month minimum, subscribers were given unlimited access to these voluminous archives. But with only 300 subscribers at the end of the first two years, the monthly revenues of $900 simply were not worth the effort.

Heeding the advice of an Internet marketing expert, Carter translated this content into a free, biweekly newsletter that is sponsored by Ask The Builder advertisers. What was a $900 piece of content is now repositioned to be a $60,000 annual revenue stream. But here's the best part: The basis of the newsletter consists of the responses to his daily deluge of e-mail. Essentially, he is leveraging his "customer service" into a significant source of income.

Although the newsletter's projected revenue figures are admirable, the bulk of the site's revenues continue to be generated from advertising.

Home improvement companies view Ask The Builder as an excellent source of sales and high-quality branding, without which they would have a hard time justifying the $330/CPM (cost-per-thousand viewing of an ad) they pay. Compare this to the industry average of $70/CPM for a well-niched site in a high-end category like finance.

Though Web advertising is based on CPM, Ask The Builder continues to successfully sell banners based on time instead of page views. In an average month, Ask The Builder logs indicate that each banner is served about 1,500 times. At a rate of $500 per month, this translates to a $330/CPM. As costly as the CPM rate may be, *click-throughs*—when visitors actually click on a banner ad and are whisked to the advertiser's site—are even dearer. An accepted average for click-through rates is about 2–3%. In this case, Ask The Builder is under par with a 1% click-through rate, an average of 15 clicks per month. Bottom line: Each click-through costs the advertiser about $40! Compare this to the industry average of 15–25 cents and you understand the truly flabbergasting nature of these figures.

Despite these unbelievably-higher-than-average ad rates, Ask The Builder's advertisers are kept completely in the know and happily renew their contracts. They are less concerned about page views and click-throughs than they are about in their prime ad placement and exclusivity, which bars their competition from advertising on the site.

Ask The Builder offers more than 130 categories in which advertisers get banner ads on the columns pertaining to their products. For example, Wicander sponsors all of Carter's columns about cork flooring. Type in the keywords "cork flooring" and the articles displayed will carry Wicander's banner. Furthermore, no other cork flooring manufacturer can advertise anywhere else on the site. Needless to say, these advertisers are heeding the real estate maxim of location, location, location.

Despite being seven times more expensive than most other ad vehicles, Carter is quick to point out that this opportunity is about value, not eyeballs. "This isn't much money for most of these companies. Compare this to a one-time ad for $10,000 in *Remodeling* magazine with a controlled circulation of 100,000. And print doesn't offer a click-through option or exclusivity."

Carter can afford to be confident of his rates. He's got the successes to support them.

The Saver Systems Synthetic Wood Sealant company owns the exterior wood sealant and the exterior masonry categories for which they paid $12,000 for one year. In the first six months they attributed $80,000 worth of sales to their Ask The Builder advertising.

Although Carter would love to assign all their success completely to the quality of his visitors, he is quick to point out that Saver Systems takes the best advantage of the medium by including their 800-number in their banner ads. "My visitors print out my columns for reference," he explains. "By including their 800-number in their banners my advertisers are providing a way for people to easily get in touch with them."

In addition to the banners served in their category, manufacturers also get views in general areas of sites where the ad inventory is equitably rotated.

Interestingly, Carter will not put a banner ad on his most trafficked area, his welcome screen. "I think it's tacky to put advertising on a home page," he says. "Think about it. You never see advertising on the front page of a newspaper."

Other sources of site income include two products for sale in Tim's General Store: Stain Solver, a multipurpose cleaner, and Gutter Guards, which function as the name implies. But these product sales are barely a blip on his money monitor, accounting for only 1.5% of his total revenue. Even though these are superlow revenue generators, he hardly considers the sales a failure.

Looking at the big picture, Carter maintains that his biggest risk to date was launching his site in the first place. It cost him $5,000. "I'm proud to say that my site cost just a little more money than what I spent on my first brand new pickup truck in 1974." But he borrowed this $5,000 from a line of credit he established on his house. Money was "very, very tight at the time," Carter remembers. "It would have really hurt my family if Ask The Builder failed."

To keep expenses down, Carter applied his do-it-yourself disposition to his Website, essentially cobuilding it with two other professionals with the goal of maintaining the basics himself, something he continues to do to this day. "I load the columns, update the sections and add all the ad banners. I do all the HTML tagging and frames, but not the CGI and Perl programming stuff."

Given the accolades, you'd never know his site is partially homespun. The design is simple, sleek, and fast—characteristics that have earned it a prestigious award. In August 1997, *WebMaster* magazine rated Ask The Builder one of the Top 50 Internet sites, beating out 850 others.

But Website design is not the only factor that keeps Carter tethered to his computer. When he launched Ask The Builder, he checked his e-mail once a day. Two years later he logs on every 90 minutes to begin fulfilling product orders (such as bid sheets), to respond to inquiries from potential advertisers and answer visitor questions. "Four years ago I was eating lunch on drywall buckets," he notes. "Now I am dripping ketchup on my keyboard."

Over time the one-man-show aspect of Ask The Builder could be Carter's biggest barrier to seven-figure success. "I don't have a full-time support staff behind the scenes. It's just me. This is going to be a big problem as more and more people want personalized service." For this reason Carter works out of the basement of his Cincinnati, Ohio home, a far less glamorous setting than his competition's.

Ask The Builder's primary Web rivalry comes from sites that are TV-related, spun from the home improvement shows "Hometime" and "This Old House." What's important to note about his competition is that neither of these sites lets visitors interact with the hosting personalities about personal remodeling issues. "Hometime" offers only a user's forum. "This Old House" lets you e-mail the hosts, but the instructions imply that all questions should relate to the show. These differences are what fuel Carter's mission.

"The newspaper column and the Website are dedicated to delivering the most accurate and authoritative building and remodeling information to homeowners. I want people to understand how and why things work in building and remodeling.

Armed with this information they can select the best products and hire the true, professional contractors."

For these reasons Carter doesn't recognize his competition as genuine competitors, online or off. "Let Bob Vila be the king of home improvement on TV and let the Carey Brothers own radio. I, Tim Carter, will own the Web."

For up-to-date information about
the success of
Ask The Builder
visit
www.StrikingItRich.com

Cassette House

DAT Tape, Blank Cassettes, Blank CD's
Recording Supplies.

Order 24 hours a day, 7 days a week!
Voice: 800-321-5738 * Fax: 800-848-5738

Secure Online Ordering

On the net since '89!

MUSIC

SPIKE!
Our 1st CD.

ON SALE!

Maxell Minidisc
from $3.25!

Maxell 120UR
type I cassette
from $1.25!

PRODUCTS

- **Internet Specials**
- Cassettes and Cassette Supplies
- Cassettes - Wholesale/Bulk
- Dat Tape, DDS Tape and Supplies
- ADAT, DA-88, Minidisc
- Blank CD's and Supplies

FEATURES

The DAT Web

Tech Info

Tape Trader Pages

Robin's-Eye View

Independent Recording Acts

Resources

Bulletin Board

PRODUCTS

- Computer Media
- Video Tape
- Storage Racks
- Books, Gifts and Misc.
- Recording Gear For Sale
- Search Catalog

Since April 1st 1995, our WEB page has been accessed 217,251 times!
Check our press! * * **Internet Magazine** * * **Nashville Business Journal**

Contact

ART MUNSON
CASSETTE HOUSE

www.tape.com

It's the stuff Internet commerce legends are made of. In April 1995 Art Munson launched his Website for a price equivalent to dinner for two at Sizzler. Less than three years later his enterprise is annually grossing close to $1 million.

Welcome to Cassette House, home to some of the best deals on the Net for name-brand recordable media such as blank cassettes, DATs, and CD-ROMs. In fact a quick perusal of their price list may make you cringe when you realize what you pay locally for the same Maxell, Sony, and BASF products.

While Munson's low prices are a definite distinction, the company's history also sets it apart. Cassette House has been online longer than most Web storefronts. Although the Website was launched in mid-1995, Cassette House has actually been online since 1989 via e-mail and discussion groups, qualifying Art Munson as a bonafide e-commerce colonist.

Cassette House began as a paper catalog in 1981, as an adjunct service to Munson's successful recording studio. In 1985 he began logging on to the Genie and CompuServe proprietary online services, and in 1989 he finally posted a commercial notice on the Genie Forum devoted to music recording techniques. Since the service frowned on such solicitations, the notice was quickly deleted, but was up long enough for an attorney/Deadhead to e-mail Munson and suggest he get on the Internet and participate in the Grateful Dead Usenet newsgroup. As Munson sees it, "Essentially a lack of netiquette launched my Internet business."

But that would be Munson's last breach of netiquette. Working proactively, he responded to posts that fit his enterprise, such as notices inquiring about the cheapest places to buy blank DATs or technical questions about recording live music. He gave a thorough response, in addition to a "by-the-way" alerting them to Cassette House with a few sample prices and an encouragement to e-mail for more info.

About 25% of the first orders came in via e-mail, with the balance to his 800-number. In 1990 his sales from the online world were about 50% of his business's gross receipts, approximately $4,500.

Sales soared and profits swelled as Cassette House's prices were considered ultracompetitive. For example, in the early 1990s a 120-minute digital audio tape (DAT) on the open market sold for $15. Munson moved the same product for $7.50 and was still making $3 profit per tape. The commodity nature of his inventory and stiff competition have since lowered his profit margin considerably to an average 25% or $.50 per tape.

A techno-guy at heart, Munson's marriage of tape to the Web was inevitable. Therefore in January 1995, armed with a $30 edition of *Laura Lemay's Teach Yourself Web Publishing with HTML in 14 Days,* Munson plunged into the design of Cassette House, deciphering the code from existing Websites and applying it to his own. Four months later, Cassette House had a new home on the Web. One year later he swapped paper for pixels and closed his catalog for good. By May 1998 he filled over 15,000 orders exclusively from the online world.

Due partly to his initial posts in the Grateful Dead areas, many of these orders can be attributed to tape traders, the core of Cassette House's clientele, accounting for over 60% of sales.

The practice of tape trading began with the Grateful Dead, who were one of the first bands to recognize that they couldn't stop unauthorized recordings of their concerts. So instead of fighting it, they embraced it and actually set up taping sections where people would openly bring in machines and record the live shows. The catch was that you were never allowed to sell the performance, but you could trade them.

Out of this sprung a network of people who traveled the country taping concerts, which, of course, record companies frown on. Yet with the Internet it's now easier than ever for tape traders to contact each other. In fact, many have Web-sites (for example, *www.deadbase.com* and *bertha.wwim-pact.com/gdtapelists*), and the practice is exploding. Although the Dead are no longer together, other heavily taped live per-formance acts such as the Dave Matthews Band, Phish, and the Smashing Pumpkins continue to fuel demand. Between the blank tape traded for prerecorded tape and the blank media required by the actual tapers, Cassette House has maintained a healthy business. At least for now.

There is one hitch in the copyright law that has allowed for this," explains Munson. "Because trading is not selling and there was a perception that no value was trading hands, the practice of trading has not been illegal. However, a 1998 fed-eral law may amend this because a value is now being per-ceived."

Munson predicts that if the law is enforced the practice will not stop, but will simply drive it underground. The network will then depend on Stealth Tapers, people who tape live shows on the QT. Nonetheless, Munson doubts this will affect his busi-ness considering the voracity with which these people tape.

To better service these avid tapers, Munson also offers con-tent on his site by way of technical papers focusing on sound engineering tips and tricks. These articles are exclusives since Munson has them specifically written for the site. "I use a free-lancer who writes for various recording magazines," he ex-plains. "The articles are about 1,000 words for which I pay $150 in cash or trade out in product." At some point Munson would like to integrate a monthly newsletter devoted entirely to recording issues.

Since not all of Munson's clients are tape traders, he spends an equal amount of time concentrating on the balance of his 5,000 customers who include the organizations repre-senting Jewel, Allman Brothers Band, and Barry Manilow, along with dozens of universities, National Public Radio (NPR) stations, and Fortune 500 companies. "I remember when I sold 700 recordable CDs to NEC," he recalls. "It made me feel like I was playing with the big guys."

From his early days posting to the Grateful Dead lists, Usenet Groups, and other forums, Munson has relied on one-to-one marketing to drive traffic to Cassette House.

He still spends time in newsgroups, although he admits "I've cut back in my newsgroup participation because it takes an inordinate amount of time. At this point there is always someone out there who can answer quicker than I. Besides," he continues, "The publicity value of posting has decreased over time. There's so much spam, fewer people are using them as a resource."

Another benefit of his informative posts are links from sites who consider Cassette House an ideal value for their audience. More than 500 sites link to him of which only 20% were re-quested and reciprocated by Munson. Even though hyperlinks may generate only a few clicks per month each, the aggregated effect is impressive. Using an average of 1,500 clicks and a modest 2% sale conversion, these innocent links can translate to up to 30 orders a month and, more importantly, 30 new cus-tomers.

Perhaps the most important links for Cassette House come from the search engines. Because his pages are static and he has been online for so long, *tape.com* is well represented in all of the navigation services. According to his logs, Yahoo sends the most people from searches on the words "DAT tape," "blank CDs," and "recording supplies."

Between the voluntary links from related sites and the visi-tors he gets for free from search engines, Munson has under-standably shied away from traditional online banner advertis-ing. Furthermore, he is not quite comfortable with the notion of paying for impressions. He will, however, gladly pay for ac-tion and has wholeheartedly embraced the low-risk, pay-per-click advertising model.

One of his favorite spots for such an arrangement is Tape-Trading.com where Munson places banner ads on individual band pages. On the average he gets 500 click-throughs a month for which he pays 10 cents each. While Munson has found that he can directly attribute few sales to these banners, he values the exposure and branding, which overall he has correlated to sales increases. "Sales of Maxell and TDK tape, the brands tape traders use, have gone up dramatically in the 40–50% range," he acknowledges.

Nonetheless, just getting people to the site is one of Munson's goals, since at least 10% of his 300 daily visitors buy, placing an average order of 50 items for a total of $100.

One of Munson's greatest marketing challenges is the nature of his inventory, which is not conducive to cross-selling. Generally blank media buyers are loyal to one format. "I don't have anything else to offer someone who buys blank DATs," explains Munson. "They generally don't buy cassettes. They have graduated away from them." Without this cross-selling option, Munson focuses on considerable price breaks to increase his profits through a greater number of units per sale. Quantity discounts start at 10 and 50 units with a price difference on the average of 50 cents between unit one and unit 51.

Realizing that he should be getting the most from each sale, Munson does plan to include videotape and computer back-up media products, with the hope that these products will appeal to his entire customer base.

Although more cross-selling options would surely boost the bottom line, Munson continues to spend most of his time nurturing his e-mail list, perhaps because his business's online presence began in electronic mail.

In the first quarter of 1998 Cassette House's e-announcement list exceeded 4,000 recipients. Along with the addresses captured from his customers who have ordered and those who have simply e-mailed Munson with a question, he has been collecting names since he began roaming online services nine years ago. "I don't consider this spam because they requested information," Munson explains. "They only get a mailing every four weeks or so and I always give them the option to take them off the list."

In fact, it's rare that recipients opt out. These e-announcements contain golden deals through Cassette House's private weekend sales. Because of their incredible effectiveness, Munson dispatches these weekly superspecials to only 25% of his list.

"The great thing about these blow-outs is the cash infusion," he says. "In 48 hours I can get rid of 3,000 recordable CDs 20% below normal low price. Nonsales time would take a couple of weeks to move this much merchandise." Even selling product very close to cost is worth it to Munson, whose motive is partially to keep his name in front of his customers. Even better, if they visit the site to buy a blow-out product, 75% of the time they purchase a regularly priced item too.

To keep building his list, Munson occasionally hosts a contest, the object of which is to guess how much a certain product has sold in a given month, such as how many 90MTR DATs. The contest is announced in newsgroups with the guesses submitted by e-mail. If the contestant is not a Cassette House mailing list member, he or she instantly becomes one. There are three prize categories and the contest costs Munson about $400–500. "This has helped build awareness of the site and creates a lot of goodwill," he contends.

One interesting note about Cassette House's clientele is that, even though they are technologically proficient, over 30% prefer to order by phone, a statistic Munson relentlessly tries to reduce to save money. As an experiment he offered free products for Web orders to encourage people to stay digital and spare him the phone charges. The decrease was negligible. What really shocked Munson, however, was that people who qualified for the free materials weren't adding it to their cart. "I put this huge free stuff logo on the homepage and in the shopping cart and even though they qualified for it they didn't include it with their order. I can't figure it out."

For the first six years, Munson answered all the 800-number calls personally, but in spring 1997 he hired an order-taking service which he credits as a major relief. He pays 85 cents per minute while the live operator is servicing the call, plus the 800-number charges. The average call for an order costs about $2.75. (To keep costs down when running his weekend specials, Munson offers only Internet ordering.)

What's important to note is the difference in the average order size between the 800-number orders and the Website orders, with the Internet-based orders about 100% higher. "Most of the Web people are repeats and therefore order larger amounts," Munson explains.

Although he may lose some upselling opportunities compared to the period when he answered his 800-number personally, Munson is thrilled that he no longer has to deal with the cacophony of inbound calls. He does, however, still answer his non-800 number, which generally services calls from his more serious buyers.

Getting an order service was the first major labor delegation Munson made since Cassette House's Web launch and one he wishes he had done sooner. "It's such a thrill to no longer have to deal with a constant phone ringing plus I now have the freedom to travel." Shortly thereafter he also hired one full-time person to handle ordering, packing, and shipping, for which he pays $10 per hour plus benefits.

Until this first employee came onboard, the business was run entirely by Munson with the invaluable help of his wife Robin. And while Cassette House reaps sizable revenues, Munson has no desire to transform Cassette House into Cassette Mansion. As a former guitarist and engineer for legends such as John Lennon and Barbra Streisand, music remains his primary focus. "I've made the conscious decision to keep the business relatively small as my first love is making music and enjoying life," he explains. In fact, in the near future Munson plans to sell his own music via Cassette House.

Since Munson is in the enviable position of not feeling pressure to constantly increase sales, he decided to not proactively pursue the international market. For one thing there is the sheer complexity of international custom laws and the complications of global delivery. "I'm amazed that some of my customers buy $25 worth of product and pay more than the cost of the product for overseas shipping." Regardless, it was an international order that is Munson's most memorable. From Kingston Springs, Tennessee, with a population of 2,600, Munson was doing business with a customer in Finland.

While international sales account for only 10% of his revenue, with orders going to the such distant spots as Fiji, Slovania, and Australia, they remain his greatest vulnerability to fraud, which he learned when he lost $600 on a deceitful order bound for Poland.

"It's too easy to get ripped off," Munson warns. "The most suspicious orders come from the Eastern bloc countries." While Munson will continue to fulfill international orders, he is not emphasizing it on his site.

In all fairness, fraud attempts are commonplace for domestic orders as well, although through his international experience he has a procedure that has so far protected him since his $600 loss.

When checking for fraud, Munson looks for two criteria: order size and delivery speed. If a new customer wants an order of $500 or more shipped overnight, this red flag is the prime indicator. He says that he gets such orders once every couple of months and 90% of the time they are frauds. "It's a lot of phony addresses where people will actually wait for FedEx to deliver," says Munson. "Some actually go to FedEx for pick ups and even use a phony FedEx account number." Since Munson has implemented a comprehensive verification procedure to accompany his intuition, he has all but eliminated fraud.

One reason Munson might be a fraud target is the fact that his Bartles and Jaymes-quality Webpage design clearly identifies Cassette House as a small business. While it might work against Munson in some instances, including people who associate slick page elements with a business' reliability, Munson loves the look and feel of his site. "I don't have an eye for designing but I enjoy it and I like coming up with neat small graphics," he says. "My pages load quickly and that was my ultimate goal."

While Munson could certainly afford to hire a professional Webmaster, his self-anointed "control freak nature" won't let him. He relishes the fact that he can instantly make adjustments to the site, like implementing a predawn brainstorm for a new sale.

Even though he is his own Webmaster, Munson is able to keep his time spent on the Cassette House site and business details to 4–5 hours a day, less than 40 hours a week. To work most efficiently, sometimes he starts at 3:00 A.M., answering the 50 e-mails he receives daily, downloading orders from his site and his 800-number service, and printing the orders that need to be fulfilled. This process takes about two hours. Later in the day, he spends another couple of hours helping with shipping or, more likely, getting a head start on paperwork.

Munson realizes that he could increase his revenues by 50% or more if he was willing to invest the time to market more aggressively. His 58-year-old wisdom has also helped him to realize that he can sell Cassette House and retire in the not-so-distant future. As he sees it he has two assets: the actual business and his domain name, tape.com, which he registered in July 1995. "I have one supplier who is interested in it, but I'm not sure how to price it," he says. "Frankly I'm surprised that I haven't heard from one of my competitors in all these years."

At this point almost nothing surprises Munson. After doing business by modem for 10 years, he is still trying to adjust to the dizzying pace of online technology and growth. "I sometimes get overwhelmed by it all," he confesses, "and long just to be a simple woodworker!"

---

*For up-to-date information about
the success of*
Cassette House
visit
www.StrikingItRich.com

Coastal Tool & Supply
The Discount Tool People
The Complete Web Source for Power Tools

Bosch, Black & Decker, Dewalt, Delta, Makita, Milwaukee, Porter-Cable, Skil, Senco, Hitachi

Drills, cordless drills, saws, routers, sanders, polishers, rotary hammer, demolition hammers, grinders, compressors, pneumatics, dust systems, vacuums, biscuit joiners, planers

Enter the Coastal Tool Shopping Plaza

Coastal Tool & Supply
248 Sisson Ave
Hartford CT 06105
sales@coastaltool.com
Toll Free 877-551-8665

TODD MOGREN

COASTAL TOOL AND SUPPLY

www.coastaltool.com

It's the online order that the folks at the offline Coastal Tool store will never forget. "A Saudi Arabian citizen, who worked for Saudi Airlines, found our Website," relates Todd Mogren, who runs the enterprise. "He e-mailed an order for about $8,000 worth of Bosch tools. Next he flew to New York on Saudi Airlines, rented a car, drove two and a half hours to our Hartford, Connecticut store, picked up his order, paid cash, drove back to the airport and flew home."

While only 10% of Coastal Tool's orders are international, this one perhaps best symbolized to the mom-and-pop tool shop that their homespun business was now part of a world arena, the result of launching a Website only a year and half earlier in October 1995.

Catering to home do-it-yourselfers, woodworkers, professional power tool users, and even the federal government, Coastal Tool boasts an online inventory of over 1,000 power tools and related supplies, from 45-cent screwdriver bits to $975 panel saws. When they launched, Coastal Tool was perhaps the first full-service consumer hardware supplier online and remains the leader, by far, having filled over 6,000 orders since their Web introduction.

On a first visit you would assume that the secret to Coastal Tool's success is their winning combination of massive inventory and deep discounts (their mark-up on power tools is 10 percent maximum). While this is certainly true, a closer look reveals a far less obvious but far more powerful mechanism: a site design that is so simple it's elegant and so elegant the purchasing process literally flows.

"Site navigation is our number one priority," explains Mogren. "It is truly amazing how many sites in the business of selling disregard this rule. I have a strict Three-Clicks-to-Buy policy. Regardless of how we organize the site, from our main shopping page, any customer should be able to add-to-cart within three mouse clicks. As the number of items at the site has grown, I always check to see if the Three-Clicks-to-Buy policy holds true. If it doesn't, I figure out a way to make it true. No exceptions."

Mogren's relentless Three-Clicks-to-Buy refrain is paying off in thrilled customers. "We get so much positive feedback about what an easy Website we have. And these customers don't know how we do it, but we do. There is a lot of text, but not a lot of graphics and you can find what you are looking for, get it in your cart, and get it ordered."

As important as it is to streamline the purchasing process, equally important is getting customers to the goods in the first place. Think about those rare times when shopping in an offline store you instantly found exactly what you wanted. Chances were that you stayed and browsed a bit before checking out and hence purchased items you might not have intended to buy before you walked in. Coastal Tool mimics this dynamic on their site by creating subsections that literally guide you through the purchasing process.

The best example is in their Gift Central area, which has subsections catering to everyone from the "hammerless" to Bob Vila wanna-be's. There's also the Best of Category Tool List along with a complementary area called Ten Gift Ideas (tools any user would love to have). Their biggest winner, however, may be their Create-a-Tool-Box option. Taking advantage of the medium, visitors interactively assemble a personalized tool assortment that makes sense for them.

The process begins by selecting your box before you begin picking tools, one-by-one, from 17 categories, which include screwdrivers, levels, pliers, wrenches, tape measures, and nail pullers. You work from a text listing for easy loading and navigation, but with one click you can see all the items in a category as one screenful, thus making it an efficient way to compare and select the best tool for your needs.

Coastal's Create-a-Tool-Box option is a winning example of unconventional content. We tend to think of content strictly as information presented as articles or reference material, such as a database of toll-free numbers. But Coastal Tool understands that the greatest value for the consumer is the result of *aggregation* (combining massive amounts of information) and *filtration* (narrowing this mass to workable choices, such as the 3–5 best in a category). While this content route is the less travelled and most underutilized application for transaction-based Websites, the results are indisputable. While there is no standard order size per se, most Webstores generally move 1–2 items per sale. Coastal Tool orders, on the other hand, average 2–3 items, totaling about $188.

Undoubtedly Mogren's astute integration of creative, interactive content accounts in part for Coastal Tool Supply's astronomical 474% growth between 1996 and 1997 with estimated earnings for 1998 exceeding $1.5 million.

Five months after Coastal Tool's launch, no one could have convinced Mogren that two years later he would be on track for seven-figure annual revenues. "We opened in late October of 1995 and our first sale was not until early 1996," he reminisces. This $199 sale for a rotary hammer was eventful enough to motivate Mogren to frame the order. Surprisingly, the slow start didn't worry him.

"The expectation was that we would do around $100,000 the first year. That may seem like a huge expectation, but it is only 800 tools or 67 tools per month, which is not very much at all. The big surprise was the amount of work that those orders needed. I am not sure what our mindset was when we began, but I realized early on that more interaction between the customer and us was needed to make the site work."

Customer service for Coastal Tool centers on e-mail, via direct questions to the site's customer service e-mail address as well as from their "Free Advice from the Tool Doctor" area. Of the 75 e-mails received each day, Mogren answers about 90%. "I'm not a Tool Doctor," he explains, "I'm the paramedic. By osmosis after the past couple years I can bang back an answer. The other 10% get printed and fielded to the in-store specialists based on their expertise."

At first, most of Coastal Tool's electronic queries related to tool repair, but Mogren found a quick and graceful solution to this avalanche of redundant messages.

"Because the topic was so popular it led us to actually type into a database every factory service center in the country for all manufacturers," Mogren notes. "It was getting to the point where I was looking up these addresses and telephone numbers around 50 times per day. I needed to free myself from that so I wrote a little PERL program to lead people to the correct page. Next I used an old DOS-based database program to generate HTML pages and the 50 e-mails on this topic were reduced to one or two per day."

This feature also lead to one of their favorite customer service stories. "A customer e-mails from a town in Michigan asking where he can find parts for a tool. I look up the nearest service center and find one in his town. We e-mail him back and reference the address. He replies that from his office he can see the repair shop."

Now that Coastal Tool had invested in building the Service Center database, Mogren decided to integrate this valuable data into their site, which you can now find leveraged as their "Search for Factory Service" area, which, when you enter your state, gives you a complete list of virtually every power tool manufacturer repair facility in your vicinity.

The crushing demands of e-mail are a harsh reality and one that Mogren feels is constantly underestimated. "It was not difficult for us to exceed our sales expectations. What we did not anticipate was the amount of work those orders needed. The sales pitch from many Internet service providers is that the customers just come. All we have to do is kick back, smoke a cigar, and ship the product. This business model doesn't exist as far as I know."

Even after years online, Mogren remains amazed at the time required to be the best. "The amount of work to maintain a site where you can establish repeat traffic and adequately serve the needs of customers is more than anyone will let on. For every order I get, I also get 10 questions. That is a steep ratio."

The bright side of this equation is that e-mail does pay off. Mogren estimates that if in an e-mail a customer asks if a specific tool can be used for a certain application and the answer is "yes" and Coastal carries the tool, the e-mailer does buy. "We see this as customer service, one at a time," he notes. "It's about establishing loyalty."

Fortunately e-mail bonding as a loyalty conduit serves Coastal well during customer service nightmares. "We misshipped an order to Alaska not once but twice. The customer was at first very distressed but in the end continued to do business with us. In fact a neighbor called just after we made the order right, and asked that we not pick his order wrong."

Of the 1,000 people a day who visit Coastal Tool online, about 2% buy online with the balance of orders moved through their nontoll-free number. "More than 50% of our Web business is done by phone," cites Mogren. And despite great strides in online security, Coastal Tool customers remain wary. "We find that many people still will not let their credit card numbers be transmitted over the Net."

To the degree that credit card security has hampered online ordering, Mogren is convinced that shopping cart technology has improved his sales. In fact he is adamant that his business would not have grown as sharply without it. "Initially the coolest thing about shopping online was creating your own order, not having to write down an order and call it in—the speed and convenience factor. That is the key. All serious sites must have online ordering or you won't get anywhere near the potential return. In 1995, we spent $1,000 on software which you can now get for less than $200."

Of course, the technology has no meaning without customers, a staggering 95% of which find the online tool store through search engines and reciprocal linking. Alta Vista is by far their biggest referrer, responsible for 45% of their traffic. Yahoo comes in second.

Despite the popularity of the search engines, one of Coastal Tool's most golden links is from WoodWorkers.com, which sends him 30–50 highly qualified visitors a day. What's amazing is that this is a no-frills listing. It simply states "Coastal Tool and Supply" and is tucked under their Mail Order Tool Houses category. The mention is without any editorial critique or rating. As a netiquette gesture, Coastal links back to Wood-Workers.com, which it does for only 11 other related sites on-line. Mogren initiated these relationships by typing keywords such as "power tools" and "drills" into the search engines and forged link relationships with the informational sites that ranked highest in the results.

For the time being, Mogren is depending on grass roots endeavors such as these to fuel his business since advertising buys have been mixed.

In that last quarter of 1997, Mogren spent $2,000 on two ad buys: one on the I-Sales Newsletter discussion list and another in the Link Exchange Digest. Together he received a total of 55 orders, about a 1% response, at a cost of about $36 per order. Admittedly, this was not targeted marketing but he wanted to test a nonspecific buy and, as an active member of the I-Sales Discussion List, also wanted to support the group.

Contrary to his general buys, when Coastal bought a focused link the results were excellent. Mogren spent $1,000 in the Power Listings section of Buyers Index, pages devoted to mail order and Web shopping sites. From this link he got a 7% click-through rate, which delivered 1,000 people in the first three months.

While customer acquisition is key, Mogren keeps a watchful eye on encouraging repeat business. He accomplishes this primarily through the *Coastal Tool Newsletter,* a monthly electronic publication that includes product reviews, tips, and the latest tool gossip.

To his credit, Mogren never harvests e-mail addresses by automatically signing up people who don't specifically request a subscription. On the other hand, Mogren makes sure that people have plenty of opportunities to join. Between the "subscribe option" on the company's homepage to the "sign up here" opportunities offered every time visitors fill out a form (catalog request, question, comment, or order), there's no way someone can miss the opportunity. Percentagewise the number of signups coming from the forms are evenly divided. In other words, the percentage of people who say yes is the same regardless of whether they are e-mailing a comment or placing an order. However, the forms generating the most signups come from catalog requests and Tool Doctor questions since they get the most activity.

At the beginning of 1998, Mogren had 5,700 newsletter subscribers with a growth rate of 900 per month. As the publication matures and his subscriber base swells, he plans to leverage the electronic publication as an additional revenue stream via sponsorships or co-op advertising.

If Todd Mogren were not writing the *Coastal Tool Newsletter*, he would certainly be reading it. And if he were not responsible for the genesis of the Coastal Tool site and had no affiliation with the company, he would undoubtedly be one of its customers.

Mogren, 36, has a computer background in database management and a love of home hardware. He managed a hardware distribution company for about eight years before joining Coastal to automate the backend business processes. While technically an employee (albeit with a revenue share of the Website), Mogren approaches Coastal Tool online with a stellar blend of entrepreneurial zeal and the process-minded orientation of a computer programmer.

When he began, his mission for the site was to build a community of tool users and to offer all the store's power tools at the same price as their mail order department. "We had very little idea what this would entail or how the site should be designed," he reflects. "In our first month online I was scanning everything I could find and thinking about how to link everything together coherently."

Mogren's decision to enter the Web fray was easy. "Robert and Karen Ludgin, the owners, and I, saw it as low risk, with a minor entry cost and a high potential return. Even if our site never resulted in a sale, the upfront expense was minimal. The budget was around $1,800 for the first year and that included site hosting and development software."

Mogren's Internet experience at this point was as up to par as anyone else launching a Website at the time. Mogren's online history began in 1985 when he became a member of CompuServe. Almost 10 years later (late 1994) he saw the Web for the first time when it started getting media attention. Within a month he decided to start his Website. He signed up for 10 megabytes of space with a local ISP (whom they still use) and bought the Complete HTML Publishing Kit for $295. He didn't even start scanning art for his site until after he launched, when he locked himself up at a friend's house for two days and scanned 500 tool pictures from catalogs. Coastal Tool has since bought a scanner.

Despite many upgrades to the site, one aspect has not changed. "Our homepage is the same one as when we started," Mogren admits. "Once you pass through it you never see it again so I never considered it important to change." While the homepage is static, the main shopping page changes weekly.

Though overwhelming at times, the pace of developing Coastal Tool and Supply on the Web has been just right. "The nature of the Net and what you can offer now you couldn't even do when we started. The learning curve was fine. It wasn't too slow or too fast. As the Internet matures our site has grown up with it at a good pace, not too far ahead or behind."

One feature that Coastal Tool implemented and then pulled was a site-wide search, meaning that you can input a keyword such as "wrench" and get a results listing linking you to related articles and items. While most sites as large as Coastal consider this feature indispensable, Coastal does not.

"We found it was useless because our items are logically assembled in a way that you could find the relevant item more easily than with a search engine.

"For example, if you want a specific drill and typed in "drill" you would come up with many more pages than are relevant to the item and you have to wade through these results. With the design of our site in two clicks you can see a page of all the drills we sell."

Mogren also realizes that in time he will have no choice but to reinstate the search feature. "When we get to the 4,500-item mark, we'll have to put it back because there will be so much stuff. Even then people will continue to look for tools either by type or by manufacturer and we present it both ways now. Remember our adage: Two clicks to find. Three clicks to buy."

The next step in Coastal's development is integrating the remaining 3,500 items from their physical store and catalog. Of the 1,000 items currently online, about 95% are actual power tools. Next they will offer the accessories and ancillary products that go with them. A simple add-on of product does not make sense to Mogren until he can integrate the additional inventory. "When someone looks at a power tool I want them to get all the items that work with that power tool," he notes. "For example, a 3/8" drill would lead to replacement chucks, chuck keys, holsters, drill bits, and so on."

For Mogren this would serve as the ultimate cross-selling solution, but getting these additional items on the site is prohibitively labor-intensive. "The only thing limiting our development is time."

This is doubly frustrating for Coastal when they consider the breadth of their potential customers. "At some point during any given year, almost everyone is looking to buy a tool either for themselves or as a gift," says Mogren. Coastal Tool also ships worldwide and their international clientele is developing nicely, as evidenced by their legendary Saudi customer as well as a Colombian citizen who ordered 100 Leatherman pocket tools along with additional orders originating from such distant destinations as Feore Island and Antarctica.

Given the ubiquity of giants such as Sears and Home Depot, one could be concerned for Coastal's future considering that the behemoth competition is online as well. But this doesn't phase Mogren. "Compared to their physical stores we are equal. Website to Website, we have a bigger selection of hand and power tools than they do. Home Depot doesn't even offer online ordering. They are just providing information."

While being the first to market is a common denominator to the success of many Webstores, there is more to it than just being first. For example, Coastal Tool committed early on to a full-line presentation. Even today most of their smaller competitors only list a few tools and instead use their Web presence as a digital brochure to encourage people to order their traditional mail order catalog.

"All of the other smaller companies that could impact us are already online and they are not doing such a great job," Mogren remarks. "They don't understand the potential. All of the major mail order catalog tool houses, of which there are five or six, are focused on catalog requests. They maybe show visitors 10 items and then tell them to call their 800-number to order."

Coastal Tool also offers a catalog for which the Website generates 50–75 requests a day. Mogren estimates that as much as 15% of the people who request the catalog eventually place an order. In fact, the purchase ratio from these Internet requests is so high that six months after they launched Coastal Tool online, the company eliminated all bulk catalog mailings.

For entering Webpreneurs Mogren's best advice is to get on a electronic discussion mailing list like I-Sales. "Spend a month or two reading all of the posts and maybe downloading a few months of archives," he suggests. "You will learn more reading what others have done than reading any book."

And the best advice he has received? "I read an article in early 1995 that was written by the workers at *Wired*. Their number one recommendation was not to treat this as mass marketing as we know it. The reach may be in the millions but the contact is one to one."

*For up-to-date information about the
success of*
Coastal Tool and Supply
visit
www.StrikingItRich.com

DISCOUNT GAMES HOMEPAGE

DISCOUNT GAMES

DGC INFO

CATALOG

PRODUCT INFO

Updating Site - S___ ___lems May Exist.

"Serious ___ ___erious Gamers"

DGC

Featuring...

- Over 21,000 items available
- Online, searchable catalog
- Up to 30% discount!
- Military, fantasy and science fiction
- Role-playing games and accessories
- Miniatures and game systems
- Collectible card games

- Board games
- T-shirts, pins, and other apparel
- Paints, brushes, and tools
- Novels, from Adventure to Reference
- Models and Trains
- Anime
- We ship worldwide
- Secure Online Ordering

Helpful Resources

| Ordering Help | View Shopping Cart | E-mail |

Keyword Search

CHUCK MOSS

DISCOUNT GAMES

www.discountgames.com

Chuck Moss could give an Internet marketing specialist a heart attack. Breaking every online retailing rule, his Webstore's business approach can only be described as contrarian. They offer photos for only 1% of their products, do not advertise, and, in an environment of stiff competition, have stopped lowering their prices. Moss, whose Webstore has filled over 10,000 orders, could be considered an e-commerce revolutionary.

The Webshop is Discount Games. Although the name implies that they carry perennial favorites such as Candyland, Sorry, and Life, they do not. Instead, their inventory is focused on adventure and role-playing games such as Dungeons & Dragons and Warhammer. In addition to the games, their core inventory is gaming accessories, of which they offer thousands.

So perhaps this is our first clue to Discount Games' success: inventory. The online store carries over 20,000 products of which 10,000 are adventure game miniatures. These tiny figurines, critical for play and role-playing games, account for 75% of their sales. The miniatures range in price from $2 and up for the standard size to as high as $60 for model size.

With 20,000 items in inventory, Moss has a more valid rationale than most Web storefronts to not have product photos, at least for now. But he feels, given the nature of his product, that this is a convention he can continue indefinitely.

"We can get away without having photos because our customers know what they are looking for," explains Moss. "They are very aware of what is going on in the adventure games arena. They've read about the product in *Dragon* or *Scrye* magazines or they have seen the products at their local stores. They also get product recommendations from the newsgroups like *rec.games.miniature* or *rec.games.roleplaying*."

And it's his clientele, the folks frequenting these newsgroups, who hold the second clue to Discount Games' Web retailing victory. While CommerceNet/Nielsen surveys continually indicate that the average online shopper is about 36 years old, Discount Games caters to a group that rarely surfaces in polls: males, ages 15–25.

Moss's first evidence that his customer base was composed primarily of teenage boys and young adult males showed up in the wording of their e-mails. Phrases such as "this miniature is so cool it rocks," along with requests to ship to dorm rooms and frat houses, were neon-bright indicators. Second, their peak order times are Saturday nights. Third, this credit-card-challenged group uses their parents' credit cards. The online order forms, although submitted with permission of the parents, are not always accurately completed and need voice verification.

"We follow the Visa guidelines and if there is any discrepancy we always call. Often the kid himself answers and 'our customer' has to put his mom on the phone … it's almost always the mother."

Despite the rebel nature associated with young boys, especially adventure gamers, Discount Games has had only one incident of credit card fraud and that was early on. Nonetheless, they are not willing to carry any more credit card risk than they have to, thus there is one customer base they always turn down: prison inmates.

"We won't ship to prisons because of the credit risk. If the credit card is fraudulent, that would be a problem and we don't want that," Moss explains. "We think they are finding out about us through their Internet access inside the pen." Moss figures that other Webstores' unwillingness to ship to prisons must be a problem for inmates. "We get e-mails from them specifically asking if we will ship to prisons."

Although Discount Games is understandably reluctant to ship to convicted criminals, they do cater to other isolated gamers around the globe.

"When we first started we heard in the newsgroups that people in other countries couldn't get these products. So we decided to make arrangements with UPS to ship internationally," says Moss. "What prompted us to go international was seeing a need for it. These people were the most vocal in these groups."

International sales account for 30% of Discount Games' business. The countries they ship to most in order of popularity are Japan, Australia, Russia, China, South Africa, and Brazil. Despite their international success, Moss has no plans to offer multilingual pages because "no one seems to be having problems." He also says he doesn't want to deal with the language-specific e-mail.

No matter the age or the destination, the average Discount Games order is eight items for a total of about $80. There are always exceptions though. "A customer in Germany once ordered about 300 miniature figures," recalls Moss. "I remember it well because it took so long to check off all of the items as we were packing it."

Fortunately, not all of Discount Games' 150 orders a week are as time-intensive as that one. Launched in January 1996, Discount Games experienced 600% growth from 1996 to 1997. With their conservative 200% estimate for 1998, they will likely break the magic $1 million mark in gross revenues.

Needless to say, these figures have far outpaced Moss' expectations. He considered his prelaunch sales projections optimistic even though they called for only making one sale a day. Because of the Web's low entry and maintenance costs, even with these diminutive sales he knew in four years he would recoup his investment, the achievement of which he considered a success.

The budget for his online store's design was $20,000, and the actual cost came in at $21,500. Discount Games built their site from the ground up, including their shopping cart system because off-the-shelf solutions did not exist then. The startup capital for the venture was a combination of a $15,000 loan and $6,500 from the Discount Games offline store called The Gamer's Inn.

In addition to finding a developer they could afford, another of Moss's criteria was hiring someone local. "We wanted to have face-to-face meetings and be able to see their facilities, what kind of equipment they were using, and how sophisticated they were behind the scenes," he recalls.

Understandably, Moss wanted to eliminate as many variables as possible. "When we decided to go online I was both excited and nervous. I knew that the Internet had a lot of potential but I didn't know much about the mail order business."

For Chuck Moss, age 32, when the store went Net-bound, the concept of cloning his offline game venture was actually the outcome of some parental advice. "My father saw an article in the newspaper about a store that was selling games on the Internet and doing very well at it," says Moss. "When I saw their online store I decided I could do it better. Convincing my business partner, Joe Durham, was another matter." But Moss puts it in perspective. "This was before the Web was considered something special and he didn't think it was going to amount to very much. Then he saw some of the places on the Web, and once he saw it, he was more comfortable with it."

From the beginning, the simplicity with which Moss approached the site design was another key to his success. While they have virtually no product photos (the 1% cited earlier are in their "gallery"), he still mandated a site that was "cool to look at and provided an easy way for customers to find what they were looking for. We've kept 'fluff' such as frames and unnecessary pictures to a minimum. I see so many sites that are so graphic-intensive that they take two minutes to load at 28.8. I think this intimidates the user."

While Discount Games continually updates their database, their opening splash page has remained the same. "We decided not to change it because it provides instant recognition." This is a sentiment that is becoming more common with other online retailers. And while the graphic on their welcome screen is one of the few instances of imagery you'll find on their pages, Moss instead focuses on what he considers the site's biggest strength: its database.

The Discount Games electronic catalog is massive, inventorying more than 20,000 products. Customers can search by keyword, category, or manufacturer and, because the output is pure text, get instantaneous results. The ease with which customers can get to the inventory may in part account for Discount Games' average eight items per order, a figure higher than most other Webstores, especially for one with no minimum order policy.

Moss believes that this simplistic shopping experience is bringing customers back and the reason he could stop cutting his prices.

"Originally we were discounting our products 30% off retail and while we have some items at 30% off, the majority are at 20%," Moss explains. "We thought that we had to discount to the bottom to get people to buy from us on the Internet and that wasn't true. We think this is the case because if you offer the customer an easy shopping experience and good service they will continue to come back." Apparently he's right. His repeat customer base is 45%.

Moss was motivated to drop prices in the first place on the assumption that the volume of business would offset the reduced revenues. "Unfortunately, we found out that the associated costs for the higher volume of business just did not leave us with any substantial profits worth justifying the higher volume of business."

The only other significant misassumption was the cost of running their online store. As veteran offline retailers, Moss figured the overhead for their Internet operation would be lower than the grounded operation, but he was wrong. "When the number of orders increased to the point that we needed more space, our costs exceeded the offline store. Running the online store is about 25% more expensive than the offline store."

Despite the higher overhead, the online store's revenues exceed the offline venture. "We had been up for about one year when our online revenues exceeded the Gamer's Inn." Today, online is 40% more than offline. And now what was a budding enterprise sprung from the dusty trenches of their Troy, Michigan store had to move to its own offices a few miles away. "We had merchandise, people, and computers and no place to put them," Moss said of the much-needed relocation. "Our original plan was to run the business from our retail store as a side venture. Within six months we grew to the point where we had to move to keep up with demand."

Because his marketing efforts can be described as scarce, most first-time visitors find Discount Games through the search engines, in all of which Moss has registered. The greatest traffic generators are Yahoo and WebCrawler, the latter associated with America Online, which are responsible for 30% of the 3,000 people who visit the site each day.

Discount Games does not advertise because the few times they did, it did nothing to spark sales. "We advertised in *Implosion* magazine and on the online magazines and none of them pulled perceptibly," Moss said. "We thought about search engine advertising but have not done it yet only because we haven't investigated it."

Despite this low profile, Discount Games is a silver-rated merchant on BizRate and listed in the 100 Hottest Sites directory. Discount Games does some cross-linking and more than 350 sites link back.

Perhaps the most significant and noteworthy marketing for Moss has come from the newsgroups, because they are the best fit with the company's customer service crusade. This is where you can find Chuck Moss for at least an hour every day.

"I like seeing what people are saying about us, our competition, what new products are coming, what they like, and what they don't like," he says. But it goes beyond mere strategic recon. Moss's eavesdropping has dramatically influenced Discount Games' inventory and their bottom line.

"For example, people would be talking about models and how they were hard to get in some areas and we decided to add them. Models now comprise 5 to 10% of our sales and are steadily growing in proportion to the number of models that we carry."

Even though customers can sway inventory decisions, Discount Games won't act on every suggestion they overhear. "We won't stray too far from our core. Essentially, we carry 'pots and pans.'" But even sales for the ordinary have perplexed Moss and his staff. "A customer once ordered 35 bags of a flocking material that looks like mulched grass. Flocking is used as scenery for miniatures and dioramas. We joked that he was probably 'astroturfing' his house."

Although Moss is cognizant enough to spend time in newsgroups to interact with his current and potential customers, Discount Games makes no effort to stay in contact with their customers after a sale: no periodic e-newsletter, no occasional announcements of special deals, zip. The only e-mail a customer ever gets from Discount Games is a confirmation of their order.

While this lack of servicing a customer list could be considered a marketing faux pas on a grand scale, Moss has his reasons. "We thought that people would not want to get random mailings from us. So at first we didn't get ourselves set up for this. Now to implement that would be cumbersome, but we do have plans to incorporate something at some point."

It's also important to note that Moss has found that a featured product on key pages does not necessarily improve sales for that product. This may be indicative of the one-to-one nature of the Net. Although there might not be much activity on featured products, product questions in general account for 75% of Discount Games' e-mail, with the balance relating to order and shipping policies. To properly handle the 50 queries a day, Discount Games dedicates one employee entirely to the task and sees the need to add another in the near future.

Moss admits that part of the reason for the heavy e-mail is attributable to the part of the site he considers the weakest, the checkout page. "Looking back I would have liked to have designed our checkout page to provide more information to the customer after the order was placed so that the customer would be more aware of the ordering process and have more confidence that their order was going to be delivered in a timely manner."

But he also realizes that e-mail is just part of the nature of the Web. "Remember that the whole world is a potential customer. Be prepared to answer lots of questions," he advises.

Moss also knows that if the world is a potential customer, it is also potential competition. Because much of their sales consist of adventure game rules and related books, Discount Games competes a bit with Amazon.com and Barnes & Noble. The only other direct competition is hobby stores, but Moss points out that those who can even consider competing are not as large. Although Moss won't name names, apparently one entity could crimp his future, but he's not overly concerned. "Without being specific, a large national chain that is willing to lose money for the first couple of years while they learn about the Internet could dent our sales."

This significant lead time gives Moss the breathing room he needs to continue as the Internet adventure game giant he has become.

Though Discount Games is a Web marketing anomaly as compared to other Net ventures, their success has come from staying true to themselves and their customers. So instead of fussing with advertising, price cutting, and product photos, Moss remains focused on his original mission statement: the best customer service, the biggest selection of merchandise, the most accurate information, and the quickest turnaround.

"The Internet is a brand new channel," Moss reminds us. "Old rules simply don't hold true."

For up-to-date information about the success of
Discount Games
visit
www.StrikingItRich.com

THE EXPERT MARKETPLACE
HOMEPAGE

▶ **Need a Consultant?** Click Here

▶ **Are You a Consultant?** Click Here

▶ **Need Quick Expert Advice?** Click Here

- ▸ Members Enter Here
- ▸ Free Membership
- ▸ About The Expert Marketplace
- ▸ Comments and Questions

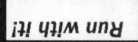

 **Microsoft**

Webmaster Magazine
THE **BEST** AND THE **BUSIEST**
Top 50 Award

The Ultimate Resource for Consulting Services
Over 200,000 Firms Listed

Home of The

In Cooperation With

Dun & Bradstreet

DAVID GOLD

THE EXPERT MARKETPLACE

www.expert-market.com

Here's proof that a person's career direction can change in an instant.

"I was at my old job flipping through a printed directory of consultants on the same desk as my computer," David Gold reflects. "I had a Web browser opened. I looked at the computer, looked at the book, pulled out the final survey results we had collected on the market barriers between consultants and small businesses, re-read the executive summary and never turned back."

Gold's consultant-meets-browser revelation is the zygote behind The Expert Marketplace, a service that provides professional consultants a virtual home and the clients in search of their services an efficient method to find them. They earn their fees from signing up consultants and their firms (known as Affiliates) as well as from a slice of the revenues from the business they refer.

In addition to a desire to capitalize on what he felt was "an enterprise with enormous profit potential," Gold, age 30 at the time, also wanted to solve a problem.

"Currently, a few large consulting firms dominate the consulting marketplace because the smaller consulting firms lack the economies of scale to compete with the Big 6," he explains. "But there are some distinct advantages to businesses using the smaller consulting firms, like more affordable, personal service, yet they are harder to locate and don't have the credibility of the Big 6 even though their services are often as high-quality or even higher-quality."

According to Gold, 80% of the consulting revenue nation-wide goes to less than 10% of the nation's 200,000 consulting firms. "The ideal market would make it easy for businesses to identify and evaluate the small to midsized consultants and allow them the opportunity to choose a smaller consulting firm, pay less, and receive high-quality services." This is the objective of The Expert Marketplace.

In the first quarter of 1998, The Expert Marketplace boasted over 45,000 members with 200 new members joining each day. Gold estimates that approximately 20% of all new visitors to The Expert Marketplace homepage sign up as members. Subscriptions are free and are used primarily by North American business people who want to take advantage of The Expert Marketplace's searchable database to find consulting firms. This directory is the largest free database of consulting firms anywhere in the world, with over 200,000 entries. It should be no surprise then that this aspect of The Expert Marketplace is so popular that a search is performed every 1.75 minutes.

A company seeking consulting services ferrets out qualified people and firms by either requesting specific information about a firm by name based on results of their database search query or placing a notice about their project in The Expert Marketplace's Contract Posting Center.

Consultants then electronically respond to these posts. These opportunities are anonymous and all communications are done by e-mail thus protecting companies from exposing their problems in a public forum. The Expert Marketplace receives 150–300 postings a month.

It must be emphasized that The Expert Marketplace is not a listing service. "There are many other directories of consultants, but that is all they are—a directory," Gold explains. "None of them have a prequalified network of firms that meet ongoing quality standards (our Premier ExpertNet Group). None of them provide serious business services for those firms; they just provide a link or two in their database."

Being listed in The Expert Marketplace database is free to any independent consultant or firm. Nonetheless, becoming a paid Affiliate has distinct advantages that, based on The Expert Marketplace's success, members find a worthwhile value.

Firms can join The Expert Marketplace as a Premier ExpertNet (PEN) Group Affiliate via one of four packages. All of them assess a one-time startup fee ranging from $795 to $2,995 along with a commission to Expert Marketplace from 0 to 15% depending on the option. The larger the startup fee, the grander the presence for the firm on The Expert Marketplace Website and the lower commission rate assessed by The Expert Marketplace on the business they generate for the consultancy.

The most popular membership is their Gold Package, chosen by 40% of their Affiliates. For $1,895 the consultancy gets: A 4,000-word multipage online brochure (linked from the database and hosted on The Expert Marketplace site). Two promoted online articles. The Expert Marketplace's commission of 2% on all business generated from The Expert Marketplace leads.

These benefits are in addition to The Expert Marketplace standard package, which includes other valuable ancillary services.

Another common denominator to all groups is that The Expert Marketplace guarantees all Affiliates one contract over their first year, a guarantee statistically The Expert Marketplace can make.

"We generate 2–6 leads per Affiliate per month," Gold points out. "That's 24–76 leads a year. How many contracts can the typical firm land from 24–76 leads? In fact it generally takes only one contract for an Affiliate to make a profit by becoming a PEN member," declares Gold.

Gold is secure with his offer, and to date no Affiliate has exercised its guarantee yet. "In the cases where a firm has not gotten a contract, they still don't want to leave," says Gold. The reason? "They get enough volume of leads that they hate to give it up." In the rare instances when a contract has not been landed, The Expert Marketplace extends the agreement for free until they get one. However, they still must pay a commission on the contracts with roots to The Expert Marketplace.

The bottom line on potential sales is this: The Expert Marketplace generates over 1,000 consulting contract leads a month for over 300 distinct consulting projects. The fees for the job range widely, from $2,000 to $100,000 plus, with an average of $15,000–20,000.

"One reason these independent, small, and midsized firms are willing to stick around, even if they don't get work, is because they are receiving leads and real business that they never would have known how to market to," says Gold.

PEN Affiliates also have a three-day head start on the Contract Posting Center leads since responses are restricted to PEN Affiliates for 72 hours. Furthermore, Affiliates only receive e-mailed alerts of new postings based on automatic keyword searches performed any time a new announcement is added. In other words, if you are a computer consultant and a post for such a job is added to The Center, an e-mail is automatically issued. With respect to database searches, Affiliates have more content and keywords in the database and therefore a higher probability of ranking higher in results listings. They also show up in larger print with checkmarks next to their names.

But beyond first opportunities for business is the cache of simply being a PEN Affiliate, which requires a thorough qualification procedure called a Performance Appraisal. The advantages of passing are added credibility for the members and added security for the firms hiring them.

About 15% of the Affiliates who apply do not pass The Expert Marketplace's Performance Appraisal. But to evaluate this figure one must factor in that the consultants who know they won't pass don't bother to apply. Regardless of the low failure rate, Gold notes that the qualification curve is rigorous and that, if they were to randomly pick 100 consultants out of the phone book—in other words, use an indiscriminate scale—the failure rate would be closer to 38%. Furthermore, the evaluations of the Affiliates are on-going.

In early 1998, The Expert Marketplace had over 200 Premier ExpertNet Affiliates, with 15–25 new firms joining every month.

David Gold, wise to the benefits of branding and credibility, recognizes that PEN Affiliation also gives the needed "credentials" in an industry where gradations of quality are nearly impossible to quantify.

Likewise, when Gold set out to launch his unknown service with just $10,000, he knew that any branding through strategic associations would be a key. So he went after and landed the big one: Dun & Bradstreet.

Gold describes The Expert Marketplace's association with Dun & Bradstreet as a "classic strategic relationship." The terms are simple. Dun & Bradstreet provides quarterly updates of all the contact information and SIC code descriptions of consulting firms nationwide. For this reason, The Expert Marketplace's database has nearly all consulting firms in existence. "In exchange, Dun & Bradstreet receives a D&B marketing channel in the small business market," Gold responds. "Now they are taking their old printed product called the Consulting Organizations Directory and creating a new way to generate revenue out of it."

David Gold initially had contact with the prestigious company when D&B was doing contract surveys for his organization in 1994. When he began developing The Expert Marketplace, he networked his way to a D&B Assistant Vice President who, after many meetings, discussions, and presentations, felt his company could benefit from the association. While The Expert Marketplace went up on the Web in December 1995, the "brought to you in cooperation with Dun & Bradstreet" banners rotated throughout the site did not appear until three months later, in March 1996.

The Dun & Bradstreet relationship has certainly been critical to The Expert Marketplace's success. The famous name and the unparalleled data they supply are crucial, but they are not the whole picture. While they may entice potential Affiliates and their future clients further into the site, the resulting customer service and other benefits close sales.

"For consulting firms our service provides them with much more than just a listing in a database or a Webpage," Gold clarifies. "It is the opportunity for them to have many of the advantages they would enjoy by being part of a megaconsulting firm without giving up their independence." This includes a steady flow of good leads, huge savings on business services, such as E&O insurance, along with free legal and long distance, to name a few.

Customer service plays an equally important role since The Expert Marketplace is, in a way, a consulting firm too. "We know that 90% of consultant–client dissatisfaction comes from poor customer service, not poor advice," Gold notes. "When PEN Affiliates join, we do almost everything for them, from handling their marketing materials, to designing their online brochures, to hiring a professional writer to work with them to write up their best success stories. Every new Affiliate has an Associate assigned to them, which makes sure that everything gets handled."

Ironically, despite the fact that the business model and technology required to make The Expert Marketplace happen would not exist without the Web, there is no online ordering and no prices listed—a combination considered almost blasphemous by Internet marketing experts.

But The Expert Marketplace is truly an exception. All their business must be done by phone. Gold explains it this way. "Our primary revenue stream comes from the consulting firms who become Affiliates and these firms virtually never sign up without at least a phone conversation. Thus, most of our sales are done by phone. Our site serves as a lead generator for consultants interested in what we offer."

Also keep in mind that this is not a one-off purchase like a book or CD. Few prospects will be willing to submit a $1,700 "order" for a service without any interaction with the company. As Gold puts it, "It's a fairly complicated decision. We also want to be able to follow up. Often the risk appears to be too high to them without being educated on the product first. We don't want to lose the opportunity to talk to them."

Another factor of the online ordering issue is The Expert Marketplace's arrangement with the credit card companies. This virtual consulting firm runs very high dollar amounts on their credit card accounts. Most are well over $1,500. Since the charges are so high they were able to negotiate a 1–2% transaction fee. Conversely, they must pay a much higher rate on low dollar items. As a result, they could lose money on these comparatively tiny sales because of the significantly higher transaction charges.

Not offering online ordering could be considered a risk, but not compared to Gold's biggest gamble, changing the company's revenue system. When The Expert Marketplace started, they charged a flat startup rate and an annual fee. While Gold had commissions integrated into his original business plan, he didn't have a mechanism to track the leads and collect them. Nonetheless, he knew it was "an appropriate way for us to have part of our revenue coming in." Gold adds, "And on top of that the consulting firms prefer to pay commissions. They don't mind paying based on success and they like the fact that we have an incentive."

The Expert Marketplace's commission tracking is a combination of technology and the honor system. For example, when a visitor elects to see detailed data about a consulting firm, they are taken to the PEN group Affiliate's microsite at The Expert Marketplace. The visitor is given all detailed information except for the phone number, which is accessible through a link that says "view phone number." When this link is clicked, the Expert Marketplace considers it a lead. Second, all Affiliates are e-mailed a quarterly declaration to be signed and returned via snail mail reporting their earnings attributable to The Expert Marketplace. To date, The Expert Marketplace says they have never caught anyone trying to avoid commissions.

Besides, instead of chasing commission-stiffers, David Gold prefers to nurture his growing business.

The roots of The Expert Marketplace's visitor bonanza are the search engines, which Gold has found is a prime means of catching consultants and business people.

Gold spends over $20,000 a month in keyword banner advertising on Hotbot, Lycos, Excite, WebCrawler, Alta Vista, and Infoseek. When a visitor types in "consulting" and other applicable derivations, The Expert Marketplace banner ad appears on the results page listing.

Perhaps for the trivia value alone, it's interesting to note what words are most commonly input to describe the one term. Out of 136,000 impressions on Alta Vista, 12% used the keyword "consultant," 26% typed the plural "consultants," with "consulting" the big winner at 62%. The only search engine The Expert Marketplace does not advertise on is Yahoo, whose advertising rates for The Expert Marketplace, are highest and click-through rates the lowest.

Gold uses banner ads to secure new members (companies looking for consultants) as well as Affiliates. He finds that he gets a two to three times higher membership conversion from visitors who click on banner ads than from those who meander onto the site through search engine queries. The cost to bring a visitor to the site is $1 from a banner ad. The direct cost of acquiring a new free member is $5 (20% of all visitors join).

While membership signup and Affiliate acquisitions have been brisk, Gold still would like to see significantly higher growth rates. "Impatience is my greatest virtue and my greatest curse," he admits. "I'm surprised I don't have an ulcer. However, the fact that I am so impatient created the impetus to get us where we are today, so rapidly, on so little cash."

Despite his impressive growth, an average of 400% in three years, it is still not as fast as Gold would like. "Honestly I expected it to grow much faster than it has! We've had tremendous growth and I now realize that I was dreaming with the projections in my original business plan."

Nevertheless, Gold expects 1998's $1.5 million in revenues to be more than double over the previous year. "So far we are ahead in our vision. When I started, I expected to be at $4–6 million with 16–20 employees in 1998, but in retrospect, it is amazing how far we've come when I consider that I started with myself and my computer."

Maybe he hasn't gotten ulcers because he is used to fast growth. Prior to founding The Expert Marketplace, David Gold was a senior manager of an organization that was building a national network of nonprofit centers focused on providing technical consulting services to very small manufacturing companies. He says that everything he learned about the barriers between consultants and companies laid the foundation for starting this business. "The fact that we grew the organization from three centers to one hundred in about three and a half years also exposed me to working in a rapid growth environment," he says.

The only regret Gold has is not getting The Expert Marketplace launched sooner. "Market research can tell you what won't work, but don't ever expect it to tell you what will work," Gold advises. "Do something small and see how it goes instead of trying to engineer the perfect gadget or service," he suggests.

And if he were consulting to a Web-based enterprise, his prime advice would be to "spend less time trying to develop the perfect business plan and more time trying to run small, careful tests in the real market."

For up-to-date information about the success of
The Expert Marketplace
visit
www.StrikingItRich.com

FRAGRANCENET HOMEPAGE

JASON APFEL

FRAGRANCENET

www.fragrancenet.com

Few 21-year-old men would even consider a career in the fragrance industry, but in 1994, Jason Apfel knew he wanted to tap into the growing gift business. "1-800-FLOWERS showed me that people increasingly want a fast and convenient way to order gifts," Apfel recalls. But he also knew he wanted to offer an 800-number alternative to the flowers, balloons, and other standard gift items. Fragrance was his solution—the only half of his business equation that would last. While perfume and cologne were excellent choices, an 800-number as the sales channel was not. Disappointing sales and a relentless advertising investment landed Jason Apfel on the World Wide Web—and put him on his way to becoming the world's largest discount fragrance retailer.

Few businesses can boast that they are the largest and best with absolute certainty, but Apfel can. FragranceNet carries over 1,000 genuine brand names at up to 70% off retail. They will not carry any imitation or knock-offs. Period. "We're not like Amazon.com where we even have close competition," Apfel points out.

But FragranceNet's unique selling proposition goes beyond brand names at discount prices. Apfel's brilliance lies in the fact that he approaches customer service with the same gusto with which he discounts. For example, every order is gift wrapped, whether or not it is a present. Personal message cards on gift orders are always included at no extra charge. During the holidays shipping and handling are free.

If your shipment is not a gift—a personal order—don't be surprised if you find that FragranceNet has included a complimentary gift for yourself tucked inside your shipment, along with a *handwritten* thank-you.

With this careful attention to detail it's no surprise that FragranceNet filled over 6,000 orders in the first six months of business, with each order averaging 1.5 items for a total cost of approximately $60.

On the Web, where customers can price compare in the nanosecond of a mouse click, the bottom line is always a consideration on a commodity item, regardless of world-class customer service. This is a point Apfel constantly considers.

"Our discounts are as good as anyone can give," Apfel emphatically states. "In fact, we make no money on Estee Lauder and Calvin Klein products even though FragranceNet offers only a 2% discount. We discount as much as humanly possible, but these companies keep the tightest lid on their distribution to keep them behind department store counters." As a comparison, Apfel notes, "If we have 100 Halston in the warehouse, we have maybe 10 CK One."

Even though he can't deep discount everything, FragranceNet prices are still so good that their "retail" prices beat many wholesalers. This explains why Apfel consistently receives large orders from a Native American tribe. "They own a large casino on a reservation in Michigan. In their casino mall they have a perfume shop that is essentially stocked by FragranceNet."

FragranceNet's overall secret to steep discounts is attributable to their low overhead. Unlike stores, a Webshop doesn't have to substantially mark up their products to cover their monthly fixed expenses.

FragranceNet averages 2,500 visitors a day, which Apfel conservatively estimates is the equivalent of five terrestrial stores in a well trafficked mall. Now figure the cost to maintain five storefronts, in rent, staff, inventory, and a 24-hour timetable (to compare it to the Web's round-the-clock day) and the comparable costs are astronomical.

Another distinct advantage for FragranceNet is that they don't have to physically carry any inventory. Instead of being locked in stock, the cash keeps flowing.

Apfel was fortunate enough to be able to make an arrangement with a large distributor who, among other personal items, carries one of the world's largest fragrance selections. Located just outside Manhattan near his office, the distributor gives Apfel access to $40 million worth of fragrance. In fact, the distributor's warehouse could be considered FragranceNet's annex.

The company's average of 70 orders a day are fulfilled and shipped directly from the distributor. But this arrangement is a variation of traditional drop shipping because Apfel actually pays for one of the distributor's people to handle his orders exclusively. This FragranceNet helper gift wraps all the orders using supplies FragranceNet pays for, but this fulfillment elf pulls the inventory from the distributor's stock on the premises. All orders are handled in 24 hours. And if you thought this situation couldn't be beat, catch this: The other occupant of the building is UPS.

The greatest benefit of this situation for Apfel is that he can carry every fragrance available, virtually, which now totals about 1,200 products. If the fragrance is being produced on any accountable scale, FragranceNet offers it.

In fact, this extensive inventory is illustrated in FragranceNet's price range. The most expensive product the Web perfumery offers is a one-ounce bottle of Knowing for $285. The least expensive is an Old Spice Gift Set of after shave and cologne for $4.40. His most consistent sellers are Cool Water by Zino Davidoff, Donna Karan's Chaos, and Calvin Klein's CK One.

Since FragranceNet's distributor/supplier has been in business so many years, chances are good that FragranceNet has scents that other stores, online or off, cannot offer (including discontinued items). With an inventory this massive, it's not unusual to have a few cases of old stock. When FragranceNet can reunite a customer with a long lost fragrance, the match can beget a tidy profit.

One day the company received an order from a disabled veteran for his favorite but nearly impossible to find fragrance, British Sterling After Shave Musk. Even though the product has been discontinued for many years, FragranceNet had access to leftover stock, which the vet bought in full, to the tune of $2,000.

To FragranceNet's benefit, perfume is a worldwide commodity. Currently 30–35% of all FragranceNet's visitors and sales are nondomestic. Australia and Japan are the most popular international shipping destinations, but FragranceNet has shipped to various exotic locales such as the Slovak Republic, Bulgaria, and even Pakistan. And always attentive to the customer's needs and concerns, FragranceNet even offers a convenient currency exchange feature on the Website.

An international clientele is something Apfel could never have aspired to with his 800-number-only service and consequently something he could not have serviced with his first Website either.

FragranceNet, as we see it now, is actually a relaunch for Apfel, who first launched the site in August 1996, about 10 months before the incarnation we know now. This first site could best be described as a digital brochure since it only listed their inventory and directed orders offline to their 800-number, a customer's only ordering option.

Despite the lack of zest in this first attempt, FragranceNet Version 1.0 inspired a profound opportunity. Shortly after the launch, an independent investor approached Apfel via e-mail. Less than a month later, the investor wrote a check for $100,000 to start the official FragranceNet site as we see it today.

Building on his experience as an independent publisher in college, Apfel budgeted $50,000 for the implementation and promotion of his forthcoming interactive site. Through judicious planning and budgeting, Apfel had already raised part of his capital before the investor even made his offer. So the $100,000 investment, although profoundly appreciated, was only minimally utilized. With steady caution, Apfel began implementing his strategy for his second full-fledged entry into the electronic commerce arena.

"The best advice we received, " Apfel remembers, "was to build a Website that was state of the art in database management and to allow any of our staff the ability to manipulate the Webstore on a minute-by-minute, hour-by-hour, day-by-day basis."

With that idea in mind, Apfel set out to research the top e-commerce sites in search of dynamic, but cost-efficient, Web design. Basing his criteria on functionality and ease of use, Apfel contacted several developers before making his final decision.

Working side by side with the developer seven days a week for almost three months, the Website he dreamed of building was officially launched. His hands-on stance really paid off, as FragranceNet's redesign came in at $40,000—$10,000 under its $50,000 budget.

Apfel's prudent use of caution in budgeting and planning was also valuable in the preliminary stages of operation. With initially low expectations, the small company was pleasantly surprised. Before June of 1997, sales generated by the static Website were pancake flat, averaging a paltry $480 monthly. However, from the launch of the FragranceNet 2.0, featuring real-time inventory, secure online ordering, and a sophisticated search device, FragranceNet has seen an average growth rate of 25% monthly through the latter part of 1997 when growth exploded into triple digits with December 1997 revenues exceeding $80,000.

During the first month after the launch of the interactive Website, Apfel spent his entire day monitoring the Website and troubleshooting content by incorporating customer feedback. The initial critiques ranged from color problems to requests for more product photographs. Apfel wisely reconfigured.

Perhaps more impactful is that, from the beginning, Apfel applied the maxim that the customer is always right, along with the caveat that every Internet user is a potential customer. "This includes all businesses and all individuals, which is why

I carry women's and men's products, as well as gifts and specials for holidays, birthdays, and anniversaries."

With FragranceNet's continued emergence as a preeminent Web enterprise with a worldwide customer base, it is no surprise that Apfel's attention to customer service would become increasingly more difficult. To this day, it's a perpetual challenge for him to keep up with technical advances while maintaining the site's integrity and ever increasing traffic. Even though he spends more time on the Website now after the initial growth, he still devotes most of his day to phone and e-mail.

Amazingly, out of the average 60 e-mails FragranceNet receives daily, Apfel manages to answer 90% himself. Over 80% of these missives are specific fragrance requests, particularly for older fragrances. "My mom is 80 years old" begins one typical e-mail, "and she wore this fragrance for 60 years. Do you carry it?"

Requests like these are also indicative of people's favorable impressions of FragranceNet as the de facto scent store, concluding that if FragranceNet can't get it, perhaps nobody can. This kind of awareness has contributed to FragranceNet's phenomenal growth.

Even with 2,500 visitors daily, expanding FragranceNet's customer base is a continual challenge. Despite the lack of serious competition, Apfel still concentrates on marketing and other growth initiatives.

Advertising, a standard growth generator for most online businesses, hasn't pulled well for FragranceNet. In the last quarter of 1997, the company bought the keywords "perfume," "cologne," "fragrance," and their plurals on the search engine Alta Vista. They paid $50 per 1,000 impressions (or CPM). Anytime these keywords were input as a search, the FragranceNet banner was placed on the results listing page. FragranceNet pulled the test three-quarters of the way through at the 60,000 impression mark. Although they initially got a 12% click-through rate, which is considered outstanding, over the period of a few months it dropped to 4%, a more standard figure. With a sell-through rate of 3% on these click-throughs, the average cost per sale ran about $20. Even with an average 50% mark-up and 40% average profit margin, there was still a negative return on the investment.

While paid advertising on search engines hasn't contributed to FragranceNet's bottom line, search engines are still the company's best source of traffic. This high-quality traffic, however, is not the result of searches, but of editorial. FragranceNet's attention to detail and satisfied customers has paid off in the form of a prime editorial listing in the shopping guides on Yahoo and Lycos, which, not surprisingly, are FragranceNet's best source of new business.

It's important to note that over half of FragranceNet's visitors come from America Online and account for 30% of the company's orders. The irony is that AOL offers a fragrance store, but, as Apfel points out, "Since the store has to pay to be there—and it's really expensive to be on AOL—they have to sell everything at retail prices. We are so far superior to their pricing it's unbelievable. We even beat their daily specials with our normal prices."

FragranceNet also offers daily specials, but they don't produce much of a sales surge for the featured product. "It's hard to talk people into a fragrance. In the same way, people generally wouldn't buy any personal care product simply because it's 40% off retail."

While the specials are not particularly sizzling, the random drawing contests for free product are hot, with 10% of his visitors entering daily. Apfel uses this information to build his database, which in just the first few months swelled to 8,000 names.

FragranceNet's Partners Program has been equally successful. In exchange for showcasing advertising banners throughout their Website, Website partners such as MasterCard, Yahoo, and Virtual Emporium get a small percentage of the gross purchases made by people they have referred to the site. This risk-neutral proposition is a favorite for Apfel. "I love it because we only pay for completed sales." Currently these transactions account for 10% of the company's revenue.

Ironically, another 10% of FragranceNet's total sales come from the analog world via phone. Based on recommendations from seasoned surfers, people who do not have Internet access order directly using FragranceNet's toll-free number, 800-98-PERFUME (the basis of their first Website). These offline orders may be his ultimate sign of success and indicative of the breadth of customers his service appeals to.

Even a cursory glance at FragranceNet's server logs tells us a lot about his customers who, based on the statistics of his site, can probably be best categorized as average consumers.

Unlike most Webstores who see sales peak during week days—presumably while people surf at work—FragranceNet's biggest selling day is Saturday. Furthermore, while peak sales times on many sites coincide with business day lunch breaks, FragranceNet sees a steady flow of customers from 9:00 A.M. through midnight. Rounding out this scenario is a customer base that is 48% female, 52% male.

Given these averages, FragranceNet is a viable resource for information related to online buying trends. It's encouraging to note how well his customer base is adapting to online ordering, a rush Apfel feels is related to secure server technology.

FragranceNet offers every payment option imaginable, including ordering online but completing payment offline via phone and fax, which is done in about 5% of all orders. Another 5–10% of their orders are paid by check or money order. To ensure customer confidence once an order is placed, a detailed confirmation is sent via e-mail within 10 seconds.

Like so many people who have taken advantage of the Internet's incipient emergence, Apfel and his company are excited by the overwhelming possibilities of electronic commerce. "We see a geometric, not arithmetic, increase in Internet commerce," Apfel expounds. "And therefore, an increase in our sales volume. If the pundits are correct, and we realize only a small fraction of the anticipated increase in e-commerce, we will be very satisfied. In actuality, we expect to get a large portion of increased e-commerce."

Despite the consistent increase in sales, Apfel is constantly improving his business. His ideas for future enhancements include offering his customers real-time order tracking and featuring more content in the form of articles of interest to fragrance shoppers. "Until browsers learn to smell, our best content is the information we provide concerning type of scent, recommended use, and other fragrance facts," Apfel laments.

Reflecting on his two-year tenure, Apfel's only regret is not going to the Web sooner. He admits that he feels he wasted a lot of time and money on his 800-number endeavor. However, now that FragranceNet has an astounding staff of five employees, Apfel's best advice is to "surround yourself with talented, experienced people. This is the most important time- and cost-saving measure."

If one had to summarize FragranceNet's formula for success, it could be Apfel's early vision that "fragrance was an entire market not being serviced." "Plus you have men," he notes, "And flowers are not traditionally sent to men."

By combining the ultimate retailing environment of the Web with an untapped market, Apfel has found his raison d'etre, a mission that includes reminding the world to "send a gift that lasts."

For up-to-date information about the success of
FragranceNet
visit
www.StrikingItRich.com

FREE GAMES

play

register

help

winners

lounge

1996

Greetings from Gamesville

Home of THE BINGO! ZONE®

FREE!

NO DOWNLOADS. NO PLUG-INS. EVER.

MORE THAN $237,000 CASH PRIZES AWARDED!

PICTURAMA

Multimedia Celebrity Trivia

NEW MULTIPLAYER CARD GAME

ACEYDEUCEY

Predict the Emmy Awards. WIN $1000 CASH!

Crystal Ball

S T E V E N   K A N E
S T U A R T   R O S E M A N
J O H N   F U R S E

GAMESVILLE™

www.gamesville.com

Few Websites can make this claim: "Our bank statements are so massive they have to be delivered by UPS." It should be no surprise that reconciling this monthly package is a full-time job, but the beleaguered bookkeeper is not poring over pages listing deposits. On the contrary, she is settling canceled checks, more than 3,500 per month. The lucky endorsers? The Website's visitors.

Welcome to Gamesville™, where people play free games and win cash prizes. Alas, this is not a casino, it's a Web game show. Advertiser-supported. Free to play. And in the vein of Jeopardy and Wheel of Fortune, a money generator not just for the contestants, but the company that produces it as well.

Gamesville is a unique online gaming venture. The games are large-scale, multiplayer, and rendered in real time. Although this proposition may sound derivative, Gamesville is unique. According to the company, Gamesville is the only site that offers cash prizes and, as such, has the most prize winners. And because all Gamesville games are free to play and the players never wager, bet, risk, or lose anything, it is *not* gambling.

Although these details are notable, the most profound fact is that Gamesville requires no downloads, no special software, no special hardware, and no particular browser.

We offer "yesterday's technology today" explains Steve Kane, 35, cofounder of Gamesville (along with Stuart Roseman and John Furse). And while Gamesville's backend technology is state of the art, they use it constantly to cater to the lowest technology denominator so that anyone who wants to play can.

As of the beginning of 1998, Gamesville had over 700,000 registered users (with 1,300 additions every day), playing their two premiere games, BingoZone™, their luck game, and Picturama™, a skill-based diversion.

"The object of winning a Gamesville game is to be the first player to successfully assemble the game clues as needed in that particular game," Kane explains.

The BingoZone is executed as you would imagine. A new ball is available every 20 seconds. Visitors click a "continue" button to get it. Using a mouse, you check off from your bingo cards any balls shown in the New Balls and Balls in Play listings. When you are ready to make a claim you click bingo. The first valid bingo claim wins. If you wrongfully click Bingo more than six times in a game, you are suspended.

Picturama is a trivia game. The object is to be the first player to assemble the pieces of a picture (usually of a celebrity) and correctly guess a scrambled word or phrase.

According to internal logs, each day Gamesville gets 40,000 players. A player count occurs each time a registrant logs in. The same person logging in twice counts as two players. Regardless, the average visitor spends an average of 27 minutes on the site. Bingo games take about 8–10 minutes to play and Picturama lasts about 7 minutes. Each is offered 45 times in an 18-hour period, but never concurrently.

"We do not run them simultaneously by design," says Kane. "We move people back and forth between games, with an intermission. We do not want them to go immediately from game to game to game." During intermission, ads might include a sponsor's own Website, special splash pages, Shockwave, Java, anything the advertisers want. "Our average intermission is two to four minutes—enough time to encourage interaction with sponsors, but not enough to lose them from the site. We send them out in frames to keep them posted as to when the next game is starting."

Advertising is the basis of Gamesville's $1-million-plus revenues, and their advertisers love them. Repped by Cox Interactive sales, Gamesville offers a mix of interstitial ads, banner ads, and newsletter advertising. They consistently attract major advertising dollars from such big players as Sony, Polygram, JC Penney, Microsoft, AT&T, and Publishers' Clearing House, along with more than 20 other high-profile companies. These sponsors pay a base minimum of $20–30 for each thousand impressions (CPM) with premiums, targeting and other considerations usually adding an additional $10–20 to the base rate.

Unlike many online publishers who avoid any mix of advertising and editorial for ethical and journalistic reasons, Gamesville welcomes it.

"In terms of advertising, there is no separation between church and state," says Kane. "We have no problem integrating the advertising right into the game. For example, during a Mr. Bean movie promotion, we had Mr. Bean's face in the center of the bingo card, another figure of him peering around the card along with a Mr. Bean banner at the top of page, and a special Mr. Bean game-over screen."

This Bean mania is so well integrated that it becomes part of the game and hence is never considered intrusive by the players. "Online games and game shows are a perfect marketing device. A neutral space that consumers and marketers are glad to be in," Kane says. Besides, after all the Bean exposure, visitors are more apt to take a look at the Mr. Bean site. "The game-over screen is premium real estate because, at the end of the game, where are they going to go?" Kane notes. "The click-through rate is high, as much as 7 to 10%."

Furthermore, Gamesville advertisers get targeting opportunities and reliable user demographics because the contestants are motivated by the cash prizes to give accurate information when they register. This accuracy is proven by Gamesville's low returned check rate. Of the 25,000 plus checks Gamesville has issued since April 1996 (one check per game for the 25,000 games played), "only 1 to 2% have been returned by the post office," says Kane. "And about half of these go back out. Someone usually has moved or made a typo and didn't know it," he says. "We always put the check in a file just in case. Usually 10 days later we get an e-mail asking about a check, look in the file and there it is. We also send it with the previous canceled enveloped to show a good faith effort. The total number of dead checks in our file right now from the beginning of our enterprise is about 600 or about 2.5%. Dead dollars are approximately $17,000 or about 10%."

This small returned check rate attests to the cleanliness of the Gamesville database. In addition to their name, address, and telephone number, registrants are also asked to provide their date of birth, occupation, and education information.

"This is loved by our sponsors who know they are getting what they pay for," says Kane. "We actively market to our players to keep their data up-to-date for prize considerations. It's a quid pro quo and that's part of the tradeoff." (Gamesville never sells or otherwise leverages this information to advertisers or uses it in any way not directly affiliated with the site.) Registrants have the option of receiving "special notice offers" of which 95% do, realizing that "yes" is the default option. For the moment, this list is used only to distribute the monthly e-newsletter, *The Gamesville Times*.

Because the database is so immaculate, Gamesville can segment their audience into custom-defined groups matching an individual sponsor's criteria. For example, Gamesville offers accurate, geographically targeted advertising.

"The U.S. Lottery is legal in only 34 states. So if you are from Alabama, for example, you won't see a U.S. Lottery banner ad." And the U.S. Lottery won't be wasting impressions on eyeballs that cannot take advantage of its offer.

In the future this geographic parsing will also serve Gamesville for time-based ads. "Theoretically NBC could buy in a time zone, let's say 30 minutes before a certain show is about to air based on their location." And while Gamesville does not have the traffic yet for mass impressions, the environment they are developing is extremely valuable.

Some players, however, are so far out of the loop geographically that they don't fit any criteria. While 95% of the visitors are from North America, the remaining 5% represent 65 countries including Serbia, the United Kingdom, Australia, and India.

While Gamesville can't really leverage this international audience, the value of these players is in the fun, novelty, and excitement for the other contestants—knowing they are competing with someone in Sweden or Argentina. "From a business point of view, currently this 5% is of no value," admits Kane. "In fact, some sponsors ask us to filter non-North American players."

While precise addressing data is helpful in filtering, it is also a boon for offers on Gamesville that require offline fulfilment. "Prodigy advertised free starter kits. So we prefilled in their address information based on the visitors' registration information." Kane says. "We got a mixed reaction. Some found it Big Brotherish, others thought they were automatically being signed up, while some simply loved the convenience."

Despite their incredible success now, Gamesville initially struggled to convince advertisers of the benefits of their entertainment initiative. "One of our biggest risks was putting together something that required selling mass market games to ad agencies and marketing as suitable content for sponsorship," Kane explains. "We do not fit the conventional image of computer games—teenage boys shooting and nuking things to death—yet we do not fit any other content categories such as sports, finance, news, and travel. However, we believe that our games will be to the Web what sitcoms are to TV."

Gamesville is familiar with the benefits of advertising from the opposite perspective as they spend money on the medium as well. To date their biggest success with search engine advertising has been on Lycos, where they bought the keyword "games."

"We try to keep a presence on an ongoing basis. We don't buy a bunch of ad banners for a week. We've bought 1 million over the course of six months," Kane reveals. "Our click-through rates are typically 1 to 2%. But we don't measure just on click-throughs because we understand the value of branding. Clicks are fantastic—each one is my friend—but we are constantly creating an aura for our brands. I don't consider one impression wasted!"

In addition to ads on search engines, Gamesville banners can be found on complementary entertainment sites such as Entertainment Asylum, The Hub, Hollywood Online, The Bingo Bugle, and Gambling.com. The advertising results of these sites are the same as those of the search engines.

With respect to their budget, Gamesville has an unconventional formula. "We spent almost as much in advertising in 1997 as we have given away in prize money," Kane says. "But one must remember that we consider prize money part of our marketing budget."

From the beginning, Kane understood that the best way to market on the Net was to integrate every marketing option available. While search engines and high-profile game sites ensure a certain amount of exposure, he also understands that the game lovers themselves—via word of keyboards—could be his best source of traffic.

With this notion, Kane began hiring college students to launch his campaign. Based in Boston, with a college student population exceeding 250,000, Gamesville had no problem putting together a qualified pool of interns for the task. The job description was simple. Surf the Web ferreting sites whose audience is compatible with Gamesville. If the site is related to gaming, trivia, bingo, or other compatible topic, the site owner would receive a personal e-mail—considered a "cold e-mail," not "spam" because it's a personalized message sent conscientiously—describing Gamesville and requesting a link. (These requested links are not reciprocal. Gamesville was not offering a return link to them as well.)

"We've had a uniformly positive response," states Kane. "Our e-mails are from a real person with a real e-mail address. We have sent probably 10,000 of these in the last two years." To date, Gamesville has over 4,000 inbound links, most of which are likely the result of this personal contact. The success of this one-to-one marketing campaign is not subject to opinion, but to fact. When new registrants are asked how they heard about Gamesville, a whopping 40% cite "word of mouth" or "friend." Because these options are far down on the drop list from which they select, it means that they can't be chosen by accident. This proves Kane's initial theory: "The Internet is very suitable for grass-roots marketing."

Kane also bases his success on what he refers to as the "virtuous circle." "The more players we have, the more sponsors. The more sponsors, the more prizes. The more prizes, the more players. This model seems to be holding true."

With more than 25,000 winners as of the beginning of 1998 and a total of $170,000 given away as prize money, Kane also has a legion of satisfied Gamesville players spreading the word. The checks may be small, on the average of $3, but cash is cash. The top Gamesville prize is $20, which is tendered once a day in each Bingo and Picturama game. The lowest is $2 and that is awarded 17 times a day. The balance of the winning amounts fluctuates, averaging $4. While it may take a long time to accumulate sizable winnings, some people come close. Picturama's all-time-winning contestant has amassed $931. The BingoZone's biggest winner to date has cashed checks worth $116.22 (35 wins total for which Kane estimates that she must have played hundreds and hundreds of times to get a figure this high).

Kane also illustrates that the odds of winning are easy to figure out. "At least one player wins every game and since players play on a level playing field, the odds of winning any particular Gamesville game are essentially determined by the number of players in that particular game." For example, he continues, "if you are one of 900 players in a game, you have a one-in-900 chance of winning that game. Yes, it really is that simple. And Gamesville games always display on the screen the number of players in a particular game."

The winnings from each game are paid in U.S. dollars, which sometimes presents a problem for international players. "Often we get e-mail from non-North America winners asking if we can hold their winnings on account," says Kane. "Often their bank levies a service charge that exceeds the token sum.

We can't hold the funds for them because it would turn us into a bank. Nonetheless, we get at least a half a dozen thank-you's a day from all over the world."

Not only does Gamesville pay, they pay promptly, further endearing themselves to their players. "Our pledge is that checks are mailed in less than five days after a win. In practice we issue checks and mail checks twice a week, cutting checks on Mondays and Fridays. So it usually takes three business days for them to receive their prize."

This attention to prize fulfillment has been a hallmark since the launch of the $200,000 venture in April 1996. "My partners and I saw a unique opportunity on the Internet for a small company to have a large presence in the media business," says Kane. "When we grow up, we want to be the King World of the Internet."

Originally called The Bingo Zone, ironically the choice of game to launch with was the last decision they made. "We wanted to do large arena multiplayer games that we would develop, but we were reluctant to launch with a game no one had ever heard of. We looked around for something to fit this paradigm of a large arena game and there are many, such as Monopoly and bridge. But we only found one truly large—meaning not four players—and that was Bingo." In October 1997, they added Picturama and changed The Bingo Zone to Gamesville.

During peak times, 7 P.M. through midnight Eastern, Gamesville hosts up to 1,600 simultaneous visitors. Their systems can handle up to 4,000 in any one game. On the average, Bingo gets 850 people per game and Picturama gets 150. Gamesville runs continuously from 10 A.M. Eastern to 4 A.M. Eastern, with no current plans to go round-the-clock. "We're going to stay with an 18-hour day for two reasons," Kane says. "Our engineers begged for a window to tinker with the site, and, secondly, it allows us to limit prize expenses when the traffic is the least."

As expected, some people play as much as possible, but Gamesville limits visitors to three wins in any 24-hour time frame. While this policy applies to all their games, it emanated from Picturama because it is a game of skill.

"We can really get the entertainment trivia savants," says Kane. "We started getting letters from people questioning the players who keep dominating the games. The fun factor is greatly reduced. The clocks starts at the first win. If your first win is at 10 A.M., then you can start again at 10 A.M. the next day to play for cash. [Three-time winners can continue to play, but cannot continue to collect prize money.] We've never had a single complaint about this policy."

Because Picturama is a skill game there is no room for cheating, but people have questioned Bingo. Kane says his standard response is, "How would we benefit by being rigged? Our advertisers and players would not be happy, and we would spend the same amount on prizes. Why would we ever risk not paying out $3 and being called a fraud and never have an advertiser again?"

"While it may not seem obvious, there is no advantage to playing Gamesville games using any particular hardware or Internet connection," Kane adds. "The Gamesville main computer makes available new game clues at the same pace for everyone (for example, one new bingo ball every 20 seconds), no matter whether you are playing on a 486 with a 14.4 modem or on the best workstation with a dedicated T1 line.

"If you request game clues or bingo balls by clicking on a 'continue' button a tad slower than the next player, no big deal. Every time you request game clues, the server sends you all the clues that have been put into play in your game since the last time you requested clues. So you can never miss a clue, regardless of whether your computer is slow, average, or fast. In Bingo, after a player has called 'bingo' but before the game is over, players get an additional 60 seconds in which to check their cards to see if they, too, have bingo. This, of course, is standard procedure in normal, everyday bingo."

If you are a consistent winner in Gamesville, you get an added bonus: a job offer. "The proposition shows up as a screen after the fourth win in a 24-hour period. Winners are informed that they have exceeded the win limit but 'we need brilliant people like you on our staff! Please contact geniuses@gamesville.com for information on career opportunities.'"

Approaching consistent winners is not Gamesville's only recruitment strategy. About once every three months someone tries to hook up a machine to play the games automatically, and, while they really can't, Gamesville is properly impressed with the people who try.

"Attempting computer play happens occasionally and we immediately offer the contestants a job," says Kane. "These people have demonstrated the interest, affinity, and skill for what we need. A good engineer takes things apart and puts them back together." Although no one has accepted one of their offers via Picturama or a hack attempt, Kane states that they "haven't gotten any hostility either." Kane has also noticed that these hackers tend to be grad students in engineering. "Graduate students make the best hackers because they have the time and access to the facilities to hack."

Students also account for a notable chunk of Gamesville's demographic, adding up to about 23% of total players. About 76% of all players have "some college or better." The gender breakdown is 58% female whose average age is 34, with a slightly younger average for men at 30. Fifty-four percent of all players are married.

According to Kane, hiring well has been critical to Gamesville's success. The company now has 11 employees and all of their technology is proprietary. They built their systems from scratch. While their focus is on their flagship site, they will license their technology and eventually move into content syndication as their venture matures.

The proprietary nature of the system and their astounding 700% growth rate makes them a prime target for companies wanting to buy into Web gaming revenues. "We won't disclose the figures of the offers," states Kane. "We haven't yet been approached by a major media company such as America Online and, to a degree, we are relieved because we wouldn't want to face that decision because we do not want to part with our company."

And what about companies not yet online who could eventually usurp their well earned premium positioning? "We are lucky that big giants move slowly. The guys who can crush us haven't because they haven't caught up, but that won't last forever."

HORSENET HOMEPAGE

Tuesday, August 04   Horse Photos by Gabrielle Boiselle

Welcome to the Internet Community for Horse People!

**Be sure to check the HomePage on each visit, and also go here
to see what's NEW on HorseNet.**

"To make a perfect horseman, three things are requisite. First, to know
how and when to help your horse. Secondly, how and when to correct
him. And thirdly, how and when to praise him and to make much of
him."

Thomas Blundeville in 1560

Visit these special areas of HorseNet	Fill out your e-mail profile and become a member of HorseNet!
Today's News Current up-to-date news **News Archives** News prior to two weeks	*All American Quarter Horse*

RICHARD LASATER
SALLY LASATER

HORSENET

www.horsenet.com

Pop quiz: Which of the following would you forego if you owned a for-profit Website?

a. Giving away site elements, such as images and programming code.

b. Appealing to an audience of which 85% are still *not* online.

c. Linking to every one of your competitors' sites.

d. All of the above.

Universally held beliefs dictate answer "d." But this is a world view of no value to Richard Lasater, 32, Director of Internet Services for HorseNet, who is bucking conventional wisdom and incorporating all of the above—with stunning results.

"We link to all our competitors, though they don't all link back," he explains. "I feel that the number of people who visit is the same for all the larger horse sites. It's really a matter of how often they come back."

To date HorseNet has never turned down a link request as long as the content of the requester is equestrian-related. "Our job is to provide useful information to our visitors. That is our editorial criterion, which means part of our job is to provide links," he explains.

Even though HorseNet links out to their competition—the in-bound links to HorseNet exceed 2,000, the result of answer a, giving away elements of the site.

The latter practice is a spiritual remnant of HorseNet's early emergence on the Net, when the din resounded in favor of community versus independence. For example, HorseNet allowed people to use their now famous "hoofprints in sand" background for their own nonprofit pages. "Most sites would freak out if this happened," says Lasater. "The upside is that we required them to link back to us from their homepage, which helps drive visitors." Ditto for images that HorseNet is no longer using. The bottom line of Lasater's philosophy is "if we can give it away free, we do!"

Little about HorseNet is traditional, including their business model. HorseNet is a true hybrid site, whose revenues are sourced from three areas: content, transaction, and ancillary services.

When HorseNet launched in December 1994 for $500, Lasater counted 28 equine-related Websites. Today he says there are thousands. In an average day they welcome over 4,000 visitors, half of which are female between the ages of 13 and 50. HorseNet, he notes, is "first and foremost an Internet community for horse people."

HorseNet has stayed ahead of the crowd through useful content that is updated several times a day, merged with pleasing design, brilliantly serving the needs of every niche of horse enthusiast, including novice and professional riders, horse owners, and horse lovers worldwide. The site even appeals to people who have never touched a horse.

"One of the things I like best about HorseNet is bringing horses to people who don't have one or can't afford them," says Lasater. "I design a lot of interactive stuff for this crowd like our chat rooms."

Meanwhile most visitors divide their time equally among all of HorseNet's content areas, with the news area and message boards just slightly ahead of the rest. Their no-charge classified ads are also extremely popular. "We have always considered the classifieds to be content," says Lasater. "That's why they are free. We bunch them together like a newspaper does to make them fun to read."

Lasater can offer free classifieds partly because the posting process is completely automated, as in most of the content on HorseNet, including the submission of horse shows and events, show results, and news releases. Because of this automatic implementation, Lasater likes to point out that "the actual users are building the site 24 hours a day."

While the visitors are creating the content, most areas are supported through advertising and sponsorships, which account for about 40% of HorseNet's revenues. A 144 × 144 pixel banner on the HorseNet homepage (equivalent to 2 inches per side) costs from $200 to $500 (depending on page location). The higher up the page, the greater the cost. HorseNet also offers "run of site" banners, which can cost as little as $75 a month with a two-month minimum. Sponsorship of key sections, such as veterinarian information and the HorseNet events calendar, begins at $2,000. On the average HorseNet has 40 sponsors at one time. Some of their most successful supporters include Vita-Flex Nutrition (equestrian supplements and vitamins), Norfields (magnetic therapy products), and Buckeye Nutrition.

In addition to creating content, another of HorseNet's revenue segments comes from building and hosting equestrian Websites, which account for over 20% of their business. Most of these HorseNet-generated sites become microsites, linked from within HorseNet and utilizing the HorseNet URL such as www.horsenet.com/nameofcompany. HorseNet has built over 100 of these microsites.

Microsite buyers and ad buyers have a great advantage with HorseNet because the company knows how to market equestrian sites and services. And Lasater charges for their expertise accordingly. "Our average hosting and other costs are about $160 a month, six times more than a local ISP," notes Lasater. But people are getting much more service and that includes a marketing plan. We offer marketing as a loss leader to entice advertising. If someone is going to spend $5,000 on ads on our site we will design a print campaign to go along with it."

Despite these steeper-than-average rates, Lasater regrets not having established more equitable fees from the beginning, billing at least two to three times higher for site-related services such as Website production and updating because of demand and labor intensity.

In addition to content sponsorships, advertising, and Web development, HorseNet also offers auxiliary services that straddle these categories. For example, anyone—business or consumer—can have a HorseNet e-mail address (name@horsenet.com) for $9 a month. Another revenue source comes from chat services for businesses that want to benefit from the interactive medium but are either not technically skilled enough to do it on their own or prefer to farm it out.

Chat services are sold by the hour with prices starting at $300 per (HorseNet offers substantial price breaks on long-term contacts). The chat is technically moderated by a HorseNet employee and occurs on the hosting company's HorseNet microsite.

For example, a horse vitamin supplement company integrated chats into their marketing plan with great success. The goal was to get vets to their site. Lasater first suggested that they advertise in veterinarian magazines announcing that on the first Monday of each month they were offering a hosted chat. The first hour of these chats is spent with an expert who answers technical questions similar to a conference roundtable, with the second hour for whatever topics the veterinarians would like to discuss as a forum.

In the case of this supplement company, the number of vets who attend vary from 10 to 100, with an average of 40. The number of attendees, Lasater says, is in complete proportion to the amount of advertising. The total cost for the vitamin manufacturer, with advertising, can run $1,000 per chat event. But it's an expense that Lasater insists must be amortized to understand the overwhelming value.

"Think of the cost for this same supplement company to send out a rep to each of these 40 people and then factor in that they are getting two hours of these vets' time."

The third section in the HorseNet revenue triumvirate is transaction. HorseNet carries over 2,000 products such as saddles, tack, nutritional supplements, clothing, and toys (including rocking horses, naturally). They have filled over 5,000 orders since they came online with an average profit of 40%. Their first order was for around $150 for three instructional videotapes, an amount that mirrors their typical order today—although they sometimes field an exceptionally large order, like the one for 750,000 pounds of chicken feed.

While HorseNet offers pricey items such as $1,500 saddles, Lasater finds overall that products that don't need to be touched beforehand do well. "Things like boots and coats, don't sell," he warns. "It's not the right medium, unless you are willing to sell cheap."

He points out that it's easier for HorseNet to sell 500 equestrian horse planners at $19 than one saddle for $1,500. "At this level of saddle, people prefer to buy in person at a show or something so they can try it out." Furthermore, 75% of HorseNet's product sales are to women, who are predispositioned to shop in person, especially for touchy-feely products such as clothing and tack.

Not surprisingly, then, HorseNet's biggest selling product category is a commodity product: videos, which are available for both sale and rental and which account for 25% of their product revenue.

This video microsite is called EquiVid and is owned by the HorseNet folks. It has the distinction of being the largest supplier of videotapes about horses and horse people in the country, with over 1,400 titles in its library, which, as the microsite's name implies, focuses exclusively on horses and horse people. Their biggest selling categories are dressage and educational/instruction by recognized professionals.

These 45–60-minute videos range in price from $14.95 to $70.00, with an average of $30. Rentals start at $10 for 1–2 tapes and $8 each for orders starting at three tapes or more for a period of 14 days from receipt of the tapes. Shipping is included in rental prices.

One of the reasons that the videotape rentals are so profitable for EquiVid is that there is a one-time lifetime membership fee of $40. Renters eventually recover this initiation with Equi-Bucks, a $1 credit given for each rental that can be applied to future video purchases or rentals. As of the second quarter of 1998, they had over 10,000 members.

One of the great benefits to both HorseNet and the renters is the "try before you buy" proposition inherent in the renting policy. If a customer wants to keep a video, EquiVid applies the rental price and bills for the balance (or the customer can return the previewed copy for an unscreened version with no penalty). This risk-neutral proposition shows that 20% of renters purchase.

In terms of sales, EquiVid's highest traffic area by far is their Video Grab Bag clearance area, which features overstocks and time-sensitive material (such as Olympic tapes). This is where visitors find videos at deep discounts, often up to 50%. Originally set up to get rid of excess, sometimes Lasater will move a title into the Grab Bag area to reposition it. For example, if they have a tape they are going to reduce by 10% from $20 to $18, Lasater will simply put it in the Grab Bag at $18, instead of showing it at a discount in the main sales area.

"These tapes sell well because people stumble upon it and think 'wow.' It's impulsive," says Lasater. "I think that people are still scared to make purchases online and the grab bag is like a garage sale. At least that's the emphasis we put behind the page."

The online purchasing wariness Lasater refers to is quantified by their most popular ordering method, their 800-number (aptly branded as 800-USA-WHOA), in which 50% of their orders are handled. This high phone rate doesn't bother Lasater, who notes that sales generated from the Web result in a lower return rate of 2% (versus 5% for their catalog). Their repeat customer rate, he estimates, is as high as 50%.

The fact that EquiVid is their transaction standout doesn't surprise Lasater or his mother, Sally. In fact it was Sally Lasater, 54, who originally thought up HorseNet.

"I first started thinking about going online when I realized that the Web would be the biggest marketing medium since

television," Sally Lasater remembers. "I wanted to more economically market HorseNet's tapes to consumers because direct mail had become prohibitively costly."

Sally and Richard soon realized that, instead of launching
EquiVid as a stand-alone enterprise, they would be better
served by being part of something bigger. In this case it meant
aligning with well branded companies in the equestrian community, businesses with hefty advertising budgets who would
attract the much needed visitors such as Equitana USA and
Premier Horse Network.

Their approach was simple and highly effective. "We practically gave away the Website design and development to entice
these high-profile companies to live on HorseNet," says Sally
Lasater. And just as they had hoped, this approach created substantial traffic for HorseNet/EquiVid without any advertising or
promotional expense, not only because the companies advertised the URL, but because instead of using a vanity domain
(www.CompanyName.com) they used a cobranded domain in
http//www.horsenet.com/CompanyName.

Because of these domain-inspired relationships, the Horse-
Net domain name has played a much larger role in the history
of this Website than it does in most others. In fact, HorseNet
has almost become a generic term. "In our industry, most online
horse-stuff is now called 'horsenet,'" says Richard Lasater. "Now
there is also horsenet.co.uk, horsenet.com.br, horsenet.com.au,
icelandichorsenet.com, and a lot that spring up in the U.S. that
we have to enforce trademark rights with. It's just a great
name." Sensing they had a great name, they filed for a trademark and service mark on it immediately upon launching.

In the years since, HorseNet has established its own brand
identity that has resulted in powerful marketing relationships,
most notably horse expos, which are huge profit makers and
traffic generators for HorseNet. "Our best months have always
coincided with marketing copromotions for large expos," says
Lasater.

According to Lasater, there are six horse expos a year at-
tended by up to 80,000 people each. HorseNet has made their
best copromotion deals with these larger events. "We have a

booth. We give Internat labs and seminars, but the greatest benefit is in the exposure," says Lasater.

He always trades out as much as possible with an average value of what he offers between $3,000 and $7,000 per event. On the flip side, Lasater estimates that a large expo will spend up to a $1 million in advertising, and, as a sponsor, HorseNet is usually part of it. Even if HorseNet's logo is not in the ads, the worse-case scenario showcases the events' URL, which is www.horsenet.com/ExpoName. Unfortunately for Lasater the expos are waking up. They realize the value of what they were trading and instead now prefer to have a vanity domain and hire HorseNet to design and implement the site. Ironically, however, the expos still request that Horsenet teach Internet seminars, for which they pay the company $500–2,000, along with a booth and other promotional perks to round out the deal.

While expos give HorseNet a ton of exposure to their core market, they are also a big believer in advertising on their own, especially in print magazines. They also barter for banner ad space on Horsenet. "Don't buy a full page ad. All you need is a URL. You can even use classifieds," he advises.

In tradeouts with other Websites, Lasater warns other Website owners to pay attention to the value of what they are offering. "Our site is very popular and the most expensive equestrian site to advertise on. So the ratio in a banner ad swap may be 3 to 1, but we deliver the impressions."

Even though Lasater is proadvertising he can't overlook the benefits of publicity. "We got our first big rush after an article in *Practical Horseman Magazine.* It wasn't a huge article, but we saw a 75% increase in traffic. Our sales in business Websites jumped 50% after a mention in a trade journal," he continues. "Our goal is to get new people, and to get previous visitors back, and magazines are effective for getting the newbies."

Search engines are the other strong referring mechanism for HorseNet. Since HorseNet has been online longer than most other equestrian sites, they naturally have more content indexed. To ensure that search results could convert to a meaningful click-through, Lasater *never* removes a page. This means that even old index entries will still bring people in. But he has one more secret that makes even better use of the search engines: making sure his classified ads are indexed as well. "This is great for keyword searches," he reveals. "If someone does a search for something superspecific like a Haflinger pony, this may be the only place on the site where they are mentioned."

While Lasater knows that Alta Vista and AOL's NetFind bring him the most visitors, he doesn't spend too much time analyzing referring percentages. "We don't consider this important information," he asserts. "What we consider important is if people weren't coming from a particular search engine. This tips us off that our pages are either not being indexed correctly or not being indexed at all."

Search engines play an important role in delivering international Web traffic since these visitors are less likely to be exposed to HorseNet's offline marketing. About 15% are non-U.S.–based, with the originating countries including Canada, Germany, Australia, Russia, Japan, and the Middle East.

"One of our first orders was from a family in Dubai for $700 worth of video tapes. Although we have had larger orders, it was our first large overseas order," says Lasater. "The fact that someone so remote, so far away, had just become our customer really impressed me. It reminded me that I live on a very small planet."

While HorseNet would like to expand more internationally—especially in Germany where horses are not a niche market—the enterprise is hindered by a dearth of talent, which limits their expansion domestically as well.

With the explosion of the Web, Lasaster says it is almost impossible to find qualified people to work. "Many times we have had to turn down or refer business away because we felt we couldn't service the customer correctly," he laments.

Nonetheless, the revenues of the company consistently surge 100% every six months, with HorseNet on track for gross profits exceeding $600,000 in 1998. And this figure will only skyrocket in the years ahead since 85% of potential HorseNet clients and visitors aren't even online yet. "I talk to people at the tradeshows and can tell from our industry trade magazine that a mere 15% of the horse world is connected."

Of those horse enthusiasts who are wired, 35% come from America Online, a statistic that causes design problems for the equestrian site. "Concentrate on the content and don't design for AOL's browser," Lasater has found. "If you are designing for their browser you are selling yourself short. Instead design without their browser and know that some things may not be usable to AOL, but at that same time you can't incorporate something important and not have them be able to see it or use it."

Having to cater to varied groups of people is a natural for Lasater given his history in video production, niche marketing, and computer programming, all of which have made HorseNet a logical and fluid career move. But it has not been without surprises.

"We figured that launching and maintaining HorseNet would be easy, cheap, and fast," he reflects. But Lasater quickly learned how the online world is different. "Instead of a real world business where you might replace your pizza oven every ten years, in the Web world you find yourself replacing your computers every 18 months."

"Building a Website is simple, but once it becomes a business all the problems are accelerated because of technology."

*For up-to-date information about the
success of*
HorseNet
visit
www.StrikingItRich.com

INTERNATIONAL GOLF OUTLET
HOMEPAGE

International Golf Outlet, Inc

"I just wanted to drop you a line and thank you for your excellent service. I normally purchase my equipment from a discount house in NC but they were unable to meet my required price for a new wedge. I "surfed" the Taylor Made web page and found your link. You had the wedge I needed at a GREAT price and delivered it to my door the next day. I am looking forward to doing future business with you!"

J McDewitt, 5/13/1998

800-444-3173 | 512-258-5225 (International)

Shop securely for over 1000 of your favorite golf products

First time visitors click here?

(please press only once)

YES

CATALOG REQUESTS

D A V I D   S C H O F M A N

INTERNATIONAL
GOLF OUTLET

www.igogolf.com

For David Schofman, choosing a domain name for his Web-bound golf shop has turned out to be one of his most memorable business decisions. "Of course I had no idea of the importance of domain names at this time," admits Schofman. "Believe it or not, *golf.com* was not even registered and was available. However, in my infinite wisdom I thought, 'what good is *golf.com*?' No one will know what we do."

Schofman says that he "feels silly now" but historically his marketing perspective was not off target. In early 1995 few suspected the value of a ordinary noun followed by a .com. A month later, however, *golf.com* was registered by the NBC television network.

But the naming story doesn't end here.

"I thought of a bunch of different names like CompuGolf, Golfshop, Proshop, and so on. However, once I decided to call the company International Golf Outlet, I felt that the initials IGO were catchy and therefore needed to be included in the domain somehow. So, I just thought that 'igogolf' worked well."

"It wasn't until about a month after we were online that a Japanese customer sent me an e-mail that said, 'I love I-GO-GOLF.' I wish I could say I was that creative, but the truth is that I never made the connection until that moment."

In retrospect, Schofman's initial naming blunder has been only a blip on the course of his business success. While he may have regrets that he didn't use *golf.com,* he accomplished his primary goal, to offer "the finest golf equipment worldwide at discount prices."

His concept is simple and noteworthy. Schofman didn't want to be just another buying service behind the technology. He wanted to lavish personal care on his customers, which means, for example, that instead of staffing his company with clueless order takers he hires bona fide golf experts. His commitment to reaching beyond the sale is seen in his swelling revenues and astronomical click-traffic.

Launched with $5,000 in October 1995, IGO's revenue growth rate began at 25–35% monthly and now stands at a steady 10%. In 1996 he grossed $600,000. In 1997 his business grew 333% with revenues exceeding $2 million. David Schofman is 26 years old.

Schofman has done many things right—some the result of his innate business savvy, others the benefit of great timing. To best understand the foundation of IGO's success, we must examine its components separately, while keeping a collective perspective, as if individually viewing the points of a star.

While most Websites are launched without any business plan, Schofman had one, the foundation of which was based on his prediction that "international customers were looking for less expensive ways to buy golf clubs." The outcome of his premise is that IGO launched as a multilingual site with pages in French, Spanish, German, and Japanese. In 1997 he added Chinese. This selection of languages covers the 140 countries to which IGO ships. Forty percent of IGO's business is international.

Since IGO carries over 2,000 products, translating their description information is prohibitively expensive. Instead, IGO's foreign language pages offer a welcome message, general information and complete shipping data. Schofman uses a Web-page translation service for all the languages and pays by the job. Their Chinese pages are translated by a professor in Taiwan with whom Schofman barters golf equipment.

Needless to say, his Japanese pages are by far the most accessed and for this reason IGO will begin offering Japanese descriptions for their top 150 products. But for Schofman, servicing the Japanese market goes far beyond offering native language pages.

For example, IGO discounts all Japan-bound orders by an additional 3 percent to cover the sporting goods tax levied on merchandise exported to the country. "Our discount was set up as a result of Japan's 3% taxation on golf clubs," Schofman explains. "This way our Japanese customers get their clubs 'tax-free.' It was essentially done as a marketing play."

Schofman is also able to move Japan-bound merchandise "duty-free," but this is because of a loophole. Golf clubs are actually tax-exempt, though many of the country's citizen's don't realize it. "In Japan the rich make the laws and the rich are golfers. Anything with the world 'golf' on it is not subject to a duty tax, but most don't know this because it doesn't apply to other items such as clothing," says Schofman.

When you combine these incentives, IGO's proposition from the perspective of a Japanese visitor is irresistible. Buying from the Texas-based Web business means their purchases are duty-free, described in their native language, discounted an extra 3% to pay for the additional taxes and available for two-day delivery to over 750 Japanese cities. It's no surprise then that 30% of IGO's international orders originate from Japan, (although their most popular non-U.S. shipping destination is Australia).

To their credit, IGO charges actual shipping costs and never assesses a handling fee on any order, including domestic deliveries.

What's interesting to note is that Schofman's international focus was a considered decision, not just a hunch. "I didn't think we had a chance in the domestic market because of competitors such as the cataloguers GolfSmith and Edwin Watts," Schofman explains. "But they were not online. My whole plan revolved around the fact that international customers will pay more because they are not willing to wait for the merchandise to get overseas. For example, a Callaway driver released in January in the United States won't get to Sweden until June.

Wealthy people overseas want Callaway drivers when they come out and don't want to wait."

While Schofman was correct in his business plan to highlight the international market, he was less accurate about subscription-based cyberspace.

Since membership to online services was heating up quick and bright at the time he was developing his business plan, Schofman assumed that services such as CompuServe were destined to be the next commerce mecca. Furthermore, the Web was still too young to be considered a contender and CompuServe's primary demographic was a nearly perfect match to IGO's developing customer profile: an international mix of rich males, ages 35–55.

Schofman actually approached CompuServe about setting up a store in their electronic mall. Considered the premiere online service at the time, CompuServe quoted their start-up fee at $150,000 plus a percentage of sales. Schofman declined. CompuServe countered with more favorable terms to which Schofman agreed and signed a contract.

A couple of months later, new market information surfaced that led Schofman to believe that his decision to work with CompuServe may not have been sound. He called CompuServe and told them that since he had not launched, he was going to renege on their arrangement. Since CompuServe knew that suing the budding entrepreneur would not serve them ultimately, instead they elected to stay in touch. They did and over the course of the following year they finally agreed to an arrangement where IGO would not be subject to the upfront fee, but CompuServe would get a percentage of sales.

Today CompuServe directs IGO customers in one of two ways. The first is located inside the proprietary service via the command *GO IGO*, which shoots people to the IGO Website from the CompuServe browser. The second is a traditional link from CompuServe's public Website at *mall.compuserve.com*.

From these links IGO gets about 6,000 visitors per month. About 5% buy, spending a total of $2,000. While this is just a fraction of the 80,000 visitors he sees in the same 30-day time frame, what Schofman likes best about this deal is the association with the well-respected service and like-minded clientele.

Interestingly, during the year that IGO was in talks with CompuServe, a dialog with America Online began as well, but in this case continued for years.

In the winter of 1995 AOL was asking for a $250,000 up-front fee to have a store on the service. In addition to the cost, store owners were responsible for programming the site using America Online's proprietary programming technology. In other words, enterprises with a Web presence could not use the same programming and in fact had to reprogram everything using AOL's special language.

After two years of discussions, AOL presented their best and final offer to IGO: $150,000 upfront, 10% commission on all sales, no exclusivity. Schofman politely declined. Shortly thereafter, Sports Discount Outlet made a deal with the service but Schofman points out that "they have to keep their prices high to make up for it."

Ironically, IGO did eventually end up on AOL, although through a back door. Members can find the International Golf Outlet link through Brands for Less (KEYWORD BRANDS-FORLESS), to whom IGO pays a commission for each order received. In addition to customers coming from Brands for Less, 20% of IGO's customer traffic originates from AOL via subscribers using the system's browser directly going to *www.igogolf.com.*

Schofman refers to his CompuServe and AOL/Brands for Less arrangements as strategic relationships. All these deals pay commissions on orders only. He has similar arrangements with AT&T WorldNet, *Golf Magazine,* Reuters, iGOLF, Virtual Emporium, and CUC's NetMarket. To complement these partnerships, IGO has also developed strategic relationships where IGO serves as the virtual store for content-centric Websites. For example, customers making purchases from the *Golf Magazine* Marketplace or from CNN/SI are actually fulfilled and serviced by IGO—a fact that is conspicuously posted to the full knowledge of customers.

"This is a good deal for everyone," Schofman points out. "We offer these high-profile sites a turnkey package that includes building the site, maintaining inventory, shipping, customer service, returns, phone, and e-mail. We take care of everything."

While the best traffic generators for IGO have been through these 12 strategic partnerships and relationships, advertising has also contributed significantly to their growth.

From IGO's launch, Schofman began advertising on Yahoo and Lycos by buying keywords like "golf," "golf bags," and "golf shoes." Ironically, Schofman has found that "the word 'golf' is not targeted enough and doesn't pull as well" (which must give him some solace with respect to passing on *golf.com*).

At first IGO owned many of these keywords, meaning they had exclusivity. If input as a search term, IGO's banner ad appears on the results page. The initial premium cost for this exclusivity on Yahoo was a mere $500 in 1995. In 1998 it's selling for as much as $20,000, hence the "exclusivity" is now divided up among several advertisers.

Even parsed out, IGO gets plenty of action. Their click-through rates on Yahoo and Lycos consistently pull a phenomenal 15–20% (against an industry average of 1–3%). Considering that Schofman is not willing to risk tinkering with a formula that is working so well, he hasn't changed the company's banner since they began advertising.

IGO's banner is nothing special. It's a straightforward digital billboard that reads "International Golf Outlet." No fancy animations. No mod colors. However, when you think about it, the IGO name is very descriptive, with three simple words relaying their entire selling proposition: "International" says "worldwide shipping," "golf" is their product, and "outlet" implies discount and selection.

Schofman has consistently kept his ad budget at $2,000 monthly. So far he has not tracked what percentage of click-throughs buy, so he hasn't yet established a return on his advertising investment or his cost to acquire a new customer.

However, being precise isn't all that important to him, as he values the benefits of branding as much as direct marketing. The same holds true with respect to his strategic alliances.

Another major traffic generator for IGO is the one business cherishes most: the media. So far, IGO has earned online accolades from Yahoo, AmeriGolf, and other high-profile sites. In offline print media, the International Golf Outlet has been featured in *Forbes* (March 1996) and *Advertising Age.*

Schofman is not always able to track the additional traffic such favorable press can motivate, but surges in visitors are sometimes undeniably linked to print coverage.

"In July 1997 a Japanese-based Internet magazine wrote up a multipage article that walked people through the site," says Schofman. At the same time *Internet Shopper Magazine* named us one of their Top Sports shop picks. Together these two increased our sales by 30% instantly and stayed that way. In fact we had to hire two more employees immediately."

Another aspect of his business acumen directly attributable to his success is the degree to which he offers extra service to customers, service with such value that IGO is a potential customer's only logical choice.

Not content with just selling great merchandise, Schofman wanted to give his customers something with even more value. One way he knew he could accomplish this was by offering custom golf club fitting.

"This brings us a ton of business," Schofman is happy to say. "If the customer has the resources themselves, they should get fitted by a PGA professional. But this costs $50–100 and they must take the time and know where to go."

"We have our customers answer 20 questions, including their shot trajectory, weight, glove size, what clubs they play with now, what they want to play with, and why. One of our experts analyzes the responses and then suggests clubs that will work best."

"If the data is contradictory, in other words the height, weight, and fingertip-to-floor length indicates he should hook the ball yet instead he slices it, one of our on-staff pros will call him and go into more depth to match the best clubs to his game."

Luckily for Schofman, custom fitting online—without the benefit of a terrestrial encounter—is working.

But this personalized attention hasn't been limited to keyboards and other virtual communications.

"I had a customer order some clubs online late on a Thursday," begins one of Schofman's favorite customer service stories. "He was from Australia and was coming to Houston on business for the weekend and flying out late Sunday. He obviously wanted to grab some clubs while he was here and had no idea that we happened to be located in Texas. It turns out that it was a set of clubs that we did not have in stock. So we ordered them Friday for next day delivery on Saturday. It also happened that I was visiting our warehouse in Houston the same weekend. On Saturday the clubs came in by UPS. I called the customer at his hotel and personally delivered them to him within the hour. He was shocked to say the least."

To the degree that his customers rely on Schofman for service, he equally relies on them. IGO is constantly integrating client feedback, most notably a version of the site that was requested by their international clientele who mostly log in at a slow 14.4 baud. Customers are also a good source of new product information, and IGO is constantly updating inventory to reflect their suggestions.

But Schofman could no longer ignore a request for one item he doesn't carry in his 2,000-plus unique item inventory: a catalog.

By January 1997, IGO literally received its 50,000th request for a catalog, even though they clearly stated that they didn't offer one. At this point Schofman realized there was a demand and spent $150,000 to design it and another $1 a piece to print. Unfortunately, he's finding that catalog sales are hard to track when you have an online presence as well, but he estimates that 5–10% of his catalog requests lead to a fulfilled order, which is good considering he estimates that his break-even point is at 3%.

Though he does not promote the catalog on the site, he still gets over 100 requests a day. When he had a "request catalog" button on the site, he accumulated 50,000 requests in 12 months. He since has sent out 100,000. Everyone who had ordered got them first, followed by those who first requested them.

Schofman considers the catalog his biggest gamble to date. "This was something we never envisioned and was a huge financial risk for us. Results are good so far, but the final analysis is still pending."

While Schofman is establishing an offline relationship now with his catalog, he continues to stay in close contact with IGO customers by personally answering most of the 350 e-mails the company receives daily. But this is changing. "I am slowly giving up the reins because it's not where my talent lies. I am delegating it to a professional golfer and this will be all he does." Nonetheless, Schofman is proud to point out that all IGO e-mail is personally responded to within 24 hours. "We use automated e-mail sparingly," says Schofman. "We try to personalize and form a relationship with each individual." This is also the case with their monthly electronic bulletins, which are individually sent to specific customers.

"We don't advertise that we do these mailings," explains Schofman. "We send e-mails to people based on what they buy. If we are having an unadvertised special we mine our database for the right fit with our best, regular buyers. They get first pick of the specials and they love it. I only send it out once a month and I only send out a few hundred. The response usually wipes out the special offer because the deals are so good. For example, we had a set of Cobra irons reduced from $799 to $499."

Schofman dips into his database only for his best deals, but he is constantly approached by direct marketers with the hope he will sell the names of anyone who has bought $5,000 or more from the Webstore. He always declines. It's an easy decision for him. IGO is not about money. David Schofman started the company because he loves the sport.

"I am a golfer. I started playing when I was about 12 and got serious at 14 when I suffered a 'career-ending' knee injury playing backyard football," Schofman explains. Though he would never play professionally, he stayed with the sport through high school and college, even working part-time at a local pro shop where he would partner years later with the owner, Jack Shanklin, to launch IGO.

After graduating from college in 1994 with a journalism degree, Schofman began working for a small advertising agency. His first client was a computer bookstore called CompuBooks. At the time CompuBooks was doing $100,000 a month in business in the CompuServe electronic mall alone. Upon learning this, Schofman started thinking, "I've got to figure out a way to get in on this deal!"

"So, one day I had the idea," relates Schofman. "I went to Yahoo and searched 'golf.' It came back with what I had hoped, nothing. Maybe 20 sites, most of them about disk golf! Immediately I starting thinking about building (replicating) the CompuBooks store but in golf. It was really a no-risk situation for me because I was so young and really had nothing to lose."

One of the key elements that made IGO possible is its fulfillment arrangement, the benefit of which comes from his business partner, who owns three golf stores in Houston.

IGO utilizes the retail stores' inventory for fulfillment. At this point IGO makes much more money than the retail stores. So one plan being considered is to close two stores and rename the third IGO to keep a retail presence in a major city. To Schofman, this is a mandatory transition. "In retail the rents are high and the margins are low."

Though he is fulfilling from Houston, IGO does drop ship from the manufacturers, though not all will participate in this arrangement. "About 30% of the companies I deal with won't drop ship because they don't consider it fair to the people who buy inventory," adds Schofman.

In their first two years on the Web, IGO has moved plenty of merchandise, fulfilling well over 12,000 orders. Their most popular items are Callaway Great Big Bertha, Callaway irons,

Cobra irons, Adams Tight Lies Woods, and Nike shoes. The average order is 1–2 items for a total price of $250. And when do they receive the most orders? "On Monday mornings," Schofman sighs. "I think that everyone who plays bad on the weekends is looking for a fix."

Now employing six people, Schofman shudders when people associate the word "successful" with his enterprise. "I never really had any expectations for IGO." In fact, it is with these "low expectations" that Schofman approached the design of his Website.

What he wanted more than anything was sensibility, "a simple layout that made sense to golfers, nothing complicated." But getting the site programmed was another matter. "At first we hired 'professionals' who took our money and produced very little. After getting burned, I decided to teach myself. For the next year or so, I did all I could to get by. Now we have a true professional programmer and designer. I still dabble a bit, but nothing serious."

Essentially there are few techoachievements on the IGO site, but the ones they do incorporate Schofman considers indispensable.

Foremost is the IGO online order tracking system, which is used by 40% of their customers. The tracking system is the result of Schofman's security fears. He is reluctant to issue a tracking number through an e-mail order confirmation because the electronic follow-up states the recipient's address and complete order. While IGO is happy to provide the tracking number by request, customers can always monitor their order through the site by clicking on the button for the express delivery service, which will display the order's exact status but, again, without a tracking number.

The tracking system was also a natural outgrowth of IGO clientele's slow but steady shift from phone orders to Web orders.

When IGO was launched, 90% of their orders came through their 800-number. Beginning in 1997, Schofman noticed a radical decline in phone activity, dropping to a total of

40% of all orders. Schofman feels that this is completely attributable to "people feeling more comfortable ordering online," to which he adds, "this is a wonderful trend."

In addition to online order tracking, IGO's other premier technofeature is a "New Visitors Click Here" button on the welcome page. This Java-gizmo grabs the e-mail address from the browser of the visitor (with permission), then automatically sends a "thank you for visiting note" from Schofman. Schofman says this $200 program has been invaluable, driving business to the site because so many people reply to the letter. "At first I was worried it would be obtrusive and put off implementing it, but I've been using it for a year and over 100 people a day click on it."

While IGOGOLF is farther ahead on the curve than any other pro shop online, Schofman remains cognizant of his competition. While he admits "there are too many to count these days," the only true challenge is GolfDiscount.com. "We know that they take business away from us because their pricing is cost plus 5%. But at the moment they have prices, not pictures, and they just started online ordering." Another reason Schofman considers GolfDiscount.com lightweight competition is because he doesn't want these customers in the first place. "We like to help people find the right clubs. We don't want to be just a price shopping source," he says. "The discounters can have these guys."

Since the beginning, building customer confidence and security has been a hallmark of IGO. "Since we had no 'brand,' customers were relying on my salesmanship and our Web presence to risk making a purchase with us."

But those who did take the risk have always been satisfied, including IGO's very first order, phoned in from a woman in a New York airport. "She was on her laptop and was searching desperately for a gift for her husband's birthday. She said he travelled a lot. So I recommended a Travel Bag. She gave me her credit card number and told me to have it to him by the time she returned so that she would be in good graces with him."

"We shipped it second-day air and she wrote me the best love letter you've ever seen once she returned from her trip. Since this was our first order for me it was like—wow—this might actually work!"

Revelations like these have come fast and furious for Schofman, including enlightening personal insights. "I'm a businessman, something I never thought I would be," he notes. "And I truly love working and building this business."

Just seven months after launching his site, Schofman started getting offers to buy IGO. "I didn't even understand why someone would think I would want to sell it," he remembers. But the offers keep coming, having now risen to seven-figure bids, numbers that Schofman can no longer ignore. "Selling IGO would mean I would never have to worry about money again," Schofman acknowledges. "That part of it is nice. But giving up my baby would be hard. I didn't build this to sell it."

For up-to-date information about the success of
International Golf Outlet
visit
www.StrikingItRich.com

iPrint
The Internet Print Shop ®

Professional Printing Over the Internet. Save Time and Money. Guaranteed.

Click Here Limited time offer...

welcome:
First Time Visitors
Information (FAQ)
Price List
Samples
Guarantee
Safe & Secure

orders & saved work:
Check Order Status
Get Saved Work or Reorder

ClickRewards™
Click. Buy. Fly.

join now:
Join Our Affiliate Network

other information:
About Us
Job Opportunities

Business Products & Stationery

Business Cards   Letterhead   Post-it® Notes   Click here for more
And More

Gift Center

Mugs   T-Shirts   Mouse Pads   Click here for more
And More

Promotional Products

Magnets   Golf Balls   Polo Shirts   Click here for more
And More

FREE **CyberStationery!** Spice up your email with an iBizCard | iAnnounce | iInvite | iNote
What is CyberStationery?

R O Y A L   P .   F A R R O S

iPRINT

www.iPrint.com

"In 1995 I was driving down highway 101 on the San Francisco Peninsula and was passing by Bay Meadows Race Track. On their digital billboard, they were advertising, http://www.RaceTrack.com. Literally, I almost pulled to a stop on the freeway and just stared. All I could think was 'Geez ... if these guys are going online, then everybody's gonna go online.' That's when I knew it made business sense to put a print shop on the Web."

Okay, so a connection between racetracks and printing might appear as a non sequitur. That is unless your name is Royal P. Farros, and your career has been revolutionizing personal printing. As the cofounder of T/Maker software, Farros, 39, was responsible for such desktop printing originals as PFS: Publisher and ClickArt, products that first introduced the world to the benefits and creative fun of desktop publishing. "Everything I have done in the past few decades is contributing to this venture," says Farros.

The Web-based print shop Farros envisioned when he drove by the racetrack came to fruition one and a half years later as iPrint, a multimillion dollar enterprise singlehandedly innovating a centuries-old industry.

iPrint offers a completely new methodology for creating and ordering professionally printed products. It is the first and only What-You-See-Is-What-You-Get publishing application on the Internet. It requires no plug-ins and no special software. Any Internet connection and popular browser will do.

Here's how it works. After entering the iPrint Website, customers select what they'd like to create—including letterhead, business cards, custom Post-it™ notes, rubber stamps, and labels. Next they are taken to a layout screen where they can choose from hundreds of different designs. The layout they choose then appears in the main iPrint Design Studio and the fun begins.

With their layout in front of them, the customer starts in-putting text, importing graphics, choosing fonts and colors, siz-ing and moving objects, viewing paper samples, changing lay-outs, whatever they desire until they have a design they are happy with. The process is completely interactive (it even has redo, undo, and save functions) and is capable of rendering just about any customer's vision. There is no time limit and the De-sign Center can host tens of thousands of customers simulta-neously. Upon completion of the order, the job is routed to one of iPrint's backend printers.

Price-wise, iPrint's product line ranges from $8.49 for a wooden handle rubber stamp to $534.99 for 2,000 bumper stickers. Accordingly, the average order amount varies from $60 for a consumer purchase to $700 for a SOHO printing job. The company expects the average consumer order price point to rise significantly once they introduce more mainstream products to the mix such as photo T-shirts and photo mouse pads. Accordingly, their profit margins fluctuate from 15% to 40%. Business cards are competitively priced in what Farros refers to as "a cut-throat manner."

With iPrint's proprietary technology, the company is creating a new printing paradigm in a $20-billion segment of the quick print industry. This distinction earned iPrint the prestigious 1997 CommerceNet VIP Award for Electronic Commerce. While some companies on the Web are doing small pieces of what iPrint does, they do it in an unsophisticated, nonautomated way. Bottom line: iPrint is reinventing an industry. There is nothing online that even resembles what they have accomplished.

"The system is designed to be as easy to use as an ATM ma-chine, so that even the newest Internet user can intuitively fig-ure out how to use the system," asserts Farros. "In fact, in the same manner that the ATM machine automated the banking industry, making the most popular transactions self-service and easy, iPrint automates the printing industry."

This shift in how we now can conduct printing transactions is iPrint's greatest asset and biggest challenge. They offer cus-tom work, not a known commodity such as a CD or book, hence customers are conditioned to handling such arrangements in person. For Farros, figuring how to best overcome this ingrained behavior is a relentless and ongoing process.

iPrint finished 1997 with over 5,000 customers and has filled more than 10,000 orders, even though their products inherently have long rebuying cycles, such as 6–18 months for business cards, their biggest selling product. What helps keep the sales consistent are some golden accounts such as the business cards for Rockwell Corporation (44,000 employees) and an Intranet shop for the IRS employees, all of whom must purchase their own business cards (along with the other 2.1 million government workers).

Even with these megacustomers and tacking on an extra 5,000 unique visitors a day on average at the beginning of 1998, Farros is always on the hunt for new customers.

What Farros knows does not work for iPrint is relying 100% on a pay-for-banner advertising strategy, the results of which have been frustrating at best. In their first year, 1997, the company bought approximately 11.5 million banner ad impressions. From this they got about 53,600 click-throughs, a total that translates to a click-to-order of $1.04 or .5% click through rate. Since iPrint's software is temporarily lacking in its tagging ability, it can't track a click-to-order ratio to determine a cost per sale. Nonetheless, they spent about $66,000 total and, because they were buying in such quantity, were able to negotiate fantastic deals as low as a $6 CPM (as compared to an average of $18 for a typical run-of-site buy).

These banners appeared on all the popular search engines and megasites such as GeoCities and Tripod. Of this group, the worst performer was Webcrawler at 0.6%, with Excite delivering the most visitors at 1.5%, a number similar to successful offline direct mail advertising.

The bright spot in advertising trials were ads that ran on Women's Wire and attracted a 2.25% click-through. Here's the notable difference between these ads and the run-of-site banners placed on the search engines. The Women's Wire spots rotated during the holidays and were designed to appeal to Women's Wire female audience. For this campaign, iPrint used softer typefaces along with holly art bordering the ad, highlighting an offer for holiday cards and invitations. Better targeting, better response.

The company also noted an increase when they moved from elementary creative such as "Design Online and Save Big Money" to more clever copy and spiffier graphics. For example, one animated banner showed a picture of Mona Lisa, a smile taking over her face and copy that read "Her Personalized Party Invitations Just Arrived in the Mail ... [second panel] "Get Yours Today at iPrint."

Even the better response with targeted advertising was not enough to convince Farros that this was the way to go. "Banner advertising is definitely something that burns cash very quickly," he warns. "While the jury's not completely back on this one, so far it looks disappointing at best."

While Farros has learned that straight advertising on a CPM basis does not work for iPrint, comarketing relationships do.

For iPrint, these comarketing relationships are essentially bounty programs, also known as pay-per-sale. Because these sites get paid only when they generate revenue for iPrint, Farros has found them far more concerned about iPrint's ad placement. His biggest success in this arena has been with the free e-mail companies HotMail and RocketMail, who receive a 2–10% commission on the revenue generated from traffic they send. These programs account for 30% of iPrint's total orders. Farros considers the match between his product and their service perfect since "once someone gets a free e-mail address, they can't wait to create a business card for it to share with others."

What's interesting to note is that visitors from these bounty programs travel to iPrint not from banner ads, but from text links or expanded buttons. Since these are equivalent to a quarter banner in size, they indicate that in the online world being in the right place with the right product doesn't necessarily require much screen real estate to drive traffic.

After an investment of 36,000 people hours and more than $1 million, iPrint was launched on December 29, 1996 at 1:30 A.M. "We tried to open the site all day and we were determined to open before the end of year and we were not going to home until we did. When we opened," Farros recalls with a smile, "we waited for traffic and we didn't have any. We stood there for 5 minutes. All we wanted was to see just one of the 20 million Internet users! It's one of those rare feelings the moment it goes live and you just wait there. The next day, however, we did get nine orders and we weren't even in the search engines."

The very first order of these initial nine was properly enshrined by Farros. "His name is Martin Peterson and his order ticket is on my wall. I remember him as being a very nice guy and excited for our service. It was a great way to start!"

While the first order was a thrill, the first order from someone famous has been the most fun for iPrint.

"It was fairly early on and we were watching each and every order pretty carefully. All of a sudden we get a whole slew of business cards and stationery from the Conservative Victory Fund, headed up by none other than Oliver North. We thought 'it can't be him,' but then how many other Oliver North's have a Conservative Victory Fund? Someone in the office worked in Washington in the 1980s and recognized a few of the other politicians' names. So we knew it was the real deal. Political affiliations aside, it was still a memorable afternoon."

The majority of iPrint's clientele is not nearly as luminous, but just as important to this Silicon Valley startup. As one might suspect, the foundation of iPrint's consumers are SOHOs. This is partly seen in iPrint's visitor traffic patterns. While iPrint sees a steady flow of business every day, there are noticeable peaks on Mondays and Tuesdays. Notes Farros, "people come back into work and are raring to take care of business."

As with most businesses, customers remain iPrint's best source of feedback. In their first year in business, the most frequently asked customer service question was about order status. "It was clear that our customers wanted to be able to watch the progress of their orders," says Farros. Seizing the opportunity, now when a customer places an order they can monitor it from the site using a reference ID and password. In fact, they can even cancel it if it has not yet been sent to the printer. A side benefit of this tracking feature has been the elimination of at least 30% of their customer service e-mail as well.

Order tracking is particularly important to iPrint's international customers who have become very dependent on this U.S. enterprise. "We ship all over the world. Americans don't know how great we have it in terms of printing with quality, good service, and good prices," Farros explains. "Try to buy printing anywhere else in the world and it's a nightmare. Literally, even after international shipping costs, these customers tell us that our total price is half of their local price. But more importantly, it is produced with much better quality." The most popular non-North America destinations are the United Kingdom, Switzerland, and Japan.

Ironically, while 10% of iPrint's customers are international, many of whom are accessing the site with a slow modem connection and iffy service, the bulk of iPrint's problems come from America Online.

"When America Online was going through its terrible time in the first part of 1997 [after they went to flat rate pricing], we were actually getting customers blaming us for not being able to log onto AOL," laments Farros. "We do know that AOL is absolutely the slowest way to use the Internet. So while we love that AOL is delivering customers, AOL customers tend to blame us—and any other site these customers visit—for their performance problems."

Not surprisingly, Farros has never considered launching iPrint on an online service such as America Online. "We are an Internet business and our first bet is placed on whether the net succeeds or fails."

A much more pivotal move for iPrint has been partnering with established brands who could also be considered his competition. These arrangements find iPrint being offered as a private label site. For example, Office Max's Copy Max Online Print Shop is essentially iPrint: same interface, similar prices, along with specials that they "will bob and weave as they see fit." Ditto for Sir Speedy.

While these are profitable relationships for iPrint, they also can wreak havoc with assumptions in its business plan. "We overestimated the traffic because some of the stores simply haven't come online yet. We had been working with Sir Speedy for over a year and were poised for their online entrance. Unfortunately their launch was delayed by six months. Our crystal ball fell apart on how fast our partners would get up to speed."

Because of the delayed entrances of their strategic partners, iPrint opened its own Web storefront. "We thought we would license our entire commerce environment to large commercial printers," Farros explains. "Unfortunately, we found that large commercial printers were sitting on the fence with the Internet, none wanting to invest in it until there was some proof it would take off. This forced us to 'be the pioneer with arrows in our back,' and that was to open our own branded online print shop."

Getting up to speed is important for iPrint who will shortly be the David wrestling with the printing Goliath, Taylor Corporation, the 800-pound gorilla in the industry, virtually the only enterprise that could dramatically affect their sales. Regardless, Farros continues to get interest from other megaplayers. "We got a note that said, 'Hi we are Mailboxes Etc. with 3,400 locations globally and we want to talk to you.'" With overtures such as these, iPrint can maintain its leadership in the online world.

Even with Taylor's entrance, Farros maintains his clear objective. "Our mission is to be the online connection between print buyers and commercial printers, thus participating in virtually every mass market printing transaction in the world."

iPrint is well on their way. Since they opened, the interactive printer has experienced 25% growth monthly, a number that constantly reminds Farros that his company must be able to adapt quickly.

"Real interactive electronic commerce is now happening," states Farros. "If you can't scale quickly, forget it. The game's over before you even get started."

For up-to-date information about the success of
iPrint
visit
www.StrikingItRich.com

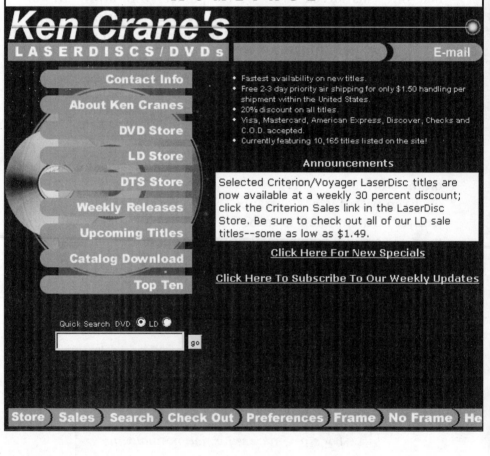

Ken Crane's
LASERDISCS/DVDs

E-mail

Contact Info

About Ken Cranes

DVD Store

LD Store

DTS Store

Weekly Releases

Upcoming Titles

Catalog Download

Top Ten

- Fastest availability on new titles.
- Free 2-3 day priority air shipping for only $1.50 handling per shipment within the United States.
- 20% discount on all titles.
- Visa, Mastercard, American Express, Discover, Checks and C.O.D. accepted.
- Currently featuring 10,165 titles listed on the site!

Announcements

Selected Criterion/Voyager LaserDisc titles are now available at a weekly 30 percent discount; click the Criterion Sales link in the LaserDisc Store. Be sure to check out all of our LD sale titles—some as low as $1.49.

Click Here For New Specials

Click Here To Subscribe To Our Weekly Updates

Quick Search DVD ⦿ LD ⦿

go

Store) Sales) Search) Check Out) Preferences) Frame) No Frame) He

KEN CRANE'S LASERDISCS

www.kencranes.com

If it weren't for two customers who kept pestering him to put his laserdisc store online, Ken Crane would have bypassed $5.1 million in additional revenue. And that's just in the first two and a half years.

"They used to just badger me," admits Crane. "Jim was a programmer for McDonnell Douglas Aircraft. Every time he would come to the store he would say, 'Are you on the Internet yet? Are you on America Online?' Then Jon, another guy, would say the same thing. 'You got to be on the Internet.' And I would say I don't have time. Then finally John said, 'Hey, I'll put something up for you and if you like it you can pay me.'"

Crane is the owner of Ken Crane's Laserdiscs in Westminster, California. Crane, 40, had never considered opening a cyberspace branch of his megasuccessful laserdisc retail store only because it hadn't occurred to him. At this point it was only July 1995, so early in the history of online retailing that the terms "Internet" and "Web" were just seeping into our national consciousness.

But Crane accepted the challenge. The result has been a financial windfall, generating over $1.6 million in 1997 and a minimum of $3 million in 1998.

The secret to Ken Crane's online success is disarmingly simple: He focuses on the basic consumer mandate of savings, selection, and service. He discounts a minimum of 20% on every disc, including new releases, and he offers every one of the over 9,000 laserdiscs available. Compare this with the 3,000 discs offered by even the largest offline retailers such as Tower and Musicland. Online, he feels, there is currently no worthy competition.

Perhaps the best part of the story is that, even though his instincts told him to go cyber, Crane was still unclear about the potential of the new medium and, in fact, had rather low expectations.

Crane figured the Web would be little more than a new vehicle for his existing advertising, with the modest hope of luring a few more customers. His reasoning was based on an elementary return on investment principle. The cost to launch his first site was $3,500 plus $2,000 in monthly maintenance fees. Compare this to the $23,000 he spent on one full-page ad in *The Los Angeles Times* that would run one day and attract a few hundred customers to his retail store. "Clearly, the Web has turned out to be our most effective advertising expenditure," he deadpans.

In retrospect, Crane can see that the Web was really just an extension of his already successful catalog business. Unlike many online retailers starting from scratch, Ken Crane's Laserdiscs already had a shipping infrastructure and a staff who understood order fulfillment. As the Web side of his business continues to explode with 300% annual growth, these very factors have become his biggest challenge. For example, from January 1996 through December 1997, Ken Crane doubled his employee base from 24 to more than 50 people. And they still aren't enough.

"And you know what the customers' responses are?" asks Crane. "If you can't answer your phone quicker, if you can't get an e-mail response to me quicker, hire more employees. Well, you can't just hire employees because it takes time for them to learn. Customers think that if you hire people tomorrow they can do the job. It's not like you just say to someone—here, put this in a box. There's a certain way to put it in a box. It's been a nightmare," he adds. "A pleasant nightmare, but a nightmare."

Although Crane's goal is to ship the same day, because of the overwhelming amount of business, the shipping time can take up to three days. If they wish, customers can get priority processing for an additional $3, and 10% choose to do so.

Despite the overload, Crane rises to the customer service challenge, boasting a phenomenal 90% repeat customer rate of his online customers, most of whom order every 10 days. Crane's client list is loaded with celebrities and other business luminaries, including one very high-profile customer. "This company ordered about a hundred movies and they asked if we would take a purchase order. We verified the name of the corporation, which was based in Seattle. However, when they paid, it wasn't a check from the name of the small company as we verified it, it was a personal check from the computer industry's biggest giant.

According to Crane, this customer ordered three times in 1997 since discovering the online disc shop late in the year, selecting about 80–100 discs at a time. "Just basic movies," Crane notes. "Nothing special."

While 80 disc orders and an occasional 125-disc order ($4,000 worth) are common, the average Ken Crane Web purchase is 3–5 discs for $90–100. For this reason Crane has found it easier to not charge for shipping. This policy not only endears him to his customers, but also sidesteps a potential paperwork ordeal.

Crane explains that if a customer orders one movie and has to pay for shipping, he's going to order two, three, or four discs. While Crane prefers the larger order, the nature of a laserdisc inventory dictates that at least one of the movies will probably not be in stock. To avoid paying extra shipping for the on-order disc, the customer will ask Ken Crane's to hold the available three until the fourth comes in.

"Then it gets to be a paper and inventory disaster," says Crane. "Now we have all four titles in stock and we ship it to him. In the meantime, his next door neighbor gave him one of the discs or he decided he didn't want one. Then he wants us to pay for the return shipping or asks us to release the discs we have been holding for him."

To avoid this, Crane decided to pay for the 2- to 3-day priority shipping. However, the customer pays a $1.50 handling fee, something he would like to eliminate but can't. "If I eliminated the handling fee I would lose money on the single-disc sale. I'm still losing some money on the single-disc sale, but then I would lose too much money." Ken Crane has no minimum purchase requirement even on his 99-cent blowout disc specials.

Because he discounts a minimum of 20% on all titles—although special buys will often result in even deeper discounts—Crane's profit on laserdiscs averages 15%. Since the average laserdisc retails between $19.98 and $31.98, Crane's profit can be as little as $3. This $3 covers the cost of his free priority shipping. Now his profit is wiped out. Then factor in fulfillment, which is extremely labor-intensive, and you understand the necessity to charge the $1.50 handling fee. Even with the charge, he is still losing money on one-disc orders.

"It takes four people to get an Internet order out the door," he explains. "There's the order entry person, the guy pulling the order, the guy processing the order, and the guy boxing the order. Now compare that to the customer who walks in the front door and picks up what he wants. He faces one person: the guy who takes his money."

That's not the only difference between the in-store Crane customer and the cyber-Crane customers. While the average in-store purchase of $80–100 for 3–5 discs mirrors the cyberspace order, the walk-ins come in as often as once or twice a week, versus once every 10 days on the Web. However, on the Net Crane notes that there are lots of preorders (ordering a title before it is released for disc sales), some for as many as 10–15 titles. Walk-ins don't preorder.

While the number of discs purchased is consistent, Crane has noticed that Web customers buy more specifically what they want, versus the walk-in customer who impulsively grabs something.

Although Web revenues are destined to eventually surpass those of his offline store, Crane says he doubts he would ever close the doors. "The walk-in business is too big," he notes. "We probably do more in-store than our biggest competitors do over the Net."

According to Crane, his 8,500-square-foot enterprise is the largest single laserdisc store in the world based on gross revenues and units sold. "We are the Amazon.com of the laserdisc industry. We have everything under one roof, except that we can let people come in through our front doors."

His business is technically part of the family-owned, eight-store chain of audio/video shops located in Southern California and founded by his father. In July 1987 Ken Crane II got bored with electronics and decided to devote himself to laserdiscs, which he had been doing on the side.

Since going online, Crane has received offers to buy the entire business several times, but he admits he has no desire to sell. "Besides," he adds. "What would I do?"

Despite the fact that his store is located in Southern California, a voracious laserdisc market, more than 50% of his 200-plus orders a day come from the East Coast, primarily New York and Florida, 3,000 miles from the glare of the famous Ken Crane name. Perhaps for this reason, out-of-town Web customers regard the offline Ken Crane's laserdisc store as a destination and the owner a celebrity.

"Our store is an attraction like Disneyland," Crane embarrassingly admits. "They come to California and they want to go where they buy their movies ... And we're talking about customers from Taiwan, Hong Kong, Singapore, and Europe ... and these people, even the ones from the States, want to have their picture taken with me. It kills me."

In addition to this fanfare, perhaps one of the biggest distinctions from most online stores is that Ken Crane's carries their own inventory—about $2 million worth at any time. There is absolutely no drop shipping. But this also is part of his next hurdle: being able to show his stock on hand in real time on the Website. This is a big issue partly because 50% of their Web orders come in when the store is closed. "If a customer placed an order the previous evening for a *Star Wars* boxed set, by the time the order is processed the next day with the other couple hundred we get, that particular title could have been sold to a walk-in customer, even another Web customer. Since my inventory is in my store, I am using the same inventory for the Web as I am for retail. There really isn't a happy way to get around this."

Unfortunately, ordering more copies from his distributor to fulfill a Web order isn't always a solution because fulfillment can vary from a few days to a year.

"Take a movie like *48 Hours*," he explains. "Pioneer, the manufacturer, will not press the disc until they have a minimum of three hundred orders for it. So now I have it on order.

The title is still available but it's not physically in stock. It's not out of print because 'out of print' means discontinued. It could be back in stock in one week or up to a year. But until they get their minimum repressing quota, who knows when it's going to be available? They don't tell us."

With respect to inventory on hand, the fact that Crane can't show real-time inventory translates to a higher-than-normal rate of orders via his 800-number at 80% along with an avalanche of 300–400 e-mails, most of which inquire about title availability.

All e-mails are responded to individually. Once disc buyers establish a relationship with Ken Crane's via the Website, many move to e-mail permanently, never returning to the cyberstore, instead relying on the company's weekly mailing of new titles, which goes out to over 22,000 customers via e-mail.

Though the mailings are a cut-and-dried list of the week's new releases, they are an integral part of Crane's repeat business. Just as the Website was started because of "demanding customers," so was the mailing list. In the second quarter of 1998, Crane began adding newsletter special deals, thus integrating a transaction element to what was once just news content. The results are outstanding. "We announced a collector's boxed set of *E.T.* at 50% off the $150 price. We sold 125 units in the first week," Crane notes.

In addition to the electronic mailings, Crane sends out a paper *Laserdisc/DVD Preview* every 30 days. Ranging from 15 to 20 pages and about the size of a *TV Guide,* Crane spends about $25,000 on printing and postage to 50,000 recipients— Ken Crane's most current purchasers including his retail customers. Interestingly, there is a palpable increase in Web orders days after the mailings, even though these same customers receive the weekly e-mail updates.

With the exception of the electronic mailing list, Ken Crane has adapted virtually no marketing initiatives online. Ken Crane's Webstore is the very definition of the oxymoron "failing upward." He's earning millions while ignoring most Internet business principles.

For example, Ken Crane offers no reciprocal linking even though more than 550 sites link to him. He does no online advertising and he doesn't participate in any of the laserdisc Usenet newsgroups, even though positive word of mouth in these discussions has shuttled many new customers to him, especially during his first year.

Despite his lack of marketing, kencranes.com gets over 3,200 visitors a day, of which about 6% buy. Hence Ken Crane has trounced his mom-and-pop competition including his nearest rival, Laser Craze, which capitulated in 1997.

In addition to the Usenet groups and relentless cyber word of mouth, Crane is aware that a good portion of his visitors also gets to him through search engines, but what percentage he is not sure. "What do I care where they come from?" he asks. "All I care about is giving them great service and keeping them once they get to us."

This attitude keeps Crane's business exploding. His dedication goes beyond modems in that he will not hesitate to personally call Internet customers to make sure their situations are satisfactorily handled. "If I get an e-mail and a customer is really upset, I will always respond to them by calling. And I'll do whatever it takes to make them happy, providing it's in reason. And generally, if it's not in reason, we give the customer the benefit of the doubt." For example, if a customer gets a movie and says that he didn't like it, they will take it back, issue a credit, and then send something else out. However, if customers take advantage of this policy, Crane charges a 15% restocking fee.

As Ken Crane is refining his current enterprise, he is also incorporating the future with a DVD (digital versatile disc) store to complement his laserdisc empire. Although both items can be found at www.kencranes.com, he has had to keep them separate to avoid customer confusion.

"Unfortunately, we have a terrible time with customers because a lot of the time they aren't even sure what they have. A customer might e-mail and say, 'Well I need that new DVD of whatever.' We send it to them and they say, 'No. I need the big one,' meaning the laserdisc."

Despite challenges such as these, Ken Crane realizes that he is in an enviable position. "We don't need to advertise. We don't need to promote. Right now we are overburdened with business ... the internal mechanism of the Webstore is maxed," he says. "If I did any promoting the wheels would come off."

For up-to-date information about the success of
Ken Crane's Laserdiscs
visit
www.StrikingItRich.com

THE KNOT HOMEPAGE

HOME | SIGN IN | CHAT | POSTINGS | FIND | REGISTRY

join now (it's free) click HERE

DECISIONS DECISIONS

engagement, wedding ideas, traditions, etiquette

DETAILS DETAILS

locations, food, contracts, planning advice

GROOMS & GUYS

proposals, rings, best men, bachelor parties

THE GREAT ESCAPE

honeymoon destinations, travel deals, tips

THE NEST

Bridal Gown Search

Dying to find your PERFECT DRESS? Search 8000 gown pictures 24 hours a day!

Aloha! Auction

Get the "hottest" vacation deals on the auction block -- click here!

The Knot Gift Registry
New! With everything from blenders to mountain bikes, you can't help but find gifts you really, really want in The Knot's very own bridal registry.

Featured: GPS Pioneer Navigational System You'll always find your way home with this GPS Pioneer Navigational System, a high-tech compass for backwood fanatics.
Start a Registry List

Search the Knot: [   ] GO

Knot Tools: Budgeter

Make your own

Knot Tools: Calendar

What do you

DRESSING UP

wedding gowns, shoes, accessories, veils

BIG DAY BEAUTY

makeup advice, hair, nails, facials, fitness

GIRLS & GUESTS

bridesmaids, moms, maids of honor, guests

LOVE ETC.

surveys, sex, relationship advice, horoscopes

GIFTS & REGISTRIES

registry lists, great

R O B   F A S S I N O
M I C H A E L   W O L F S O N
C A R L E Y   R O N E Y
D A V I D   L I U

THE KNOT

www.theknot.com and AOL Keyword: Knot

The founders of The Knot had no consuming desire to have an online presence. Their ambition was only to launch a new brand, and they smartly saw the online world as a means to an end. While most companies extend to the Web to leverage their content, The Knot's business plan focused on using the digital arena to pipe their brand into offline media. And it worked. Within 18 months of their launch, they secured a three-book publishing deal with an imprint of Bantam Doubleday Dell, and a 13-part PBS series. Meanwhile, a national print magazine in partnership with a major publisher is in the works. All this and the mind share of their audience that other content creators could only dream of.

"The Knot: Weddings for the Real World" is the number one online wedding resource in the world. Available on both the Web and America Online, The Knot quickly became the destination for to-be-wed women and men seeking practical wedding advice. In less than two years they have surpassed all their competitors online—including the high-profile bridal magazines—in terms of traffic, advertising, and retail sales.

To understand The Knot's stunning success requires nothing more than recognizing what makes them different. "We are a constant source of ideas, tips, and sympathy," says cofounder Rob Fassino. "But what sets us apart is that our advice is based on the world couples really live in—a place where tradition and etiquette don't always apply, where people have full-time jobs in addition to planning their weddings, and where money is all too often an object."

In addition to community features such as chat and bulletin boards, The Knot is bursting with content, from their more than 3,000 original wedding-related articles to their database of 8,000 bridal gowns complete with images. All this comes with a custom budgeter and calendar program that allows visitors to create, save, and later modify their wedding budgets and schedules. It should be no surprise that with this colossal collection of content, the average Knot user spends four hours a month with the brand.

Because The Knot is positioned to appeal to what they term "the post Emily Post crowd," everything in their approach was weighed and considered, particularly their offbeat name.

"We needed a name that reflected our unique editorial tone—something new that spoke to this new generation," says Knot cofounder Carley Roney. "We had a big battle with our first investor, America Online, who preferred names like Wedding Land, Wedding 101, and Weddings Channel, but we fought for it. The Knot may take an extra second when you are calling someone, but once the person gets it, they never forget it. And our audience thinks they have found some secret special club called The Knot."

The Knot's audience is both what you expect—engaged females 18–34—and what you might not expect—20% male. "I think the advantage of our positioning is that we can really debunk the myth that men don't have anything to do with weddings," say cofounder Michael Wolfson. "If someone says something in general like, 'men don't get involved,' we see a serious backlash from the grooms who respond via the community postings who say, 'Hey wait a minute.'"

But being different was always their objective, from the attitude of their site to their business plan.

The Knot began with seed funding from AOL's Greenhouse Project. Started in 1995, this America Online initiative provided the new venture with seven-figure funding in exchange for a minority equity stake plus a percentage of advertising revenue and usage from The Knot's AOL presence. At the time, America Online content areas made money through usage fees, usually 20% of the $2.95 members paid per hour. This was before AOL's switch to flat rate pricing in December 1996, when content area revenues plummeted as much as 90%. Even though users were spending more time online, the content area got only a small percentage of the total fees collected, which were substantially less. To offset this loss of revenue, America Online began introducing advertising.

The Knot cofounders always believed they had a better fit with an advertising model and introduced the concept to their content areas months before other AOL content providers would have no choice. Because they were so far ahead of the curve, while other AOL content area revenues ground to a halt, The Knot benefitted from the flat rate pricing structure because people were now spending more time in their areas, looking at more ads.

In addition to the fact that even selling ads on AOL was revolutionary at that time, how they sold them was different as well. The Knot was not selling ads based on a CPM model, but instead on a sponsorship model, $32,000 for three months, with a three-month minimum.

Since the online world has a tendency to relate online ad rates to offline, compare this to the $40,000 cost for one full-page ad in *Bride's Magazine.* "We felt the sponsorship model would produce better results for our advertisers," says Fassino. "They get exclusivity and a unique advertiser area, both of which have produced great results as demonstrated by our audience's direct response." Fassino points out that the vast majority of advertisers renew their contracts, usually extending their buys up to one year.

With loyal sponsors such as these, the fact that The Knot generated $187,000 in ad revenue just in January 1998 should not be a surprise. By the beginning of 1998 The Knot completely sold out their ad inventory available on AOL through the second quarter, with the Website following close behind. Approximately 60% of The Knot's income comes from AOL with the balance from the Web. But these numbers are shifting dramatically. In 1997 there was a 80/20 split in favor of AOL, but in 1999 they expect the Web to surpass the online service.

Even though advertisers are buying time-based sponsorships rather than impressions, banners on The Knot/AOL and The Knot Website get an average 3.8% click-through, which is excellent even for a niche site and about double the industry average for ads appearing as "run-of-site" at a general interest destination.

As an added benefit, many of The Knot's sponsors have dedicated areas on The Knot's dual services. They therefore include The Knot's AOL keyword and Web address in their advertising, giving the online nuptial resource additional branding for free.

Even though The Knot advertisers must look at response rates, they also place a high value on their connection with The Knot's image. "We have heard from the people at Lenox China's ad agency that for them it's also about brand association," says Roney. "A lot of bridal advertisers prefer to be brought to the bride and groom via the hip new wedding group than be presented to them by their mother or a bridal magazine." Lenox is so pleased with their relationship with The Knot that they now buy their ad contracts a year at a time.

The Lenox story is the norm, since most Knot advertisers have had a phenomenal response over bridal publications, including companies like a major travel advertiser who say that their response rate is 400% better with The Knot than with bridal print.

While The Knot's content is certainly the main reason these companies do well, there is another advantage over all other bridal publications. "We have the bride and groom significantly longer than the bridal magazines because our audience is the type of people who go online and look for information long before they go out and purchase bridal magazines," says Roney. "Because we are the first place people go, that's one of our great sales to our advertisers." The Knot has also learned through surveying their users that 34% of them don't even read the top four bridal publications, and hence would never be exposed to many of The Knot's sponsors if they didn't log on. While this statistic was uncovered after their launch, it validates what the four partners knew intuitively. It was the motivation for them to explore weddings as their content focus in the first place.

"We chose weddings because the market was huge—$35 billion annually, the existing brands tired, the advertising dollars large, and the competitive framework at the time practically nonexistent," says Fassino.

The foursome could never have imagined when they met in film school that this would be their destiny. "You have to understand that we didn't all come to this because we were four wedding aficionados," adds Roney. "We came here because it was a good business. For the first couple of weeks, I would even mumble that I was in the wedding industry because it wasn't very hip."

Roney's self-consciousness wore off quickly as their plan took shape. In fact she and the other partners, all of whom are in their early thirties, became more steadfast to the wedding genre and even refined their original business plan to reflect this. "We originally thought we would launch The Knot brand to launch subsequent brands," says Fassino. "But we quickly realized that the bridal category was so substantial that moving into other brands wasn't practical."

Although The Knot partners want to stay focused exclusively on weddings, their audience is demanding otherwise. The average Knot visitor spends time with the service for 14 months, from their engagement through their wedding day. But they build such a relationship with the brand and The Knot community that they don't want to leave. So The Knot has started to integrate newlywed features such as a chat hour and newsletter. Furthermore, The Knot is considering a living/shelter line extension (think hip Martha Stewart), partly because of the popularity of the content on the existing site.

The Knot community has influenced the media venture in more ways than just with their business plan. The Knot is first and foremost a community. The audience, both on America Online (120,000 unique users/month) and at TheKnot.com (200,000 unique visits per month), lets the partners know exactly what they want—and The Knot makes it happen.

"They all wanted more etiquette. Etiquette. Etiquette. Etiquette. They wanted every aspect of it broken down into categories more than anything else," says Roney. "So we did. From reception etiquette (throwing the bouquet) to having male bridesmaids. They also asked for vows message boards and more information on handling interfaith weddings. They get it all."

Sometimes new editorial content is the result of eavesdropping on chat sessions. "We heard from our chat hosts that people wanted shower games. We had never thought about that. So we immediately had an article written," says Roney.

Because of the dynamic, interactive nature of The Knot, visitors can get more involved and be instantly helpful, unlike an offline publication. The Knot always emphasizes community over authority. While they have some of the best wedding advice experts providing content, The Knot is always about their visitors. As such, the visitors consider The Knot their greatest resource. For example, when one women broke her leg days before her wedding, she was frantic and posted to the boards asking for suggestions, fearing that her big day was ruined. She got hundreds of responses, including one from The Knot partners (which she used) advising her to have her father and brother carry her down the aisle.

This relationship with their audience also lets The Knot be far more in touch than, and thus editorially light years ahead of, the print bridal magazines because, through their message boards and chat rooms, The Knot staff knows exactly what is important to their audience. "It's an amazing focus group," Wolfson remarks.

Such high-quality feedback enhances every aspect of The Knot, but more importantly it helps them maximize their revenue streams including their merchandise sales. Of the 500 products they offer, their two biggest selling items are disposable wedding cameras (very hard to find outside of May and June) and wedding gown catalog bundles. The latter is not only popular, but also their most lucrative item since every cent of the selling price is profit.

"We get them for free from the manufacturers," notes co-founder Michael Wolfson. "Brides have no way of getting these catalogs and the companies have no way of distributing them to the brides and here we are in the middle. Our audience would easily pay $50 for them, but we only charge $19."

Until The Knot's intervention, the only way women could possibly get these catalogs was by going to bridal shops or responding to a designer's 800-number in an ad. Hence The Knot's pack is a superconvenience for both the manufacturer and the bride-to-be. "We are aggregating them in one spot at one time, when women want to see all the gowns—just when they are thinking about weddings," says Liu. The number of catalogs in each pack varies according to the season, but on the average features at least 3–8 catalogs.

While disposable cameras and catalogs are The Knot's biggest seller by item count, their highest dollar value comes from their travel auction.

A quick study of their approach to travel sales once again demonstrates The Knot founders' ingenuity. Their competitors set up booking services through deals with Microsoft's Expedia and Preview Travel. The Knot partners, however, realized that travel booking was a low margin business and felt they weren't adding any value for their users. They wanted to do something unique that provided a huge value proposition for the specific needs of a bride and groom. So they partnered with *Honeymoon Magazine* and launched The Aloha Travel Auction, where visitors bid on trips to romantic resorts the world over. The best part is that the winner receives a voucher good for the trip at a time that works for them. They are not buying upfront for a specific date. To take all the risk out of the proposition, The Knot guarantees that if winners can't get reservations for the time they want, The Knot will either give them an alternative trip or refund their money.

The deals their audience gets are amazing: a $4,000 exclusive Fiji resort vacation for $2,300 or a $1,700 Lake Tahoe Honeymoon for $1,000. The response has been unbelievable—and so have the profits.

"We generally make 50% of the sale and it's a great deal for everybody," says Wolfson. "We've cut deals with some of the biggest chains and resorts directly so that we are the liquidator. Not only do they get the opportunity to liquidate their inventory but also unparalleled exposure. For every three packages we sell a week, a thousand people are looking at it. Can you imagine a more qualified promotional opportunity?"

These great deals also strengthen The Knot's relationship with their users. The Knot partners feel that doing transactions this way further endears them to their audience because it shows them that The Knot is on their side. Conversely, it has also shown The Knot how much trust their audience has in them.

"Literally within a month of the launch, we were selling packages for well over $2,000 a piece," says David Liu. "Keep in mind we are talking about three tiny GIF photos and a page and a half of text and people are plunking down $2,000. That showed us that we have a tremendously loyal and trusting audience." It also showed something to AOL. These auctions are promoted on both the Web and the online service, but AOL has noted that The Knot is generating the highest transactions for a noncomputer product.

The Travel Auction subsection is the perfect example of how The Knot team has a better understanding than most Websites of how to make a revenue-share model work. And, given their refreshing approach to every aspect of e-commerce, they know when it's to their advantage to forfeit profits—not revenue-share at all—in favor of a more beneficial strategic alliance.

"Rather than taking a small percentage of sales from a large retail partner, we've negotiated promotional relationships where The Knot waives the customary referral fee in exchange for prominent branding and cross-promotion from the vendor's Website," explains Fassino. "For example, we will be the exclusive wedding resource of a major online bookstore."

As an adjunct promotional opportunity, if The Knot is not giving away their commission, they will gladly supply content for additional exposure. The Knot aggressively pursues distribution of their content through additional Knot satellite sites and cross-links. "We've leveraged our exclusive position on America Online to become the service's wedding resource, distributing Knot Wedding content on dozens of partner and AOL Network areas including Love@AOL, Astronet, and the Lifestyles and Interests Channels. For example, enter the keyword "black" and you'll find Afrocentric Weddings by The Knot; enter "Personal Finance" and you'll find The Knot's Money and Marriage screen. The payoff of these alliances has been undeniable. After polling their AOL audience, The Knot learned that more than half of their users found them through one of these relationships.

On the Web, The Knot is pursuing the same strategy with dozens of content and commerce partners including Intuit, WebTV, and Yahoo. "For example, with Yahoo we are developing a series of four promotions tentatively entitled 'YaHitched,'" says Wolfson. "We get brand positioning links back to The Knot in exchange for our tools and our extensive content."

No cash is exchanged and in this particular deal Yahoo keeps 100% of the ad revenue. But cash is not the point. With deals such as these, The Knot has been able to build themselves into the number one online wedding resource brand by putting their content wherever they can.

"As a startup we don't have the money to go out there and buy a persistent presence. Instead we are using our most valuable currency, our content, and creating satellite content syndication areas, which cost us no money but provide far better exposure than any ad banner buy," notes Wolfson.

Despite a preference for strategic relationships, The Knot occasionally makes ad buys in traditional media. In 1997 they spent $130,000 running full-page ads in the magazines *Bride's,*

Modern Bride, and *Martha Stewart Weddings.* These ads served two purposes: first to introduce The Knot to consumer audiences and second to introduce The Knot to bridal advertisers. (Unlike many industries, in the bridal industry the major consumer publications also serve as the major trade publications.)

Based on response rates to an 800-number to get a Knot-branded AOL signup disk, *Modern Bride* and *Bride* were not great successes. However, the *Martha Stewart* run was, not because of response rates, but because it generated a lot of interest from advertisers.

Perhaps because of their mainstream media goals, The Knot's founding partners are constantly forging relationships to extend their brand offline. One of the highest-profile relationships was a sweepstakes they hosted for the hit film *The Wedding Singer,* in which the prize was a trip to Barbados.

In their relentless pursuit to extend the brand, The Knot constantly examines TV, film, and music release schedules looking for wedding tie-ins. "We spent seven months bugging *The Wedding Singer*'s distributor, New Line Cinema. We showed them the benefit of vertical content." For example, one of the content areas The Knot supplied was a fun, historical look at weddings in 1984, the time period of the film as compared to 1998, when the film was released.

"This was a great success," notes Wolfson. "We had exposure on *The Wedding Singer* Website and the URL was featured in their Super Bowl ad. In the first three weeks of the promotion we got 97,000 entries. This cost us nothing.

To their credit The Knot underpromised, overdelivered, and executed their promised plan for New Line flawlessly. It should be no surprise, then, that when the film company was making plans for *The Wedding Singer* video release in December 1998, the film company approached them. The Knot proposed a national sweepstakes to find a gold ticket that would be tucked in one of the tapes and redeemable for a $10,000 diamond. This would mean that every video has Knot branding. "The Knot will get a great promotion, New Line will get a great contest, all at no cost to The Knot."

While it would seem as though everything The Knot has thought of has been a success, they have had one flop. When they initially launched the site, they integrated a 26-part cybersitcom that centered on an engaged couple going through the travails of to-be-wed life. "We spent a lot of time and money on this entertainment-oriented content of The Knot to find out that our users couldn't have cared less," says Wolfson.

Although the day-to-day existence of The Knot team is centered on enterprise and profits, from time to time they are happily reminded of the impact of their brand.

"We were cynical media people," say Liu. "But now we never forget that these people are spending a hell of a lot of money throwing the biggest party of their lives. It's a completely emotional period. They are desperate for help. When we hear some of the success stores we get goose bumps and chills. It's then that we realize that not only do we have a good business on our hands, we are actually providing a service for people too."

For up-to-date information about the success of
The Knot
visit
www.StrikingItRich.com

KOREALINK HOMEPAGE

ENGLISH 한글판

CHAT BBS JOIN HELP

Tuesday
August 04, 1998

Lucky Numbers
07 18 35 40 48 49

$aver!
Coming Soon!

Establish Credit
Apply Click Here
Online
Click to Apply!

○ KoreaLink
○ Internet

GO

Powered by

Online Community

Public Forum — Live Chat — Scratch Pad
대화의광장 — 라이브채팅 — 낙서장

Single Link — Pen Pals — Kimchi People
싱글링크 — 펜팔링크 — 김치피플

Online Channel

Today's News — Business Center — Travel Guide
오늘의톱뉴스 — 사업자료실 — 여행가이드

Korean Links — Super Store — Classifieds
한국웹사이트 — 쇼핑 — 안내광고

A17 Forum	Music Forum	Movie & TV

Super Deals!

* Unionway Pro Pack OEM $59
* Hangul 97 $89
* Let's Learn Korean $119
* Korean Keyboard Label $4.95
* KoreaLink T-Shirts $9.95

Lowest Price Guaranteed!
If you find that KoreaLink offers the exact item that you purchased through us at a lower price within 15 days from the date of your order, we will gladly give you a full credit for the difference in price.

My Town

Let's talk about what's happening in your town!

* L A KoreaTown

JOE CHEON

KOREALINK

www.korealink.com

When the Hyundai Corporation offered KoreaLink founder Joe Cheon $800,000 for a 20% stake in his service, it took the 28-year-old entrepreneur about a month to consider and eventually decide against it. But during that month Cheon could revel that a multinational corporation was valuing his company at $4 million. Quite an achievement, considering he launched KoreaLink with birthday gift money he had saved since he was 16.

"It was a complicated deal. It wasn't a simple investment. It just didn't make sense for us at that time."

To understand Hyundai's high six-figure offer, just look at KoreaLink's extraordinary success. Broadly defined, KoreaLink is a registered-user–based content service niched to Koreans offering news, commerce, and community, through message boards, personal ads, and live chat. As such, KoreaLink provides a space for Koreans to interact with each other worldwide. To all this there is one important footnote: KoreaLink is in English.

Despite the non-native language, KoreaLink is by far the world's largest Asian online community. As such, it is also one of the Web's most visited sites regardless of genre. Month after month KoreaLink has made both PC Meter's MediaMetrix 500 as well as the Web Hot 100—as high as number 35—which is based exclusively on traffic.

So how much traffic is that? In 1998 KoreaLink will have served up 80 million pageviews. They get more than 25,000 unique visitors a day (from a base of 150,000 registered users), which generates more than $1.5 million through subscription fees (40%), advertising (40%), and electronic commerce (20%).

What's even more amazing is their demographic. Over 80% of KoreaLink's members are 30 or younger. This range fits perfectly with KoreaLink's peak activity, Monday nights beginning at 8:00 P.M. "About 75% of our members are students," says Cheon. "They are busy on the weekends but in the evening, in the early part of the week, they have more free time at home. They haven't started their homework yet."

Not everyone who visits KoreaLink is Korean. According to an in-depth poll taken by the service, about 20% of KoreaLink's members are Caucasian. This figure thrills Joe Cheon, who has always viewed KoreaLink as a way to expand Korean culture beyond the Korean community.

The core of KoreaLink is interactivity—a perfect fit with their young demographic. This is why their public message discussion boards, live chat, and SinglesLink personal ads are by far their most popular areas, the latter even responsible for several marriages.

"We have been told of at least four marriages, but we know it's more than that. They just haven't told us," says Cheon. "The women write us—never the men—and say thanks. But there are a lot of couples who have just dated and didn't get married. Again it's the women who let us know. They are very appreciative."

Because the KoreaLink membership is 76% male, the personal ads are free for females to post in an attempt to keep a decent proportion of activity. A typical count is 11,000 male ads and 2,800 female. But the small percentage of female posts is not just because they make up only 24% of the service. "Asian women are shier and less outgoing than non-Asian women," says Cheon. "Therefore they would be less apt to do this. Some might also be afraid that their friends or parents would see their ad."

To circumvent this stigma, many of the women place ads in KoreaLink's pen pals section, which Cheon describes as "more casual" than the personals. Women post in this area to the same degree that they post in the personals forum.

Regardless of where they post, the average female receives 100 responses per month, and the men receive about 5–10 e-mails, which according to Cheon, "depends largely on how well they write."

Cheon is very protective of his female audience, not only because they attract paying male members but out of a genuine concern for the women's safety. Because of his protective nature he began a fee-based membership program not only as a revenue source but as a security measure.

"We need a full profile of the males to safeguard the females," Cheon explains. "We can get the full profile if they are paying members since they must use a credit card. This way we are sure we have a bona fide person. We use an address verification system to match to the credit card. We never have to worry about fake people with their Hotmail e-mail addresses.... The women know that if there is a problem, we know how to find these guys."

KoreaLink has two tiers of membership. All visitors are asked to become registered members, and registration is free. However, if they want to use SinglesLink, Pen Pals, or the classified ad areas—the service's most popular—they must pay a subscription fee called a "Gold Membership," which costs $9 a month plus a $19 setup fee.

Just under 10% of all registered users become Gold Members, although hundreds sign up each month. The attrition rate is less than 10%. While the base monthly charge is $9, there are price breaks for longer prebilled terms at three months, six months, and one year. Most forfeit the savings and choose the month-to-month option.

One of the ironies of KoreaLink's membership program is that guests—people who don't register at all—have almost the same benefits and access as the nonpaying registered members. But they sign up anyway. "I don't know why but I think it's because they want to officially be a part of KoreaLink," say Cheon. "They think that if they come to the site more often it's better to register."

Needless to say, it benefits KoreaLink to have people registered because it provides valuable demographic data that they use to attract advertisers.

Five months after he launched the site in January 1996, KoreaLink began accepting advertising, which has been a consistent profit center, accounting for 40% of their total revenue.

At any one time KoreaLink has 10–15 sponsors. The higher-profile names include Citibank, Microsoft, Apple, IBM, and Alta Vista. Most are utilizing the service to specifically reach a Korean audience. Apple, for example, advertised a Korean language kit for the Mac, which allows any Mac program to display the Korean character set. Microsoft is looking for KoreaLink members' international travel business by advertising their Expedia travel service. Alta Vista promotes Alta Vista Asia. The ad rates paid vary based on banner size, placement, and term, but they run as high as $11,500 a month.

Not only does KoreaLink deliver the precise audience these advertisers want to connect with, they are also providing the click-throughs at an average rate of 2%. Some advertisers, such as Cyberian Outpost, have seen click-throughs as high as 4%. Again, it's the quality of the click-throughs that makes these advertising relationships winners for the sponsors.

Because of KoreaLink's enormous traffic and winning reputation, Cheon does not have to spend time soliciting advertisers; they come to him, either directly or through agencies. The primary disadvantage to agencies is that he often has to pay commissions of up to 40% on large-dollar, short-term contracts. On the flip side, sometimes the commissions are as little as 20% for longer-term contracts or those that come from small companies represented by equally small agencies.

When KoreaLink has remnant inventory, Cheon turns it over to ad brokers to firesale it at an average of $8/CPM for run-of-site. Approximately 500,000, 25%, of the 2 million impressions each month are sold on this basis. Typically the remainders are bought by companies like Amazon.com, books.com, and students.net.

Cheon understands the value of online advertising to his sponsors because he aggressively advertises KoreaLink as well, on the Web and off.

KoreaLink's success offline in print magazines has been difficult to quantify because it's so hard to measure. Accordingly, Cheon has not been able to "see a direct financial result." He spends about $3,000 a month for six full-color ads in Korean computer and Internet magazines, and he views this expense as more of a brand awareness opportunity than a method to secure paid memberships.

Since KoreaLink caters to a niche group, determining the best sites to match with is easy. KoreaLink advertises on other Korean-oriented sites such as OpenTown.com where they pay about $2,000 a month for a banner ad and get an astounding 12% click-through.

Even with this click-through rate, Cheon feels his best advertising expenditures have been with Alta Vista, where he spent about $6,000 on keyword buys using the words "Korea," "Korean," and "Seoul." With a 7% click-through rate, they got approximately 300 Gold Members and 4,000 (free) registered users. The gross value of the paid subscribers for the first month with the $19 setup fee was $8,400, clearly demonstrating the value of this buy.

Although the paid members produce consistent revenue for KoreaLink, Cheon realizes the value of the registered users with respect to his e-commerce objectives. As of the second quarter of 1998, approximately 20% of KoreaLink's revenues came from product sales, particularly their Hanme Hamgul software, which allows popular browsers to read the Korean character set.

Because of a unique arrangement, selling the software is a pure profit proposition. Cheon simply swapped banner ads with the company. Cheon bartered six months' worth of ads valued at well over $100,000 for hundreds of cases of packaged software, which sell for $60/piece. Fortunately for Cheon this software is not only his highest-profit item, it's also his most popular. In addition, Cheon sells other Korean-oriented products, most of which have a 50% profit margin and include videos and textbooks to teach basic Korean. One of these sets was bought by a man of Korean descent living in the United Arab Emirates. "He told us that he would need to travel on his camel to pick up his order at the post office," Cheon remembers. "All that work, and the delivery charge was more than the items."

In addition to paid advertising, Cheon draws new users through his current member base. In fact, word of mouth accounts for over 30% of his new registrants. How he accomplishes this is a win-win, providing value to both the visitor and KoreaLink.

"In our Kimchi People area we offer a free link to anyone's personal homepage," Cheon explains. "In exchange for the link they have to include our logo on their homepage, which is hotlinked to our site." To make sure people comply, Cheon has delegated one of his four staff members to a logo patrol, making sure the 300 new submissions they get each month are honoring their agreement. On the average about 90% do, which means that over 2,000 sites link back from this arrangement.

Another 30% of KoreaLink's traffic comes from the search engines, particularly AOL's Webcrawler, Infoseek, Alta Vista, and Yahoo, in that order. In addition to traffic from AOL's default search engine WebCrawler, KoreaLink also has premium positioning on the service. In the International Channel's Web recommendations, KoreaLink is listed number one. Since this is an editorial mention, Cheon does not pay for the exposure. In part due to this high profile, 20% of KoreaLink's visitors come from America Online.

One of the advantages Cheon created for himself is demonstrated by the traffic he gets from AOL: He chose a name that aptly describes the nature of his service. "I was thinking how great it would be if Koreans from all over the world could come together; as I was thinking about this, I thought 'KoreaLink.'" The main benefit of this name is that it clearly identifies the service as a people place versus information about the country, which is exactly what one finds if they type in korea.com. Perhaps this proves that a noun plus ".com" is not always the best domain name choice.

Knowing he has a good name, not to mention a bona fide brand, Cheon made only a slight modification to the domain when launching the Korean version of KoreaLink in June 1998, which can be found at www.korealink.net (versus the ".com" for the English version).

Actually Cheon had plans for a Korean version of KoreaLink when he first launched the English edition. He always knew he would complete the circle of his venture, but he also wanted to get the first KoreaLink firmly rooted. "I wanted to get the complete inbound and outbound users," says Cheon. "With an English version of KoreaLink we can promote Korean companies, but we cannot promote American companies. The last time AT&T advertised on KoreaLink they told us they also wanted Korean speaking persons." This gave Cheon some comfort knowing that his high-profile advertisers would be waiting on the ".net" side as well.

KoreaLink.net is similar to KoreaLink.com in its context, but not its content. In other words, they have nearly identical subsections, but ".net" is not a translated version of ".com." The content is unique to each. Since 67% of KoreaLink.com's users speak both languages, it actually would make sense for them to belong to both since the content is different. Even so, Cheon estimates that 99% of the members will originate from South Korea, versus the heavy Los Angeles population responsible for frequenting ".com." "Los Angeles is the number one biggest population of Koreans outside of Korea," says Cheon. "It never surprised me that that many visitors would come from L.A."

Perhaps fitting the profile of his users, Cheon's family moved to Los Angeles when he was 15 years old. His father once ran the Korean version of *Time Magazine* and was a journalist for a major Korean newspaper. During a period of instability, his father wanted to ensure a better education for his children and a better life. He and the family emigrated to the

United States and became citizens. His father now runs a successful print shop.

The parallel is interesting, since his son is essentially in the same business only digitally. Furthermore, he is preserving the culture he had to escape as a child. "Korea is about 5,000 miles away from Los Angeles," laments Cheon. "I feel I have lost touch with my culture and KoreaLink is how I want to preserve it … uniting Korean people."

This, however, was not an initiative shared by his co-workers. When Cheon graduated from San Diego State University with a B.S. in electrical engineering in 1993, he started a company focused on computer consulting and networking. Even though he was the President, Cheon's staff were constantly miffed by his relentless surfing and chatting on the Internet.

At this point Cheon suggested they start an online service; they balked. This forced Cheon to dip into his birthday savings. "I had about three staff in my company at the time and they did not want to cooperate. I had to buy a server and I didn't have any choice for funding." Even more amazing is that Cheon couldn't think of any way to make money from his venture at the time he was launching. "Banner ads had not occurred to me. Even so I never thought my site would become this popular. It was one of my hobbies. I was making enough money from the networking and software side of my business that it didn't matter."

Now Cheon has a total staff of nine people. Five of them help run his original business, with the other four devoted to KoreaLink. None of them hassle him for spending so much time online.

Now that he has had such success, Cheon is noticing that it influences every aspect of his life. "I've learned to trust my intuition and go like a bulldozer when it comes to ideas I think may fly."

For up-to-date information about the success of
KoreaLink
visit
www.StrikingItRich.com

LONG ISLAND HOT TUBS
HOMEPAGE

Long Island Hot Tubs   516.395.5900   Paramount Pools

Virtual Pool & Spa Store

Virtual Pool and Spa Store Main Navigation Bar

Home **Spas** Pools **Info/Tips** Shopping **Email** Services **Orders** Mailing List **Help**

The World's Largest Internet Pool & Spa Store

Voted Best Pool & Spa Retail Web Site - National Spa & Pool Institute 1997
"Electronic commerce at its finest on the Internet" - CNET's The Web TV Show 1998
Undisputedly the World's Largest Internet Pool and Spa Store - L.A. Times reporter Jaclyn Easton 1998
Retail Marketing Professional Excellence Award - Pool & Spa News Magazine 1996
Voted one of the top 100 Pool & Spa Companies in the entire USA - Aqua Magazine 1998
Top Shopping Site Award - All Internet Shopping Directory 1996, 1997, 1998
The Best of the Best of the Web Award Winner 1996, 1997, 1998
Aqua 100 Award Winner 1990, 1996, 1997

"We bring the world of Pools and Spas right to your door!"
Call us Toll Free at 1- 877- HOTTUBS
Over 50,000 Pool and Spa related items - worldwide shipping !

DANIEL HARRISON

LONG ISLAND HOT TUBS

www.lihottubs.com

Years after the verdict, the specter of O. J. Simpson continues to drive traffic to a Website that sells pool and hot tub supplies.

"It's a short article called 'Jacuzzis and the O .J. Trial,'" explains Dan Harrison, the site's owner. "The article makes the point that if Kato had not forgotten to turn off the jets on the Jacuzzi, O. J. would never have gone to his guest house and they probably would not have gone to McDonald's together. This whole series of seemingly small and insignificant events made Kato famous and helped the prosecution's case against O. J. Simpson. And all because he left the Jacuzzi jets on!"

Such details might be overlooked by the untubbed masses, but spa owners find the concept riveting and continue to descend on the site to read the short piece that was originally posted in 1996.

We should probably consider this a not-so-gentle reminder of the accepted belief that even transaction sites should have high-quality content. If the content is not highly informative, then it should at least evoke a lot of curiosity.

Content is certainly a nonissue for Long Island Hot Tubs and Paramount Pools' Virtual Pool and Spa Store, whose 400-page Website undisputably makes it the "The World's Largest Internet Pool and Spa Store." Launched as an adjunct to their successful mail order business and physical store on tony Long Island in New York, this Internet destination has such a massive presence it all but owns the spa supplies category online. With over 7,000 Web orders and over $600,000 in annual revenues, their claim would be hard to dispute.

Long Island Hot Tubs' site boasts a massive 50,000-item inventory, which ranges from 39-cent spa knobs to $1,800 swimming pool covers. The only spa items they don't sell are the spas themselves. "I don't need another headache," Harrison confesses. "I did it for 18 years and I don't have the stomach for it anymore."

While he doesn't care to focus on the component that drives the rest of his business, he does pay more attention to his spa category than pool supplies because he has found it to be a more profitable segment.

"Spa customers are more valuable than pool customers because there are tens of thousands of pool stores and this is in addition to Home Depot where they can also get pool stuff," Harrison explains. "There are only a couple hundred spa-only stores in the U.S. It's a very niche market. Also, spas are year-round and pools are not. So they need more chemicals and parts, and, since they are electronic, they break down more," he adds.

With less competition, Harrison has room for higher profit margins. Mark-ups of 100–400% are not unusual, partly because these are highly seasonal products. A $200 chemical order can yield a $140 profit. Parts have the lowest profit margin at 100%. Furthermore, Long Island Hot Tubs does not discount. "Our prices are reasonable," Harrison maintains. "Other sites charge about the same."

Combining spa supplies and the Web makes a lot of sense when you consider the clientele. According to Harrison, the typical spa owner is over 35 and earning a minimum of $66,500 annually—a demographic consistent with the online world.

Long Island Hot Tubs is in an enviable position because so few stores carry spa parts. They have an extensive inventory, which is detailed in over 60 Web pages complete with line drawings so that customers can easily identify what they need.

Despite the less erratic nature of hot tubs, Harrison still sees seasonal spikes in his online business. During the 1997 season, his site averaged 400–600 visitors per day, 4,000 pageviews, and at least 30 orders. Off season, those numbers are about halved. Though he consistently grosses more than

$10,000 per week, these seasonal shifts make it difficult for him to estimate an "average order" amount, but, if forced, he settles on the figure of $80, with the caveat that $30 orders can be as common as $1,000 orders. Then, of course, there are the occasional mega-orders.

"We got an online order for 50,000 rubber ducks. The customer was using them for a charity duck race," he explains. "They number the ducks and people get to buy one for $5. They put all the ducks in a river and the one that gets across the finish line first wins a truck." This $60,000 order has been Long Island Hot Tubs' biggest and required them to import containers of yellow duckies from Taiwan to fulfill the request. Thank heavens for drop shipping.

What has greatly benefited Harrison is that he is less myopic than most who have a catalog and a Web presence. While most mail order folks migrating to the Web dream of eventually dumping their print catalog and converting to a totally digital medium, Harrison is pumping his mailing list. He sees a profitable union between the two and an important cycle inherent in an offline catalog and a Web presence. They feed on each other, creating a profit vortex.

For example, mail order sales for Harrison are boosted bimonthly via his paper newsletter *Hot Tub Life*. In his first 17 years of business, he accumulated 2,000 names. In 1997, via the Website, he added 5,000 more. In 12 months he was able to add more than two and a half times what previously took him 17 years to build up.

Even though Long Island Hot Tub's Website grosses mid-six-figures annually, Harrison considers his biggest success to date these newsletter signups. "Mailing lists of hot tub owners are not available for sale," he explains. "Pools require permits, so list brokers can get names that way. Without the Web there would be no other way that we could have grown our mailing list like this."

Because his sales are seasonal and cyclical, accounting for what is motivating sales is difficult to measure. "People find us online, sign up for a newsletter or catalog, and then a year later phone in an order. It is really hard to track," Harrison explains. Of one figure he is certain: His repeat business rate from the Web exceeds 80%.

Regardless of the interactivity of the site, according to Harrison, even if a customer does all his online research on the site, over 90% still call in their orders to the company's non-800 number. Despite highly detailed information on his pages, people still need and want more data. "We are not selling tires," Dan points out. "We are selling spa stuff and many people don't know what they need or want, and they have to call."

That could be, but Long Island Hot Tubs does not use any shopping cart technology. This means that customers must jot down product numbers or print out pages to refer to when completing the static order form, a process that is incongruous with the convenience of Web shopping.

"To date we haven't added a shopping cart because I was my Internet service provider's only client who needed one," Harrison explains. "Customers were calling and complaining. So I am paying to have the software installed."

Besides customers who call, others e-mail. "In season, we get at least 200 e-mails a day," Harrison sighs. "Our New Year's resolution for this year is to try to answer all e-mails every day. This year we were not able to do that. During the busy season, there were times when people had to wait up to two weeks for a reply. There was just no way that we could keep up."

"Obviously we always pull out the online e-mail orders daily and process those items right away. But the Ask the Pool Guy and Ask the Spa Guy e-mails would mount up at times."

Part of this is due to a smart move rarely seen on most Websites. In addition to securing new customers, posing a question to the Spa and Pool Guys virtually ensures a new mailing list entry, since folks are encouraged to give their physical mailing address information via the form they are using to pose their questions.

What is so incredible is that, despite the fact that he has built up this snail mail list, he does not service his e-mail addresses. "I have all the addresses and will start servicing the list when we have the time to devote to it, but it simply has not been high priority," Harrison acknowledges. "This whole Internet thing took off much faster than we had thought. We were simply unprepared."

Most of Long Island Hot Tubs' new customers come from search engines, with 50% specifically coming from Alta Vista. So you can imagine the impact it had on Harrison when Long Island Hot Tubs was temporarily pulled from the Alta Vista database.

As Harrison told an Internet trade publication, being cut from Alta Vista had catastrophic results. "Our revenues were like—boom!—cut two-thirds for two weeks."

According to Harrison, in April 1997, Long Island Hot Tubs was wrongly accused of "spamming" the Alta Vista search engine and was stripped from the search service's database. Essentially, no search results could reference Long Island Hot Tubs. It was as though the site did not exist. Alta Vista claimed Harrison was removed because he submitted too many pages containing the same kinds of words. That may have been the case, but the removal was done unbeknownst to him.

When Harrison launched his megasite, he used a popular submission service called PostMaster, which he ironically found via the Alta Vista homepage. One of the services PostMaster offered was "deep submit," which individually submits each page of a site to all the search engines. The benefit to the site is that, the more individual pages (and their unique URLs) are listed, the better the chances are that their site will get listed higher up and more often on a results page.

"Since our site contains over 400 pages of pool and spa information and products, it stands to reason that our site would appear very frequently in Alta Vista when someone searched for pool- or spa-related terms," Harrison recounts. "Unfortunately, when someone from Alta Vista was reviewing their listings, they decided that we were illegally 'spamming' them when, in fact, we were merely using a submission service listed on their service."

What bothered Harrison most was that "as a judge, jury and executioner, they deleted all references to our site." Apparently repeated attempts to explain why Long Island Hot Tubs felt they had been "wrongly accused" failed and, after some trade press, were eventually handled.

Long Island Hot Tubs has since been reinstated, but the memory of the Alta Vista debacle still irritates Harrison. "I wish that there were some sort of governing body that a company could turn to if one has problems with a search engine. Our experience with Alta Vista showed us how much ultimate power they wield and how strongly they affect Internet commerce—all according to their unregulated whim."

Fortunately many months later, typing in "hot tubs" still finds Harrison's Webshop in the fifth, ninth, and tenth position in the results and the query "spa parts" shows them in positions one, four, and five. All is well.

Harrison is so dependent on search engines partly because his advertising experiences have not fared well. He spent $2,600 advertising in offline pool magazines before he gave up on that venue, and another $5,000 on local cable TV touting the Website, which did not work either. Since the search engine results listings rank him so high, keyword buys make no sense. In other online advertising opportunities, Long Island Hot Tubs became a Link Exchange member but stopped after 2.5 years and dismal results.

"The Link Exchange banners were slowing down our page loads, and we were only able to attribute a pathetic amount of traffic to them. Out of the 600,000 banners our site served, we got maybe 100 click-throughs from reciprocal ads."

Despite infinitesimal click-through rates, Harrison had a more pressing consideration, making his pages work for the least powerful technology. "I wanted to give priority to the speed that it took my pages to load," Harrison notes. "I wanted people at 14.4 from AOL at peak times to be able load our site."

America Online members are critical to Long Island Hot Tubs' success, with over 50% of their visitors originating from the service.

In addition to the AOL considerations, from the moment Harrison launched his online enterprise he has been virtually obsessed with his site's design and functionality. While most online catalogs with the depth of Long Island Hot Tubs would be database-driven, Harrison's is not. Today, most large sites use database technology, which creates pages in real time. Harrison's pages, on the other hand, are separately designed and programmed. This means that if Long Island Hot Tubs wants to make a change that would appear on every page, it has to be programmed 400 times.

This explains why any changes are such a herculean task. "During the off season, we have three people who spend all day and all night working on the site." When Long Island Hot Tubs was launched online, their site was 150 pages deep. It took over six months to plan, develop, and program. Harrison estimates that, if he had contracted it out, it would have easily cost him more than $100,000.

"Our site started early in the history of the Web. We couldn't even do intersite searches at first," he explains. "But we are rebuilding the site from the ground up, and we're on track to completely reconfigure how we are approach this."

Regardless of the backend technology, within months of his launch he started winning awards. To date Long Island Hot Tubs has earned dozens, including the National Pool & Spa Institute's Consumer Influence Award for Best Pool & Spa Retail Web Site, Best of the Best on the Web award, and a Top Internet Shopping Site seal.

Many of the awards are attributed to the site's content, which is divided into various sections including Hot Tubs & Spas, Pools and Home Service, and the Java Gaming Center, the latter of which includes nonaquatic categories like blackjack and biorhythm charts. The site also features messages boards and chat.

"The more things on the site that are fun and interesting, I figure the more that would keep them coming back," theorizes Harrison. "Actually under 5% play the games."

While visitors might not be playing games, Harrison figured that surely they would be interested in live chats and message boards, but he was wrong.

"I truly thought there would have been more activity on the message boards. A lot of people read them, but not many post. In eight months we got a couple hundred messages, but based on the thousands of visitors we get, this was really low. We realized that because we have the Ask the Pool Guy and Ask the Spa Guy areas there isn't a whole lot of reason for people to post on the boards. If I am having a traumatic spa problem, I would prefer going directly to an expert than depending on the advice of someone I don't know."

So to get right to an expert, Harrison launched weekly chats, but these didn't fare well either. Harrison announced Ask the Spa Guy Live with announcements on Long Island Hot Tubs' five most active pages and even offered discounts during the chats. This results were disappointing. "At the peak of it we had six people in the six-week trial run. When people want info, they want it now; they are not going to wait for Wednesday," he explains. But there was a bright spot. "The people who did come were prepared with great questions and they loved it. I'll never forget the woman who finally got her foamy water questions answered."

What Dan Harrison may have also learned is that simply posting notices on a few pages on a site, without follow-up reminders the day of the event via e-mail, may be expecting too much proactivity on the part of customers.

One area where Long Island Hot Tubs' business is bound to expand is the international market, which currently accounts for only 1% of their sales. However, his first foreign sale was promising, a $1,500 spa equipment pack to Norway.

"The U.S. is in the forefront of spa equipment and sales account for 75% of the world market, mostly because the manufacturers are in the U.S. For this reason we get a lot of e-mail from places like Malaysia and India, and a place called Yap or Yop, looking for basics like chlorine."

To some degree Harrison must have been a bit psychic. He started on CompuServe a couple of years before he saw the Web. In late 1994 he produced a catalog on disc before the launch of Long Island Hot Tubs in June 1995.

"It was too expensive to print a color catalog and we knew that we were not presenting our products in the best light," Harrison explains. "We found a program that lets you place all your products with full-color pictures on one floppy. To date, we have had about 800 requests for the disc catalog delivered by postal mail and about 300–400 people a month download it off the Website. It includes an order form. So we know that people with the disc order more than those who don't have the disc."

Perhaps because of this disc experience, Harrison knew when he started hearing about the Internet it was the answer to expand his spa chemical and accessory mail order business nationwide for a very small investment, since national advertising was prohibitively expensive.

While he practically has a lock on the spa supply online category, Harrison is cognizant of the competition, especially if the Web sees a launch by Leslie's Pool Supply, a national retail pool store with around 400 stores countrywide. "This could hurt the chemical end of my business," confesses Harrison.

While their presence could make a dent in Long Island Hot Tubs' sales, Harrison also knows that there is plenty of business for everyone. "When we first started, our hope was that we would get a few new customers and increase our mail order. We clearly underestimated the power of the Web. I cannot even begin to imagine how big this is going to get once 50% of the U.S. gets online. Just the thought makes me want to go pick out a Ferrari!"

For up-to-date information about the
success of
Long Island Hot Tubs
visit
www.StrikingItRich.com

MOTORCYCLE ONLINE

Daily News
What's New?
Come Meet MO
Product Reviews
New Products
Bike Reviews

Noriyuki Haga

Yamaha YZ400F

99 Ducati 900SS

New '99 Harleys

'98 SBK Photos

BMW R1100S

Bartels' Performance Products

Motorcycle Rentals

| SEARCH | BREAKIN' THE LAW | OFF ROAD | MANUFACTURER'S ROW | AD INFO | MULTIMEDIA ARCHIVE | CLASSIFIED |
| RACING | PRODUCT REVIEWS | TOURING WORLD | NUTS & BOLTS | ABOUT MO | VIRTUAL MUSEUM | DATABASE |

"The World's Largest and Most-Read Digital Motorcycle Magazine"
iyuki Haga | Yamaha YZ400F | Ducati 900SS | '99 Harleys | World Superbike | BMW R110(
Daily News | What's New | Bike Reviews | Product Reviews | Multimedia Archive | Racing
Nuts & Bolts | Touring The World | Manufacturer's Row | New-Model Database
Search | Breakin' The Law | Off-Road | Classifieds | Museum
Editorial Feedback | Advertising Inquiries | Staff
Events Calendar | New Products
© 1998 Motorcycle Online, Inc.

BRENT PLUMMER

MOTORCYCLE ONLINE

www.motorcycle.com

Few 29-year-olds get to do exactly what they want. Brent Plummer is one of them.

As the publisher of *Motorcycle Online,* one of the most successful Web-based publications in history, he has the ultimate freedom. "Each day it doesn't matter what I want to do. I now have a staff that can run *Motorcycle Online* without me," Plummer remarks. "I don't even have to answer to my advertisers. If any of them left, it would not be a big deal because we have enough of them. Everybody is making a lot of money, and we are all very happy."

Happy indeed. According to Plummer, *Motorcycle Online* was the first profitable online magazine ever and the only profitable motor sports e-zine to date. "We've been 100% earned-revenue–supported since 1995. Thus, we've been profitable longer than most sites have been online." Funded primarily by ad banner revenues since their launch in August 1994, Plummer states that he has never heard of an e-zine showing a profit before 1997. "It's entirely speculation," he admits, "but a fair hunch."

Launched on his 26th birthday, *Motorcycle Online* is the largest digital motorcycle magazine on the Web—bigger than all their competitors combined, a position it has enjoyed since its inception. In a typical day the site is visited by more than 17,000 people to whom it delivers 83,000 pageviews. In fact, *Motorcycle Online*'s 1997 server logs clearly show that they have more readers than *Popular Mechanics* online.

Most of *Motorcycle Online*'s extraordinary popularity has to do with their completely unbiased editorial, which is the core of Plummer's mission statement.

"In this industry, the money end of the business has a lot of say in the editorial end. So everything turns out 'good' but nothing is 'horrible' or 'the worst product in its class,'" Plummer explains. "We're not like that. We tell it how it is. While this initially hurt ad sales, eventually it earned the e-zine massive readership. I figured that a magazine that held to strict ethical publishing standards could build a hugely loyal readership, and then, with the largest reader base in the world, advertisers would have to pay attention."

Plummer's hypothesis was correct. Approximately 80% of *Motorcycle Online*'s advertisers, about 18 companies, have purchased long-term contracts of a year or more. The remaining 20% are monthly deals and are often for time-bound propositions.

For example, the New Zealand–based Thunder Bike company runs surveys and randomly picks a respondent who wins a free trip. Thunder Bikes then uses the data to build up their physical and e-mail address list of people interested in their products. Since Thunder Bikes wants to build an international ad base, this arrangement is perfect, costing them only $1 net per person to augment their list. But *Motorcycle Online* has very strict terms with Thunder Bikes. "They cannot rent the e-mail or physical address list for any reason," maintains Plummer.

Back in August 1994, *Motorcycle Online*'s first advertiser was Graves Motor Sports, who paid "a 'whopping' $200 per month in addition to the *Motorcycle Online* staff's having unlimited access to their mechanical shop, which is about 15 miles away," Plummer remembers. Today the same ad would cost nearly five times as much. Graves' contract, along with all the other charter advertisers, stated that their rates would not rise for the first three years. While this agreement has now expired, Graves remains a loyal and satisfied advertiser.

Not all of *Motorcycle Online*'s ad banner revenue is a monthly flat fee, however. They also have integrated commission-based arrangements that have been wildly successful.

With one advertiser moving to a pay-per-sale and pay-per-lead model on an after-market part, the magazine netted over $100,000 in one year. From this positive experience they have

decided to make similar arrangements with motorcycle manufacturers. The terms are simple. If one of the banner ads on
Motorcycle Online actually moves a bike for a big name manufacturer, they will get paid a commission on the sale. If *Motorcycle Online* is responsible for only a referral, they will also be
paid a fee. Plummer states that the amount is confidential but
more than $10.

If an advertiser balks at the *Motorcycle Online* rate card,
the e-zine considers offering them a pay-per-click arrangement.
The irony is that many of these advertisers would wind up paying much more with this arrangement. "Our standard rate card
for the homepage is $13,500 per month," says Plummer. "If
Bartels' Harley-Davidson were paying $1 a click-through, they
would have paid $100,000 instead. In fact, after they made
their quota in two days we moved them to a flat rate."

Motorcycle Online started a similar pay-per-click program
in 1995. Plummer says that his potential advertisers didn't understand the concept then, still don't, and it frustrates him.
"They're so used to paying $75-and-more-CPM rates for one-
page ads with no guarantee on how many people see that particular page despite the rate being based on total number of
magazines printed. They have an entirely skewed image of how
many people were seeing their print ads and the return per dollar spent."

But the companies that do understand the advantages of
Web advertising are spending their marketing dollars in one
place only: *Motorcycle Online.* "We are larger than all our competition combined and have some 95% of all online motorcycle
industry revenues concentrated at *Motorcycle Online,*" boasts
Plummer. "This is where people read about their bikes first. I
have waited four years for the Big 5 [Harley, Honda, Yamaha,
Suzuki, and Kawasaki] to get around to advertising with us."

Despite these inroads, Plummer would prefer to move away
from industry advertisers entirely. "We are focusing on revenue
sharing with Dell Computer and closing deals with companies
like Dodge Trucks—52% of bikers own trucks. Then we'll move
to audio and alcohol," says Plummer. "We're attempting to

have over 50% of our revenues from outside our industry within two years. Direct sales of computers and trucks is really what we're hoping will be our cash cow."

There is only one feature of advertising on the e-zine that annoys advertisers: *Motorcycle Online* knows the exact degree of their success on the site. Since the sales take place on the *Motorcycle Online*'s secure servers, the e-zine is cognizant of the advertisers' grosses. Ditto for click-throughs on banner ads. "The only thing my advertisers are not happy about is that we track how much they make and how well their ads perform. So they don't have a lot of leverage when it comes to negotiating their deals." Staying true to his audience, Plummer will not accept advertising from companies whose products detract from motorcycling or are harmful, such as attorneys. "We are not here to get rich. We are here to make motorcycling better," he contends.

While *Motorcycle Online*'s revenues rely on advertising, paradoxically the Website does very little advertising for itself. Currently Plummer advertises *Motorcycle Online* on one Website, the Daily Bikini, a start page that features a different bikini-clad model along with links to categories of interest such as news and sports, the latter featuring the *Motorcycle Online* link.

The traffic the Daily Bikini sends to Plummer's site proves that there is an ideal match between the two. "We spent 10% of what we did on Yahoo and get 2,000 referrals a month from it." While Plummer is reluctant to reveal the rate he pays the Daily Bikini, he did confess that it works out to an inconsequential amount when amortized by the amount of traffic it generates. He has signed a multiyear contract.

In addition to the Daily Bikini, Plummer had dabbled in traditional banner advertising with Yahoo, exclusively owning the Recreation/Motorcycles area and buying the keywords "motorcycle" and "motorcycles" in various search engines. Somewhat blocking the disappointing experience, Plummer says that all he can remember is that he spent $45/CPM and that "it wasn't worth it."

If you were to examine *Motorcycle Online*'s referrer logs (stats that show from which site people arrived to get to yours), advertising on search engines probably would not make sense. While most sites have a double-digit dependency on search engines for their traffic, *Motorcycle Online* finds that the major navigation services account for an infinitesimal 1% of their traffic.

Better than advertising, 12% of *Motorcycle Online*'s traffic is generated from links on pages of motorsport enthusiasts. These are not reciprocal links either. *Motorcycle Online* links only to paid advertisements and occasional points of interest referred to in their daily news. Despite the lack of reciprocity, over 4,500 sites are linking to *Motorcycle Online*, a substantial figure that, when first presented to Plummer, surprised even him. "We've been here since August of 1994," he responds. "People respect what we do."

In what was a marketing coup without knowing it, Plummer has an another advantage: the ultimate domain name in motorcycle.com.

The Netscape browser, which didn't even exist at the time he was registering his domain, has a keystroke-saving feature that automatically adds the www. and the .com to whatever word is typed in the address field. This means that users in the know need only type in the critical "middle word." The result is that the address automatically expands to include the other components. For example, simply typing "motorcycle" automatically expands to *Motorcycle Online*'s address: http://www.motorcycle.com.

According to Plummer this drives 12% of his traffic.

Securing motorcycle.com was a marketing decision for Plummer before anyone considered such an entity an asset. Plummer was miles ahead of the curve, registering the address in mid-1994, early enough in the history of the commercial use of the Internet that the few domain names requests made each day were actually processed by hand. Furthermore, you had to give the Internic, the registering body at the time, a reasonable reason to have one. This is part of the reason Plummer did not register the plural, motorcycles.com, as well. (It was later registered by Honda Motorcycles who were not actively using it as of the first quarter of 1998.) Plummer, however, has no regrets that he didn't secure the plural at the same time. "Back in those days the Net was tiny and you were respectful and cool. You didn't take more than what you needed," he reflects. "If I were hoarding names I would have taken motorcyclist.com and cycleworld.com also." Nonetheless he also owns motorcycle.net and motorcycle.org.

While he was certainly not stockpiling domains, Plummer was clearly thinking of the future. Around the same time, he also registered bicycle.com, vehicle.com, and whitetrash.com, along with eight others. Despite the fact that he continually gets six-figure offers for the Net names, he has never sold any of them.

While Plummer eventually plans to fully develop the concepts which the domains represent—though whitetrash.com currently points people to *Motorcycle Online*—his focus remains on *Motorcycle Online*. Part of the reason is the nearly perfect fit between the demographic of his readers and the Internet. *Motorcycle Online* visitors are 97% male, ages 35–44. Approximately 61% earn more than $51,000 annually and 89% have some college or better. We can also assume most of them are reading the magazine during business hours since *Motorcycle Online*'s West-coast–based servers are consistently their busiest between 7:00 A.M. and 7:00 P.M., Monday through Friday.

When asked to describe his site in three sentences, Plummer answers in two words: "It rules." Even a quick trip to motorcycle.com from a nonenthusiast could cause one to think, if content is king, then *Motorcycle Online* is majestic.

Thanks to a clean and simple design, navigating *Motorcycle Online*'s 14 content areas is easy. In fact, the online magazine has won virtually every online award there is. And, against convention, they have not changed their homepage layout and design in almost one and a half years. "We post so much that if we were changing the context all the time, people would get intimidated. We never get complaints."

Access to this of silo of content, which features over 2,886 stories, is simplified by a robust database. This search program, which allows for multiple keyword searches, retrieves information from anywhere on the *Motorcycle Online* site, including its voluminous archives. The database handles over 1,500 queries a day. These queries also include search requests from other motorcycle sites.

As a traffic generator, *Motorcycle Online* offers the code that lets people on another site input a keyword search term, but the search is actually performed at *Motorcycle Online*. The results listing from the search then moves the visitor over to *Motorcycle Online*. Plummer estimates that 10% of the searches originate from other sites, accounting for an equal amount of his traffic.

In yet another popular *Motorcycle Online* database, a search feature can deliver information on any motorcycle produced by a major manufacturer since model year 1994. Visitors can search by maker, model, price range, displacement, and seat height.

Both of these databases are clearly winners for *Motorcycle Online,* and the multibike shootouts (motorcycle comparisons) and the homepage are certainly the site's most popular areas. Because of the wonder of technology, a quick perusal of the *Motorcycle Online* server logs instantly tells Plummer exactly what people like most and least, data a print publisher would die for.

"We base much of our editorial focus on watching our log files constantly to catch reader preferences. This is a huge advantage over print mags, which never really know what people read the most. Thus, we're always ahead of trends and the print mags are always behind."

The influence of *Motorcycle Online*'s readership trends on future editorial direction was something Plummer paid attention to from the start. For example, Plummer says that sportbikes were all the rage in 1994 and *Motorcycle Online* saw big increases in cruiser-style stories. So they focused on them long before the big print mags did. Then they saw the trend revert to sportbikes and adjusted their editorial instantly.

One reader trend even influenced a major marketing/public relations position for *Motorcycle Online*. "We noticed that racing results tanked. So we stopped covering races in blow-by-blow action and instead focused on racing features and interviews with leading racers," Plummer explains. Realizing the interest in racers in general, Plummer decided to take his biggest marketing gamble to date, one that has resulted in huge dividends.

"Our most risky marketing move was to fund a national road race team, which cost us over $110,000 in 1997 alone. In 1997 we won a National Championship and got a ton of press coverage. Now we pitch the race team as a public relations medium to companies for associate sponsorship. Seemingly, it's a subtle difference from the standard marketing proposals for racing, but PR is typically a lot more flexible with budgets than marketing, which has to go through media buyers, ad agencies, and eternal delays."

Plummer notes that in 1998 the team will become a profit center. In addition to providing supplementary revenue, the team generates publicity and good will in the industry that is nearly impossible to quantify. *Motorcycle Online* is the only magazine, online or off, that funds a race team, and, according to Plummer, most in the industry appreciate that the publication isn't pocketing all their profits, but is actually giving back to the sport.

The racing team is another example of how *Motorcycle Online* is slowly diversifying their revenue streams. While banner ads will always remain the prime money generator, the site continues to experiment with alternatives, especially if they provide better service for the visitor.

For instance, although classified ads account for only a scant 1% of *Motorcycle Online*'s revenue, the e-zine offers them on the honor system.

The ads stay up from two weeks to one month based on the board in which they are posted. The site gets about 8,000 ads a month. When the ad is automatically deleted, an e-mail notice from *grovel@motorcycle.com* is automatically sent requesting the poster to remit $10 if the item sold. The site averages about $800 per month from this.

"The classifieds cost us nothing to operate," Plummer says. "The program was written by our board member Eric Murray and I decided to adapt it. We added autodelete and other features over time." One of the aspects that Plummer attributes to the paltry 1% compliance rate is that the poster must manually send a check. To overcome this, *Motorcycle Online* is starting to allow people to pay by credit card, with payment requested up front as a donation. Plummer does not want to make payment a requirement because enforcing it isn't worth their time.

Considering the extraordinary success of *Motorcycle Online*, the people weaseling out of a $10 classified fee have no meaning to an enterprise whose conservative estimate for profits in 1998 is over $200,000.

But this level of success also begets regrets. "I thought it would be all fun and games. Instead our growth has been so high everyone smells money around us. So the vultures are always swarming," explains Plummer. "Money is not what I'm after. I've turned down a $3.5-million offer already."

Plummer also recognizes that a few entities could come online and usurp his position, if they were willing to spend the money. "Flynt Publications could affect *Motorcycle Online* because they have inroads with companies like Dodge and people with real money. But it would be easier for them to buy us than to start from scratch."

To his credit Plummer doesn't consider anyone competition. For this reason he is extremely forthcoming about the figures related to his success. "We don't keep secrets," states Plummer. "Knowing how much we make shows our competitors how much they would have to spend to beat us. Part of this is our momentum for having been online so many years."

Anyone attempting to dethrone *Motorcycle Online* would clearly have to understand the scope of what the e-zine has established. They are the largest online motorcycle magazine in the world, technically giving it the largest reach of any motorcycle publication.

Their other primary competition is *Cycleworld*, a print magazine that Plummer feels *Motorcycle Online* can always beat editorially. "We provide stories on new bikes before anyone in the world," says Plummer. "We get them at the same time but our turnaround is one week after testing finishes. Their lead time is three months."

Motorcycle Online also has a geographic advantage too. When certain motorcycles are released in Europe first, *Motorcycle Online* has a team of freelance testers and writers in Denmark, Spain, and Israel to evaluate them immediately.

Between their dedication to covering European bikes and their 22% non-U.S. readership, *Motorcycle Online* has an opportunity to capitalize on its international audience, but for the time being probably won't. One challenge is that no one other language has enough value in terms of readership numbers to mandate a translation. Plummer also points out that the cheap way of using automatic translation software won't work. "Motorcycling uses so many proprietary words," he relates. "For instance, 'backing it in' is a technique used to spin the rear tire at a corner entry to turn the bike faster. That wouldn't translate well."

Even as an English-only Web publication, *Motorcycle Online*'s readership continues to swell as more enthusiasts come online, thus keeping them on their triple-digit growth rate track.

Motorcycle Online's readership scope is even more extraordinary when you consider that the venture was started with $28,000: his life savings of $11,000 combined with $17,000 from his publisher Erika Waechter. There is no way that his dream could have come to fruition had Brent Plummer attempted to do this in print, but this hurdle put Plummer and his enterprise on a road less traveled, but paved with opportunity.

"I was going to do my motorcycle magazine on paper but no one was willing to give a 25-year-old white male a loan. A major bank turned me down twice, both times suggesting that I move company ownership to a minority or female. That sucked! Mosaic [the precursor to Netscape] was making a big stir. So it just dawned on me do it online."

Moving to the online world actually made perfect sense for Plummer, who was able to blend his troika of talent and make the e-zine work initially as a solo enterprise. Plummer is an ace computer/network system administrator and passionate motorcyclist whose career prior to *Motorcycle Online* was as a freelance writer, photographer, and graphic designer. This was helpful in the very beginning since he was essentially a one-man magazine, writing all the stories in addition to editing, photos, and layout.

"In those first few months I never really woke up because I never went to sleep. I was working 20-hour days, seven days a week," Plummer reminisces. "Now, I still work 60 to 80 hours per week. I close all the big deals, set the editorial schedule, and generally try to look important in meetings. But I also get to ride around on the latest motorcycles and spend time with my racing team, if you call that work."

While he admits this is not a very "rule the world and make a fortune" ideal, he's still achieving exactly what he set out to do. "I just wanted to get paid to play with nice, new toys."

For up-to-date information about the
success of
Motorcycle Online
visit
www.StrikingItRich.com

Tuesday, August 04, 1998

Skiing
Extreme's Video

Snowboarding
Outreach Society

News
Archives

Free Magazine
Subscription

Check out today's Snow Reports

Marketplace
We sell stuff. Click here.

audio video showcase

YOU SET THE PRICE
Mountain Zone AUCTIONS
GREAT GEAR

snowboarding | skiing | mountain biking | hiking | photography | climbing

site map
news
contests
weather
snow reports
gear reviews
calendar
national parks
resort directory
Marketplace
Bookstore
Gear Store
Map Store
Video Store
letters
all about us

Racing to Kingdom's Crown

Crazy weather, new faces and a brand new venue combined to bring the '98 NORBA mountain biking season one step away from the end. Huge photo gallery, DH, XC, and DS action from **Breckenridge, Colorado**.

A Trip to Shangri-La

A stunning journey through Bhutan, from the precariously perched monasteries to the valleys 1000 feet below. Story and photos from **the doorstep of the Himalaya**.

Climbing Mount Adams

Follow a first time summitter as she climbs for a cause. Story, photos and audio from **The Mount Adams Climb to Fight Breast Cancer**.

SKIP FRANKLIN
GREG PROSL
TODD TIBBETTS

THE MOUNTAIN ZONE

www.mountainzone.com

"There were a lot of pundits who said that a site like ours, which is heavy on content, wouldn't make it," says Greg Prosl, cofounder of The Mountain Zone. "But we've had over 3.5 million people visit our site in the last two years and our revenues for 1998 are forecasted to exceed $1 million. All this because we did one thing: We stuck to our plan."

Prosl and his partners' plan was a clear-cut strategy. "We refer to it as our three Cs: content, community, and commerce," he explains. "Everything we do is focused on these three objectives."

Their content is best described by their motto, "If it's in the mountains, it's in The Mountain Zone." To that end, the editorial content is divided into six primary sections: snow boarding, skiing, mountain biking, hiking, climbing, and special topics (snow reports, directories, etc.). During the winter, skiing and snowboarding vie as the most active content areas, while in the summer activity shifts to mountain biking and climbing. As of the second quarter of 1998, the six areas housed more than 30,000 pages of information with approximately 200 pages added daily.

Just like their content, The Mountain Zone's commerce offerings possess the same wow factor. They have over 6,000 retail products, some of which are exclusives, many of which are just hard to find, but all of which are in tune with their audience.

In fact, The Mountain Zone may be the Web's most elegant execution of a content and commerce combination. There is so much content of such high quality that commerce functions as a watermark—accenting the information without distracting. Most important in this context, the product offerings are always in harmony with the content with which they are associated. Then there is the last element, which even most online retailers overlook, but The Mountain Zone has not. They see their job as not only aggregating products of sincere interest to mountain lovers, but filtering these product options and selecting those of the best quality and value. With a selection of more than 6,000 items, some would argue that The Mountain Zone has done a better job than a site devoted to transactions.

Despite this heavy emphasis on commerce, The Mountain Zone is considered primarily a content destination, which racks up over 500,000 unique visits a month. Their audience consists of 63% males and 37% females who earn $30,000 a year or more (34% earn over $50,000). Seventy-one percent participate in mountain sports 1–3 times a month. Since their launch in March 1996, the company has received over 18 awards or "prime picks" by media notables such as *USA Today* and *The Los Angeles Times*.

This avalanche of accolades should not be a surprise since The Mountain Zone invests heavily in unique and exclusive content and was far ahead of the curve in this arena. "We think that it's worth the investment to have staff members cover live events, such as the Winter Olympics in Nagano or the U.S. Snowboarding Championships, in order to give our visitors our own spin on events," Prosl remarks.

One event that they covered resulted in a stampede of visitors. Yet it was a bittersweet occurrence for Prosl and the rest of The Mountain Zone team because the circumstances begat fatalities.

One year after the tragic 1996 Mount Everest climb, chronicled in the megabest-selling book, *Into Thin Air* by Jon Krauker, The Mountain Zone got the rights to launch the Official 1997 American Mount Everest site and dispatched their publisher Peter Potterfield to cover the expedition from Everest base camp.

Unfortunately in 1997 more people perished as they attempted to ascend the world's tallest summit. Todd Burleson, the expedition's lead climber and partner of The Mountain Zone, was stationed about 12,000 feet away in base camp. Since Burleson was equipped with a satellite phone, he was able to provide live coverage and interviews as the tragic events unfolded.

"We broke the story," says Prosl. "We were the first media to report those events and then major media came to us. The first was CNN, followed by NBC Nightly News, Good Morning America, and the Today Show. Since they were all using our news reports, they would say 'as reported by Peter Potterfield from The Mountain Zone.'"

Prosl explains these reports suddenly transformed mountain climbing into a human interest story, with people from all cross-sections of life and all over the world wanting to better understand this deadly passion. To find out more they went straight to www.mountainzone.com.

In 1998 The Mountain Zone again was the official American Everest Expedition site. During this three-month period, they updated the section at least once a day with a daily dispatch and daily audio. In fact, the Everest area is a multimedia mecca with dozens of Real Video clips documenting some of Everest's greatest challenges, thus giving the visitor as much of an in-depth experience as possible via the Internet's limited bandwidth. Perhaps because of these bandwidth-intense applications, The Mountain Zone's peak visitor time is between 10 A.M. and 2:00 P.M. Pacific time, Monday through Thursday. People are surfing from work benefiting from the high-speed lines common in many offices.

In addition to attracting new visitors, premier content such as the Everest area creates significant revenue streams through sponsorships. In 1997 Microsoft was the exclusive sponsor of the area as a tie-in for their Internet Explorer browser. In a mid-five-figure cash deal, Microsoft got their name on the subsite, banners throughout the event coverage, and an additional one million impressions running through The Mountain Zone.

Ironically it was a similar arrangement a year earlier that actually launched The Mountain Zone. After obtaining sponsorship for a live cybercast of the U.S. Snowboarding Championships in Stratton, Vermont, Prosl and partners started programming the site. As Prosl puts it, "Essentially, it was a case of 'if you come, we will build it.'" But the decision was far more deliberate than it may seem. Prosl was already a cybercasting pioneer, having done some of the first ever including Handel's *Messiah* from the Kennedy Center in Washington D.C. in the fall of 1995.

However, instead of launching a general information site, Prosl (age 34), along with cofounders Skip Franklin (42) and Todd Tibbetts (30), wanted to approach their site differently, specifically as vertical market communities. "It was then that we spent a good deal of time figuring out the right market to tap into," Prosl says. Because Tibbetts was a graphic designer, their initial launch costs were several thousand dollars. Over time the figure would build to $182,000, of which two-thirds came from the cofounders and the balance from private investment.

"We knew that it had to be a growing market, and something that was large, at least 100 million people worldwide, in order to have enough of an online population. The three of us have a great passion for the outdoors, and we just kept coming back to this idea of a mountain/outdoor site. Combining this passion with the recognition of the huge opportunity represented by the Web, it seemed like an ideal business venture."

While many sites are now incorporating products as an afterthought, The Mountain Zone launched with an integrated commerce initiative. Their product categories include videos, books, maps, posters, apparel, and equipment. They get about 24 orders a day, with an average price point of $46. About 1–2% of the visitors to their marketplace area purchase. To spark sales, they occasionally offer a superdeal to get the commerce dollars flowing.

"Before the 1997 holiday season we were selling the hardcover edition of *Into Thin Air* for about $10," says Prosl. "This was basically a promotional tool and it generated a lot of excitement. We wanted our audience to have the experience of buying from us. Since we were basically selling the book at cost, we attributed it as a marketing expense."

While The Mountain Zone items for sale range from 80-cent lightbulbs for flashlights to $4,995 satellite telephones, as a product category, books represent 50% of their virtual inventory at 3,000 titles as well as being their highest-profit item at an average of 44%. Books are also The Mountain Zone's biggest seller, which Prosl feels is because they are easy to order online with a reasonable price point and a low-risk factor.

While The Mountain Zone is open about their statistics of the book sales, they will not discuss fulfillment, demonstrating what a highly competitive niche this has become.

"All products are drop shipped in The Mountain Zone packaging," says Prosl. "I will not reveal who is doing our book fulfillment. That's highly competitive information. Amazon.com would love to know that because they do not have access to some of the titles that we carry because their suppliers don't carry them." Prosl goes on to explain that in The Mountain Zone's specialty categories, many are self-published or small press prints, which make up for about 50% of the titles that they carry. "Amazon could get those books if they wanted, but it would require them to make deals with every one of the micropublishers or get their distributors to get them at great expense. The fact that The Mountain Zone has a single distributor who has aggregated these titles for them gives them a tremendous advantage, an advantage Prosl has secured, guaranteeing The Mountain Zone that they will not distribute for any other outdoor site.

Books, along with over 500 videos and the rest of their commerce offerings, are available via their niche stores—map store, gear store—and marketplace, but their most successful sales occur when they feature a product along with germane content, a practice Prosl refers to as "context-sensitive merchandising."

"Within each page that contains a feature story, we carefully select a product that matches the subject of the story," he explains. "If the story is about snowboarding, we might spotlight a great snowboarding poster or book or video. For example, on the snowboarding home page you might find a video called *Quest: The Ultimate Ride Video* for $26.95." By carefully examining their server logs, the company can increase sales by putting their best-selling products on their most visited pages.

What's important to note is the subtlety of these offers. These are not traditional, large banner ads, relentlessly animated to the point of distraction. Quite the contrary. They are small square buttons just large enough to distinguish a photo of the product. Underneath the image is a description of less than ten words that is hot-linked to more information. These petite billboards are situated in The Mountain Zone's left side navigation bar, thus preserving valuable screen real estate.

As might be expected, The Mountain Zone has found that featuring products this way has improved sales of the highlighted products dramatically. In fact, this is how most sales are generated.

Although The Mountain Zone offers a simple shopping cart system—off-the-shelf software refined to reduce 12 clicks to order a product to 3—about 40% of their orders come through their 800 number. While phone orders are more expensive, The Mountain Zone found an up side and uses the inbound calls as an opportunity for quality feedback. "We take advantage of these phone calls to find out where customers found us and a little bit of information about them," say Prosl. "This is how we found out that they wanted an electronic confirmation that their order was received."

Their 800-number is also the conduit for their customer service, an aspect of their commerce initiative that they consider as important as sales, even when the customer is at fault. Case in point: "A visitor ordered a book that was returned to sender three times! After many phone calls with her, we had our supplier return the package to our office. It turns out that she inadvertently typed in the wrong suite number, but the amazing part is that the address is right across the street from us. Nonetheless, we still wanted to make up for her trouble. She had ordered *Into Thin Air* by Jon Krakauer. We had an autographed copy in our office. So we exchanged her book for a signed edition, which our customer service manager delivered personally."

In addition to customer service, the other commerce challenge is merchandising because of the extraordinary variety. According to Prosl, sales of outdoor equipment and accessories are several billion dollars a year and growing. While this is good news, the number is so high because there are so many product options, up to 100,000. Prosl finds a simple and easy navigation through this much inventory a barrier. Furthermore, the industry is still shying away from the Web world, not understanding the benefits of online retailing. Afraid of disrupting the current infrastructure, which for them works well, manufacturers are hesitant to jeopardize their relationships with their existing retailers on what they consider a still unproven medium.

The Mountain Zone is proving that the Web is the perfect terrain for selling outdoor gear, as evidenced by the popularity of the online auction—bidding online for outdoor gear below retail prices. Rapidly becoming a major part of their commerce revenues, the auction offers deals secured by winning bids, such as a $550 snowboard for $200. They also auction one-of-a-kind merchandise such as a pair of specialty skis signed by extreme ski legend Scott Schmidt. They sold for $700.

In 1998 commerce accounted for half of The Mountain Zone's revenues, but by the end of 1999 they expect it to account for 40% of their $6 million in projected revenues.

Although commerce has been a major source of revenue, The Mountain Zone remains the envy of any Website that is even semidependent on ad revenue. Because of their niche audience and outstanding content, they usually sell out their entire ad inventory. Their high-profile advertisers include Chevy Trucks, BMW, Lycos, and Microsoft. Ironically, sports equipment king REI also advertises heavily despite the fact that the companies could be considered competitors because some of their product offerings overlap.

The cost of banner ads runs about $35 per CPM. Most advertisers get a 1–2% click-through, which is right on the industry average, with the exception of one advertiser who got

4%. "It was this horrendously ugly banner—pink with big red lips," Prosl recalls. "It was a promotion for a Valentine's Day e-card."

Because they sell out their banner ad inventory, The Mountain Zone can spend extra time on sponsorships and strategic marketing relationships, which have the multiple benefit of generating revenue, increasing brand awareness, or both.

One deal that combines both these elements occurred with CNET. First they supply content to CNET's Snap Service, providing stories wherever key Mountain Zone sports appear on the service. The Mountain Zone gets a percentage of the revenue of the banners that run in their areas, along with prominently displayed links back to The Mountain Zone.

The Mountain Zone has made a similar deal, only in reverse, with Deja News, the premier Website that aggregates all the Usenet Newsgroup postings with the added benefit of filtering out the spam. The Mountain Zone now hosts a Usenet group feed of discussions pertinent to Zoners such as rec.skiing.alpine and rec.climbing. The Mountain Zone splits the banners' ad revenue 50/50. Both Deja News and The Mountain Zone sell the ads.

The Mountain Zone was also CNET's first distribution partner by having cobranded The Mountain Zone/Snap CD-ROMS, which were put together by Earthlink. Intended for people just getting started on the Web, people who use these signups constantly have The Mountain Zone brand in front of them. Wherever they go online, The Mountain Zone logo follows them, linking back to The Mountain Zone start page. Furthermore, The Mountain Zone gets a $15 bounty from Earthlink for each signup. "We include these CD-ROMs in polybag giveaways at all the events we cover," says Prosl.

The Mountain Zone also enters into many soft dollar sponsorship deals, trading branding opportunities for services. For example, The Outrigger Hotel in Hawaii became a sponsor of The Mountain Zone's site section devoted to the 1998 Hawaii Mountain Bike Tour. In exchange for the sponsorship, The Mountain Zone received a combination of promotional opportunities, such as physical banners on the actual course, a booth, and lodging for Mountain Zone correspondents covering the event.

While The Mountain Zone has made advertising work for them, it was the one aspect of their business plan that was slightly off the mark.

"The assumption we made that was correct was that commerce would be one of our more significant revenue sources," says Prosl. "The assumption we made that wasn't correct was that advertising would evolve more rapidly than it has. Advertising hasn't come along as quickly as predicted. I think the predictions were all hyped. If you go back and look at some of the early forecasts, they are way off. And that's the thing, we were relying on the accuracy of these forecasts ourselves. So we thought it would happen quicker."

Because The Mountain Zone executives are so savvy with marketing and publicity, they don't need to do much advertising themselves. But when they see a buy that is a perfect match, even if it is outside their prime medium, they grab it, including television.

To date they have done TV spots on the Fox show *Boardwild* and on ABC during the airing of the made-for-TV movie of *Into Thin Air*. It was a 15-second spot run in selected markets such as San Francisco, Portland, Seattle, Denver, and New York. The ads cost about $20,000 plus the creative, which was significantly less than it would have been because they traded Web development for the work. "We did see an increase in traffic but it was hard to discern, because we had some print press at that time ... but we feel strongly about TV," notes Prosl.

Another successful marketing program for The Mountain Zone has been contests. They particularly enjoy doing them because they provide fresh content and help build community, all while driving traffic to the site. They usually partner with other companies for the prizes. For example, they were able to give away a Nissan Pathfinder in conjunction with Warren Miller Entertainment, the legend of action sports filmmaking. But there is one caveat to all their contests according to Prosl:

"They have to be mountain-oriented and of real value to our visitors."

Perhaps the most successful marketing program is the one that costs the least for them to execute: their periodic electronic mailings, of which they have three. Their primary missive is the weekly *Mountain Mailing.* Distributed to over 90,000 people, these dispatches inform The Mountain Zone visitors of current new features, upcoming cybercasts, chats, and other notable content. After a mailing, The Mountain Zone sees an immediate 15% increase in traffic, which lasts an average of four days.

To increase signups for the newsletter, The Mountain Zone started offering a free Everest screen saver, which increased signups by 40% to about 500 per day. The important correlating statistic is that, even though signups are induced by an incentive, The Mountain Zone has a minuscule attrition rate of less than 2% per mailing.

In addition to *Mountain Mailing,* The Mountain Zone offers a biweekly *Gear Alert,* highlighting the marketplace blowouts and close-outs, as well as an *Auction Alert* featuring upcoming lists of their hottest auction items. Both of these mailings have a similar traffic and sales benefit as they do with *Mountain Mailing.*

When examining even a smattering of The Mountain Zone's marketing programs, you can clearly see how they market themselves so brilliantly. In doing so, they also differentiate themselves from their competition. Their exclusive relationships with such high-profile entities as Warren Miller and acclaimed artist Art Wolfe are two examples of big names in mountain sports that are now also associated with The Mountain Zone. Because they have positioned themselves as a year-round destination, they have essentially squelched their near competitors.

"Our biggest competition is *Times Mirrors'* The Skiing Company's Skinet.com and twsnow.com. These sites are very narrow in that they cover only skiing and/or snowboarding. We're really the only site that comprehensively covers all the mountain sports. However, these sites are backed by a company with very deep pockets," say Prosl.

While niche marketing is important and often more profitable than appealing to a general audience, The Mountain Zone founders were smart to see that their vertical market is seasonal but they could rotate and serve their audience year round. For instance, Prosl points out that more than 80% of the people who snowboard also mountain bike. This essentially doubles the number of companies their advertising can service.

The same theory applies to their future venture. The Mountain Zone is actually part of a bigger picture called The Zone Network (TZN), which will eventually host other content sites germane to the outdoors.

As The Mountain Zone starts to expand into more zones, they are also leveraging their existing one. At the moment about 9% of their sales are international, including such faraway places as Jakarta, Indonesia, and China. Recognizing their worldwide popularity, they are in the throes of translating parts, but not all, of their content. First on the list is Japanese, with German next because of the high proportion of Germans on the Web and their love of mountain sports.

To their credit, The Mountain Zone founders have always positioned themselves as a global provider of mountain sports information. And that aim is at the core of their future plans as they continue to report from around the world and integrate more multimedia via Real Audio and Real Video.

So where do they see themselves in the year 2000? Prosl instantly responds: "In Sydney, Australia cybercasting the summer Olympics. Where else?"

---

*For up-to-date information about
the success of*
The Mountain Zone
visit
www.StrikingItRich.com

PRACTICAL ONLINE WEIGHTLOSS CLINIC HOMEPAGE

A personalized weight-loss program...

PRACTICAL
Online Diet Clinic

Over 27,000 Online Members

A custom weight-loss program is created from your personal profile!
Expect to <u>lose two pounds a week</u>.. every week!
Private <u>online delivery</u>...any time...any day.
<u>Safe</u> supermarket foods!... Plus, a <u>personal shopping list!</u>

Free Personal Profile

This is our <u>free no-obligation offer</u> to you!

dietcity.com

Over 250,000
subscribers!

❶ Complete a profile questionnaire

❷ Receive **free**... a <u>personal weight-loss profile</u>, a subscription
to **dietcity.com**, and a professional weight-loss recommendation.

❸ Join Practical for just $2 a week... receive a new plan and shopping list each week!
Lose 2 pounds a week... Attend online meetings... get motivated!
<u>Questions?</u>... our Hotline is 1-800-265-6170

Click Here for Free Offer

D A V I D   H U M B L E

PRACTICAL ONLINE WEIGHTLOSS CLINIC

www.practicalprogram.com

What would you do if you decided to redirect your company's business plan to an Internet-only strategy and your employees revolted? Welcome to the world of David Humble, 63, President of Self/help Technologies. "I called a staff meeting to tell everyone we were going to put up a site and market our program via the Internet and there was instant rejection," says Humble. "A group even attempted to organize the other employees to stop the strategy."

This was not a good start.

In fact 50% of the staff were so dead-set against the proposition that they quit. Sadly, their opposition had to do with venturing into an unknown business abyss known as the Web, which in January 1997 still had a short track record as a viable conduit for business.

"The employees had bought into our original offline strategy," Humble reflects. "We did lots of market research and focus group studies, and it looked like we were right on target. Any change in this plan was a trauma."

While research may have indicated that they had a winner, reality proved otherwise. At the point Humble decided to move to the Web, it was his last hope. Either he marketed his product exclusively online or shut his business down entirely.

Humble's original concept was to install kiosks in supermarkets to deliver personalized diet programs to consumers. "After all, everyone that is ever interested in a diet frequents a supermarket, right?" Humble surmised. "We produced the expert-based software to create the individualized programs, built a high-tech kiosk, created the interactive video presentation, and installed it in our first store. The results were not good. In fact, the results were zero."

Humble conservatively expected 1,500 people to pass the kiosk each day with approximately 1.5 people purchasing the program. "Roll this out to 5,000 stores and you have a substantial business," he believed.

While he did see the traffic he predicted, Humble did not see the sales. "The results were so bad that I did not even try to figure out why they were bad. The patient was DOA."

Fortunately part of Self/help's original business plan included a test of its expert-based software to a broad base of consumers, something that was not practical in a one-store supermarket test. "We had learned that the supermarket idea was a stupid idea, at least for now, but we discovered that a personalized weight-loss program on the Web was good and that it could be a cost-efficient distribution channel."

Despite employee dissension, in the first quarter of 1997 Self/help Technologies officially launched Practical Program, which began Humble's foray into direct marketing of a subscription program online.

Few Web businesses are harder to launch than a subscription-based endeavor. In fact, few are known to be profitable and those that are tend to be highly branded entities, such as *The Wall Street Journal Online* and *Disney's Daily Blast.*

The belief is that most consumers can get what they want on the Net for free, therefore you better have something mighty compelling to lure them into a subscription arrangement. In fact, many experts argue—and can usually prove—that most subscription-based sites can make more money in a model based on advertising and transaction than on monthly fees. "Free" means significantly more visitors, making it a viable advertising medium, and the substantial increase in traffic results in statistically better opportunities for sales of goods. In Practical Program's competition, many participants give away nonpersonalized plans while offering diet pills and other aids for sale.

Despite conventional wisdom and indisputable statistics, David Humble has proved otherwise. With a subscription base that exceeds 13,000, he is proving that if you have the right product with a unique value there is an audience. Humble's success is even more inspiring when you realize that 80% of his clientele are women. Only recently has the Net balanced gender-wise. When Practical Program was launched in early 1997, it was believed that about only 25% of the Web population were women, making it that much more difficult to sell.

Practical Program is a simple concept executed with care and consideration. For a $9.95 signup fee and $19.95 a month for a minimum of three months, subscribers get a completely personalized weight-loss program based on lifestyle, food preferences, and goals. The program costs less than half of the fee for Weight Watchers (which costs up to $14 per week) and, in addition to the significant cost savings, doesn't require time-consuming mandatory meetings. (For those who enjoy working in a group environment, Practical Program offers free online meetings for members who like the camaraderie.)

Unlike Weight Watchers or Jenny Craig—neither of which offer cyber versions of their programs—Practical Program is 100% personalized. Members begin by choosing a course based on their goals, such as the amount of attention they want to give the process. For example, the highly motivated would choose The Max, while those who care to eat a bit more and who are comfortable with the process taking a bit little longer may choose Just One Pound.

Each week subscribers receive step-by-step instructions and a personal shopping list to buy everything they need at the supermarket. The instructions and list are based on additional data from a detailed personal profile. What's extra nifty about the weekly programs is that they are further personalized based on the prior week's progress. The entire program is supervised by a top-notch registered nutritionist who is also available for members' questions. Essentially the value proposition is technology as a tool for one-to-one counseling. And it works. According to Humble, the average member loses 1.8 pounds per week.

As a way to convert visitors to subscribers, all visitors are encouraged to fill out the free personal profile, which asks enough questions that the prospective member can view a sample day of exactly what their program would be like. They also get a professional course recommendation, a body mass indicator, and a list of the 100 best supermarket foods (using a criterion of nutritional value and taste) based on the profile responses. Approximately 65% of Practical Program's visitors complete the profile, of which anywhere from .3% to 3% purchase. Humble says the huge variance is related to the originating site delivering the visitor, the time of the month, even the browser.

As much as Practical Program would like as many subscribers as possible, they will not accept anyone whose weight is considered normal or anyone with medical conditions such as diabetes. But this is not a barrier for Practical Program. The way the system is designed, no human is required to screen participants. "Our computer will not create a program for anyone who does not fit within the envelope. So it is an automatic process," says Humble. If the prospective member qualifies, her personalized program is issued the moment her credit card number is taken.

Since Practical Program is a direct marketing enterprise, it relies almost entirely on advertising. Consequently, Humble continues to refine or, more appropriately, tries to crack the secret code that will deliver the most sales with the lowest investment. So far his approach has involved three entities: (1) America Online, (2) banner ads on content sites and search engines, and (3) a content site he launched as "advertorial" for Practical.

To date, America Online has been Practical Program's most effective sales tool. Humble arranged to have Practical Program sponsor a weight-loss section on Thrive, an AOL Greenhouse site popular with women. The site promoted the section on their main page, the AOL Health Channel and the main America Online welcome screen, easily the most desirable screen real estate on the service. In addition, Humble purchased a large block of banners. "We paid a special rate for the banners with 30% of our sales from the ads going to Thrive, the area which hosted our banners," he explains. Despite the initial success of the program, unfortunately the experience for Humble was bittersweet. "Clearly, the objective of this site was not to help their customer succeed and after being exposed to a number of what I call 'cheap online tricks,' we were forced to terminate the relationship."

The package as described cost $8,000 per month, which included one million banners plus promotion such as an editorial message pointing to the Practical Program–sponsored page. Content appeared on the page along with banners promoting Practical. The idea was to drive traffic to the editorial areas sponsored by Practical Program. Because of an AOL shift in strategy, the site lost access to the AOL welcome screen and unfortunately could not deliver on the contracted promise.

Humble says that from this experience he learned not to count on sites he contracts with to "deliver tomorrow what they are delivering today. Your page position can move, the frequency can change, page one today can be page three tomorrow," he warns. "All of the above will be blamed on corporate policy, a change in strategy, technical problems, et cetera. At least that's the way it is on AOL."

Due to this experience, Humble strongly advises others to ask for a "make good" policy and have that put in the contract. "Some sites are good about this. Others aren't. Yahoo is excellent."

Because so much traffic is generated from AOL, Humble is happy to have the business, but he can't help but curse the online service. "The AOL browser does not present our Website at its best and our customers complain they are knocked offline while they wait for their printer to print their weekly program," he protests. "We had to develop a special site for AOL traffic with nonscrolling screens that fit the AOL window, in addition to a special download procedure. However, our number one complaint from our customers is AOL technical–related."

And it gets worse. "If you are dependent upon AOL for commerce and it involves your customer to download and

print, lower the revenue you expect from this area by 20%,"
Humble warns. "Because these subscribers constantly get
knocked off and eventually cancel."

For the time being Humble is learning to live with AOL's in-
efficiencies for one reason only: They deliver customers. For
Practical Program, America Online advertising pulls higher than
the Net, even when comparing apples to apples. The AOL channel where Practical advertised also has a Web presence on
which Humble has also advertised. Using the same content and
the same banner ads, the AOL site pulled twice as much as the
Website. In fact, the best sales day in the history of Practical
Program occurred when the content area they were sponsoring
was featured on the America Online welcome screen, as a result
of which they were enrolling as many as 100 people an hour.

Since there is more to cyberspace than America Online,
Humble constantly advertises on Web-only ventures such as
search engines and content sites to fuel the growing number of
new visitors, which in the first quarter of 1998 was averaging
3,000 per day.

On search engines, Humble buys keywords such as "diet,"
"diets," "weight loss," and "nutrition." In most cases he owns
these keywords exclusively. Humble has found that he is much
better off with keyword advertising, where his banner ad is displayed on the results page of a search, than with category advertising. The latter is most common with Yahoo, which is technically considered more a directory rather than a search engine
because it organizes its information by topic. If a person drills
their way down hierarchically to a particular subcategory,
Humble's banner ad would be displayed. Through trial and
error, Humble discovered that he gets a 7% click-through on
keyword advertising and only a 3.5% click-through on category
placement. "I would have bet the opposite," he says. "In fact I
have dropped all category advertising."

Coming from a direct marketing perspective, Practical Program keeps careful track of all ads by assigning a code to each
banner or selling site location. Every day they compile a report
of the number of unique visitors to Practical Program from

these various selling locations and calculate the conversion to sales. Humble has found that there is quite a conversion variance between different selling locations, banners, time of month, time of year, and, as he puts it "who knows what else."

"Basically, we do not believe all the numbers and look at a general trend," he explains. "The banner reports from the advertising sources never agree with our click-through numbers and, as a group, are off about 20% in favor of—you guessed it—the search engine or content site." Humble says that this is just one more of the Web's unsolved mysteries.

In his effort to hold his advertising costs at 35% of sales, find a better mechanism than paying an average $30 per CPM for banners, and to come up with the perfect niche site, Humble decided to launch his own: Dietcity.com, a central resource for weight loss and other nutritional information. Dietcity.com features weekly articles by Practical Program's nutritionist, diet book reviews, Website suggestions, and other helpful information. While positioned as an informational site, Practical Program members can get their weekly programs here in addition to housing the member-only online meetings and bulletin boards.

All the banner ads on the site are for Practical Program, in addition to loads of advertorial and other clickable links, which lead people to the free profile with the hope of closing a sale. Approximately 10% of all Practical Program signups come from Dietcity.com. The site costs about $2,500 a month to maintain, which is equivalent to what he would spend for 83,000 banner ads. If only 20 people a week become subscribers via DietCity.com, the site has paid for itself. For these reasons, Humble believes that in time DietCity.com will be his lowest-cost method to generate sales.

While the Net is a global presence, only 1% of Practical's subscribers are internationally based. Due to the limited availability of many of the food products in foreign countries, overseas sales aren't much of a market for Humble to pursue. For the time being, non-U.S. members e-mail Practical when they need to request substitutions, which are handled along with the average 275 e-mails Practical receives each day. Most of the inquiries are specific to an individual's diet or special request. One of their favorite messages came from a member requesting that they figure out a way to incorporate 1 pint of ice cream per day, hot dogs, and chocolate bars. Other e-mails are upbeat notes offering recipe suggestions and progress updates.

In addition to client feedback, there was one trend in the e-mails that Humble could not overlook and that subsequently had a huge impact on his bottom line: There were virtually no complaints about the program being too expensive. So he raised his prices 40% with no negative effect on sales. Humble has played with Practical's prices four times, incrementally raising them. Here's the pricing chronology from first to most recent:

- First month free, $19.95 for next two months
- $19.95 for three months
- $19.95 registration and $9.95 month
- $9.95 registration and $19.95 month for three months (minimum)

Looking at the trend, his original startup fee moved from $39.90 to $69.80, a 57% increase—great news for Humble! This proved to him that his subscribers are not price-sensitive.

In addition to constantly adjusting pricing, Humble redesigned his site 12 times in its first 14 months. The major difference between each were look and content. Humble started with a clinical format featuring a factual explanation of their program, slowly evolving to a kind of direct mail message where he talked *to* consumers instead of talking *at* them. They plan to improve on this content as well. The initial costs to launch the Practical Program site were about $300,000, which does not include marketing costs.

Humble realizes that he never could have tweaked his product in any other venue. "In my opinion, one of the least publicized benefits of the Net is the ability to put a selling presentation in front of a broad base of customers today, have the sales results today, and change the presentation today," he attests. "Compare this to the time it takes for a direct mail marketer to test and finalize a standard print mailing."

This instantaneous advantage of the Web should only help Humble reach his ultimate goal that much quicker: to displace Weight Watchers as the number one provider of weight-management services. But he realizes that he has more challenges to face before he overtakes the diet giant despite his current success.

"This is my third startup and there is little that prepares you for Webonomics other than a penchant for going down dead-ends, spending money in totally wasted ways, and experiencing many trials and errors," Humble advises. "It's essential to maintain a strong belief in your concept, but be prepared to make major shifts in your strategy."

For up-to-date information about the success of
Practical Online Weightloss Clinic
visit
www.StrikingItRich.com

Welcome to DogToys.com

Over 400 toys...you can browse by breed!

Holiday Gifts

Stocking Gift Packs

Food Gift Packs

Toys by Breed

Toys by Dog Size

Toys by "Squeak"

Popular Brands

Fleece & Plush Toys

Best Selling Toys

Toy Blowouts

Chews & Snacks

Balls/Ropes/Rubber

Funny Cards & Gifts

Looking for Cat Toys?

Customer Service

Special Programs

Tell a Friend

Toy Newsletter

Show My Order

Toy Search

Toys by Breed

Featuring 151 breeds and their favorite dog toys. What breed of dog do you have? **FREE stocking with purchase.**

Holiday Hats & Collars

Jingle bell collars and Santa hats. **Hey, someone has to wear the Santa hat!**

Toy Boxes

"Put your toys in your toy box please." Teach your dog a new trick. Bone-shaped toy boxes come in two sizes.

Chews & Snacks

We offer only the highest quality treats for your dog - **pre-made or make them yourself.**

Toys by Dog Size

Toy recommendations for big dogs, little dogs, and puppies.

Stocking Gift Packs

Featured on **The Oprah Winfrey Show** *** Holiday **DELIVERY** available. ***

Holiday Gifts

Celebrating our 3rd Holiday Season online with hundreds of great Holiday gifts.

Deluxe Holiday Toys

Great Gift Idea When only the best toys will do - these are the toys for you.

Original Toy Inventors

DECEMBER'S toy inventor is John K. Curry, creator of the **Holiday Paw Stocking.** Learn the history of the coolest dog toys - and their inventors.

Gift Certificates

Give a DogToys.com Gift Certificate this year. Say "Happy Holidays" starting at $25.00.

JILL GIZZIO
DOGTOYS.COM
www.dogtoys.com

If the most reliable assurance of success on the Web is to be the first retailer in the category in which you are selling, Jill Gizzio guaranteed her victory by creating a new category. In other words, DogToys.com was not the first e-tailer to sell dog toys (there were a number of Web-based pet stores at the time she launched which stocked canine playthings), but DogToys.com was the first to sell nothing but dog toys, thus creating a new category in a retailing wilderness so deep, it seemed there couldn't possibly be any categories left.

But Gizzio's dog toy emporium goes far beyond the obvious. In addition to knowing the importance of being first, the 43-year-old entrepreneur also understands the need to be the best, and because her site always exceeds visitors' expectations, it is remembered, talked about, and generously featured in the press. If you abide by the adage that it's more about the sizzle than the steak, imagine what happens when you have both.

The steak in this instance is Gizzio's extensive inventory. While most pet stores, online or off, sell 25, 30, or at best 40 products, DogToys.com features over 400, ten times that of their nearest competitor. In the Web world of customer acquisition, when your next client can enter and exit in a nano-second, being able to position yourself as best is imperative, and the only way to do that *instantly* and *objectively* is through the depth of your inventory. If you have substantially more product for sale than your closest competitor, it supports your credibility as the de facto choice for that product.

Speaking in broad strokes, depth of inventory is easy to accomplish. But let's consider what business guru Tom Peters would refer to as a "wow factor"—that element of the enterprise that is so fresh, so different, it is noticed and never forgotten.

The sizzle for DogToys.com is how they organize their inventory and one of the many ways in which the e-store over-delivers on their retailing promise. The primary unique selling proposition of DogToys.com is that you can browse their 400 toys *by breed*. Got a Poodle? Great. You can click and get right to a page that features toys enjoyed most by Poodles. Ditto for Bull Terriers, Airedales, Pekinese, Labradors, and over 146 others for a total breed count of 151.

"My dog loves every toy you recommend," begins a typical e-mail. "What a wonderful service." According to Gizzio, "people respond to the convenience and certainty of the 'by breed' section, even if they only buy one toy from the list."

Ironically when DogToys.com launched in 1997, the "by breed" category was a mere footnote, listed ninth on the navigation bar's ten choices. Shortly thereafter a marketing expert told Gizzio she thought the "by breed" section was a marketing bonanza. Once this was pointed out to Gizzio, the seasoned entrepreneur saw the value in what was a "last minute thought category" and began expanding it.

Gizzio started the "by breed" research by gleaning her dog toy orders which always ask what breed of dog the purchased toys are for. In addition, Gizzio began offering a toy survey on the site which included questions about what toys were favorites and why. Furthermore, Gizzio consulted the book *Legacy of the Dog*, a comprehensive reference work which discusses the physical build and personality of each breed, key characteristics for toy matching. "Toys are my passion," says Gizzio, "and I have instincts I can rely on which also helps."

After months and months of research and data analysis the 151-choice "by breed" section was offered. Ironically, it was after she launched "toys by breed" that Gizzio realized she inadvertently omitted the most popular class of dogs: mixed breeds (usually referred to as "mutts"). Gizzio, always quick with a marketing solution, instantly launched "Toys by Dog Size." Visitors have since made this section their second most favorite, just behind "by breed."

With the "by breed" and "by size" sections on DogToys.com navigation bar, Gizzio was quickly learning about the importance of product organization for a Webstore, a vital success component since the Internet's slow load times make it less than conducive for browsing. With a new appreciation for how the Web allows her to organize inventory in a way that an offline store never could, Gizzio added several more categories including "bestsellers," which turns out to be toys that, according to Gizzio, "are less about fun and more about quality."

In addition to bestsellers, Gizzio added one additional category just for fun: "toys by squeak." One customer wrote Gizzio to explain that she has her dog sit in her lap while she clicks on the sound icon for each toy. "Whichever squeak gets the dog's attention the most is the toy I buy."

For most e-store owners, constantly tinkering with categories, adding and subtracting products, and other tweaking results in site design and maintenance bills so high it would make such experimentation impossible. But Gizzio found a solution a few months after her initial launch.

"I drafted the original site in Microsoft's Powerpoint and handed the pages to a Web developer. That was the end of my involvement," Gizzio explains. While the developer made it come to life with a back-end database, credit card processing, and other transparent technology, the site only lasted seven months. "I was frustrated because I couldn't easily add products or make changes," laments Gizzio. This initial site cost $10,000 for a Webstore about 15 pages deep.

Despite the frustration, Gizzio didn't know of any other solution. She dabbled with iCat's e-commerce design software, but because she's not technically inclined, simply got frustrated and resigned herself to "be paying my Web developer until I died because I was not going to learn it."

In the midst of her angst, a friend told Gizzio about Yahoo! Store, an all-in-one solution simple enough for novices. It allows one to effortlessly build a sophisticated online retailing venture, complete with hosting, credit card processing, built-in database, and much more for a small monthly fee. "She was rather emphatic that I try it," Gizzio recalls. "My biggest concern was that it wasn't going to look like my $10,000 custommade store and I refused to be stuck in some cookie-cutter template." Determined to show Gizzio the light, the friend built a mini DogToys.com Yahoo! Store which demonstrated that

DogToys.com on Yahoo! Stores could look amazingly similar to her original design. "It wasn't exact, but it was close enough to what I had."

But there was still the hurdle of being one's own designer, despite the extreme user friendliness of Yahoo's technology. "I didn't understand how to import an image so I hired a young guy just getting started in page design, but more technically inclined than I, to get the store up and its hundreds of images imported. Gizzio kept the old store online during the 60 days her new one was being built.

"I was chomping at the bit," says Gizzio. "It couldn't happen fast enough. I couldn't wait to get out of relying on someone else and get on with what was finally starting to feel like my own store—my store to add and change items at will." Unfortunately during the 60-day gestation phase that her Yahoo! Store was being put together, DogToys.com got a generous mention on CNBC's hit show "Power Lunch." "The activity it generated brought my server down. It showed me how much I needed something like Yahoo! Stores which can instantly scale to handle a surge of people."

Relaunched on Yahoo! Store in February 1999, it was at this point that Gizzio expanded DogToys.com's "by breed" section to the depth she wanted. "If I had my previous designer handle the 151 breeds, it would have cost me at least $37,000—not to mention many months waiting for him to get around to it."

Now with complete control over her cyber-retailing enterprise, Gizzio finally felt as though her dream of DogToys.com was a reality. After establishing her core categories (toys by breed, toys by size, toys by squeak, bestsellers, and toy blowouts), Gizzio concentrated on marketing, especially getting new visitors to DogToys.com.

At present, 40% of DogToys.com's customers come from search engines (Yahoo first, followed by MSN, AltaVista, and Excite). Another 40% of her customers come from her affiliates, a group of dog-related content sites who link out to Dog-Toys.com for a 10–20% commission on each sale they send. The only advertising Gizzio does is on one site, an extremely well established dog-related content destination, where, for a $1,000 investment to date, she's gotten over 25,000 visitors.

Promotional opportunities also come easily to Gizzio. Because of the novelty of DogToys.com, she has received exposure in *Reader's Digest,* the Land's End Catalog, *U.S. News & World Report,* and other prominent outlets just from journalists stumbling on DogToys.com as they surf the Net.

While promotion and marketing is extremely important to Gizzio, golden customer service factors into her success formula too and helps account for her 4,000 ecstatic customers. "Even though DogToys.com is unbelievably profitable, I consider the fact that my customers like what we are doing even more important in defining its success," Gizzio relates.

Though Gizzio has a staff of seven employees, she is the only one who responds to each day's average of 30 e-mails and 30 phone calls, never alerting the inquirers to the fact that she is the business's owner. "I want them to know that I see them as a person, not just a credit card."

It is this personalized attention that immediately ingratiates new customers and keeps her steady ones happy as well. "Our best customer is a woman named Fran who calls about every three weeks from her car phone to buy toys for her twin mini schnauzer puppies," Gizzio explains. "She always asks 'what is absolutely adorable that I must have?' so I pack up the box with two of the exact same of everything."

This example also shows how most DogToys.com customers are not price-sensitive. Interestingly the company's least expensive and most expensive items are both on the DogToys.com bestseller list: the mint-flavored tennis balls (pack of 2 for $2.59) and the treat dispensing Buster Cube ($18.95). "Dogs have very specific needs like children," Gizzio points out. "For this reason price is less important than product." This is especially true when the product is hard to find, which Gizzio discovered when Harvard University's Primate Research Lab ordered 24 flashing dog balls for their monkeys.

With an average customer repeat rate of 15%, the typical DogToys.com customer is female purchasing $31 worth of toys every two months, most of whom are returning to buy Dog-Toys.com's number one most popular item, Liver Biscotti.

"We give away samples of Liver Biscotti with every shipment," Gizzio explains. "But the key is the fact that we don't give one or two sample bags. We give at least three. The idea is this: Once the box of toys arrives, the dog's owner will usually dole out a couple bags—especially if there is more than one dog—because the dog has sniffed out the treat when the sealed box arrived. Then the third bag goes on the kitchen counter which is when the big brown eyes start and the dog waits patiently till the next day for that snack again. Basically we've just created a Pavlovian behavior. Now there are no more samples, so the owner is guilted into buying more. You can't do this with one sample."

Gizzio's "Biscotti Conditioning Theorem" is just one of many samples of her marketing creativity, in which Gizzio tends to go where few, if any, online retailers have gone before, one example of which is DogToys.com's Fundraising Is Fun opportunity.

Loosely based on the Girl Scout cookie paradigm, Fundraising Is Fun is a simple premise. DogToys.com provides fundraising catalogs to a school or nonprofit's members and volunteers. The toys are presold via order forms with the money collected by the sponsoring organization, which keeps 30% of the total sales with the balance forwarded to DogToys.com.

Gizzio has found that selling pet toys is a refreshing change of pace from traditional fundraising products like candy and raffle tickets. With earnings between $2.10–$6.00 *per toy* it is also a great revenue generator for the sponsoring organization.

Because Gizzio gives such a high percentage of the revenue to the nonprofit, DogToys.com makes only 10%, which basically covers costs. In other words, this program is less about making money and more about altruism and customer acquisition. It's a pretty safe bet for Gizzio who notes "after their dog chews up the Silly Squirrel, where are they going to get another one?"

In addition to Fundraising Is Fun, DogToys.com also offers prepackaged toy selections for donation to local dog shelters and rescue organizations. Making it easy for their customers to donate, purchasers need only indicate which shelter they want the donation made to, along with the size of the pack ranging in price from $59.95 to $119.95. With each shipment Dog-Toys.com includes a letter explaining where the toys come from along with the name and contact information of the donor.

For this cause, DogToys.com deeply discounts their products, reducing their markup to a mere 15%. Once you factor in the free shipping, the result for DogToys.com is a tad above breakeven. This is just fine with Gizzio. "Shelters desperately need toys," she explains. "I consider it on par with donating toys for homeless children."

Despite the leanings toward philanthropic endeavors, Gizzio does focus on pure profit concepts as well, one of which started when eBay's popularity began to rise and Amazon.com decided to join in the auction fray.

"For about eight weeks we conducted 300 auctions, mostly on Amazon.com, with the sole goal of acquiring new customers," Gizzio remembers. In addition to preferring the Amazon.com clientele, she liked the bulk loading template which makes it much easier to upload dozens and dozens of product offers. At first most of the bidders were new to auctions so it made it a pleasant experience, but once the seasoned auction bidders got going on Amazon.com, they out-clevered the novices, taking all the toys for themselves. "I had one buyer get 17 of the 40 items one week and 21 of 50 the next. We were trying to attract new customers … not have a few who 'hog' the experience."

Since auctioning individual toys held little profit potential for Gizzio, she included an incentive for every winner: Buy at least one additional item at the DogToys.com store and the shipping was free for both the auctioned item and any other toy the auction-acquired customer wanted to buy. A whopping 80% took Gizzio up on this offer.

Because she began bids at her cost, Gizzio's auction was never a financial risk and every winner essentially cost nothing to acquire. However, for Gizzio the labor was too intensive and despite the 15% conversion rate to full-time customer, she no longer participates in auctions but still recommends them for new online retailers seeking exposure.

Amazingly, when Gizzio began she knew nothing about dog toys except that her dog Brownie was crazy about them. One night, while attempting to tire the terrier at 11:30 P.M., the name DogToys.com popped into her head. "I ran to the computer to see if it was available," remembers Gizzio. "I was shocked that it was because it's such a great name."

Fortified with the proceeds of a $20,000 second mortgage, Gizzio started approaching dog toy manufacturers. "When I started calling I got a mixed reception." The problem for Gizzio was that the dot-com frenzy was still in its infancy and the manufacturers didn't understand the Net or how to classify Dog-Toys.com, since it had no offline presence via a store or catalog.

The solution came when Asten Pet Products, makers of the famous Booda Burger, suggested she designate herself as a mail order catalog, thus making her eligible to buy directly from the manufacturer.

"This was the clue I needed," says Gizzio who immediately recontacted the manufacturers which now allowed her to start buying direct. Not only did she get to buy from the source, but eliminating the distributor instantly doubled her markup, resulting in a net profit of 25%. DogToys.com and a few of the mega-pet sites, such as Pets.com, are the only pure play Internet companies allowed to purchase directly from the manufacturer. For this reason Gizzio opened RetailPets.com, a site devoted to wholesaling pet toys. "Early on I knew wholesale sales would garner 4–5 times the profits of our retail sites. In fact a wholesale account will yield an average profit of $150–$200 per order while my consumer sales average $10–$15 per order."

Whether she is retailing or wholesaling, DogToys.com's growth is through the roof in the quadruple digits—1,800% to be exact—for 1999. But the surge isn't just financial.

In September 1999, Gizzio moved her office from her home to a 4,000-square-foot warehouse, holding her inventory of approximately 20,000 toys—a space that she has already outgrown. Nonetheless, the move couldn't have come soon enough. Shortly after relocating, Gizzio received an order she had previously placed for 96 Crazy Rings (a plush toy with a hole center). The problem was that the order was misread and

DogToys.com got 96 *cases*—2,304 rings in all. "Imagine if I had been working out of my home!"

Regardless of the fact that Gizzio is now buying and selling just like the big guys, she still doesn't consider e-tailers such as petsmart.com and pets.com competition. The difference is that neither one of these online stores has the depth of inventory or the specialization. "They've got the same stuff that you find in the supermarket or chain stores," notes Gizzio. "There's nothing unique about their product selection or organization."

Besides, competition is nothing new to Gizzio for whom DogToys.com is her third business. "I like starting new ventures," she confesses, which partly explains why in August 1999 Gizzio didn't hesitate to launch a site catering to the U.S.'s number one pet: CatToys.com. With sections such as "Toys by Breed" and "Toys by Personality," it's easy to identify the sibling-like relationship.

Given her affection for her dogs, Terriers Willie and Brownie, DogToys.com remains the crown jewel in her online pet toy retailing empire.

"It's the same joy as selling toys to kids," explains Gizzio, whose personal favorite items are the plush, singing birthday cake and the Bungee Weiner Dog. "My customers love their dogs. They kiss them, sleep with them, even take them on vacation," Gizzio points out. "This is just another way for them to show their dogs how much they care. Besides, who doesn't love toys? Toys touch the child in everyone."

For up-to-date information about the
success of
DogToys.com
visit
www.StrikingItRich.com

REEL.COM HOMEPAGE

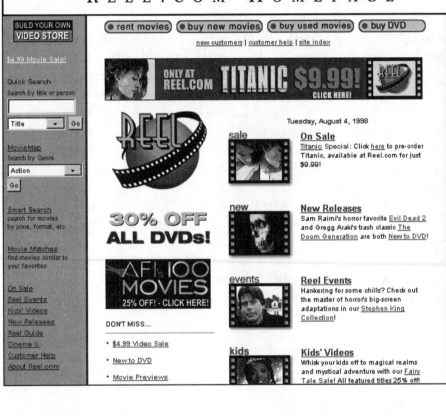

BUILD YOUR OWN VIDEO STORE

(● rent movies) (● buy new movies) (● buy used movies) (● buy DVD)

new customers | customer help | site index

$4.99 Movie Sale!

Quick Search
Search by title or person

[Title ▾] [Go]

MovieMap
Search by Genre

[Action ▾]

[Go]

Smart Search
search for movies
by price, format, etc.

Movie Matches
find movies similar to
your favorites

On Sale
Reel Events
Kids' Videos
New Releases
Reel Guide
Cinema U.
Customer Help
About Reel.com

ONLY AT REEL.COM TITANIC $9.99! **CLICK HERE!**

30% OFF ALL DVDs!

AFI's 100 MOVIES 25% OFF! · CLICK HERE!

DON'T MISS...

* $4.99 Video Sale
* New to DVD
* Movie Previews

Tuesday, August 4, 1998

sale
On Sale
Titanic Special: Click here to pre-order
Titanic, available at Reel.com for just
$9.99!

new
New Releases
Sam Raimi's horror favorite Evil Dead 2
and Gregg Araki's trash classic The
Doom Generation are both New to DVD!

events
Reel Events
Hankering for some chills? Check out
the master of horror's big-screen
adaptations in our Stephen King
Collection!

kids
Kids' Videos
Whisk your kids off to magical realms
and mystical adventure with our Fairy
Tale Sale! All featured titles 25% off!

S T U A R T   S K O R M A N

REEL.COM

www.reel.com

While thousands of offline retailers are opening cyber versions of their stores on the Web, Reel.com has the distinction of being the first known Internet retailer to expand in the opposite direction and open a store offline. In fact, the 8,000-square-foot terrestrial offshoot occurred only four months after this online video retailer launched what was intended to be a Web-only enterprise.

"We thought we needed one physical store to connect with the people," says Stuart Skorman, Reel.com's founder. "We didn't want to just know our customers through e-mail. We think combining the physical and virtual worlds is strong. We use the Website as an advertisement for the store and the store as an ad for the Website."

Actually the combination proposes a wild mix. If you are in the mood for a truly cybersurreal experience, while you are in the offline Reel.com you can access the Reel.com Website via in-store Internet terminals.

By foot or by mouse, Reel.com remains "the planet's biggest movie store," boasting an inventory of 85,000 videos, which are cross-referenced into 320 categories. About 35,000 of these titles are available for rent by mail. In addition, the site features so much content via their Movie Guide, it could qualify as a separate site. Because of their endless inventory and useful content, Reel.com has bonded with film enthusiasts to the same degree that Amazon.com has won the heart of book lovers.

Much of the loyalty stems from the particulars of Reel.com's inventory, which features not only new movies, but also used movies (at bargain prices) and rare films. In fact,

Reel.com is so determined to offer every film ever available on video, that they challenge visitors with an unusual guarantee: If you can't find it at Reel.com and you find it somewhere else, Reel.com will pay for it.

This depth of selection is the core attraction for much of Reel.com's 35,000 customers: film connoisseurs looking for hard-to-find and independent films; film directors, actors, and actresses ordering their own movies; folks living in small towns who rely on the Webstore for purchases and rentals. A typical example of the latter is an Alaskan resident who lives 80 miles from the nearest town and loves how he can get his movies delivered and, using the site's Movie Guide, generate new ideas for things to watch over the long Alaskan winter.

This Movie Guide is Reel.com's primary content area, the goal of which is to "Help you discover your next favorite movie." One of the Movie Guide's most nifty sections is Movie Matches, a system that suggests titles based on an existing favorite film. Type in *Bull Durham* and Movie Matches will suggest Close Matches, which in this example include *Tin Cup* and *A League of Their Own*. Balancing the obvious, however, Reel.com also offers Creative Matches, which are either lesser known movies or older films someone in the mainstream might not otherwise have heard of or even considered. In the case of *Bull Durham*, one of the Closest Matches is the Spencer Tracy/Katherine Hepburn classic, *Pat and Mike*. What makes this service truly extraordinary is that, while these suggestions are stored in a computerized database, the actual matches are selected by a human committee. "These matches are not based on the personal opinion of the Reel.com staff. Instead the staff mirrors the opinions of what our customers are likely to think," says Skorman. "This is an important distinction."

Skorman says that they have done Movie Matches for 5,000 of their 85,000 films and are adding them at a rate of 400–500 per week.

This same personal touch is behind the Movie Guide's Movie Anatomy section, which, using a graph, highlights 14 essential elements of a movie, such as the degree of sex, violence, and humor, with the goal of accurately indicating whether the film fits your mood or interests.

Movie Anatomy and Movie Matches represent just a small slice of Reel.com's Movie Guide content options and also illustrates the strength of their inventive and proprietary content, giving them a distinct retailing advantage. "Unlike a physical store where a customer usurps an employee's time, there is virtually no cost for us to serve this information if someone doesn't make a purchase," explains Skorman. "Because of this advantage we like to encourage our customers to think of us as a resource, not just a proprietor."

These golden databases also are enhancing Reel.com's bottom line, as the retailer is leveraging the content as a revenue stream. "We're talking to search engines and other online content sites as a cobranded venture. For example, you may see it on the Web version of *TV Guide*." In return, Reel.com gets a share of the banner ad revenues, terms that will vary depending on the sites.

The *TV Guide* arrangement is one example of Reel.com's successful alliances in which the cyber video store has established partnerships with high-profile content sites that complement the Reel.com audience. Other examples include Film.com, Mr. Showbiz, Yahoo, and The Internet Movie Database. While the results have been more than worthwhile, Skorman admits, "We have paid dearly with generous revenue sharing in order to establish these deals." In some cases Skorman says the price has been worth it and others less so. Regardless, he values the traffic and branding opportunity these extraordinarily popular sites provide.

In addition to these partnerships, Reel.com does additional advertising on search engines where he has bought such less-than-common keywords and phrases such as "Blade Runner," "Star Trek," "Quentin Tarantino," "Woody Allen," "The Crow," "horror movies," "David Lynch," "Martin Scorsese," "home video," "Terminator," "science fiction," and "Citizen Kane." As demonstrated by his keyword choices, Skorman insists on focusing exclusively on his segment. He refuses a scatterbrain approach and therefore does no advertising that is run-of-site. "We are a niche business with a really limited ad budget. We believe we are better reaching one person five times than five people once." The results of his advertising buys are this: On average Reel.com gets a 3% click-through on which 3.5% buy, bringing his total cost per sale with banner ads to $30.

As an antidote to these acquisition costs and perhaps taking a cue from Amazon.com's wildly successful Associates program, in the first quarter of 1998, Reel.com initiated an affiliates program aimed at the mom-and-pop sites. The sites are paid a 5% commission on the total sale, which brings his cost per sale for Reel.com to about a dollar.

While the average order is similar in size and price to sales made from advertising and other lures to entice visitors, Skorman is adamant that his affiliates program is a conduit not for cash but for awareness and visibility. "This is a branding game, not a money game," he says. "All the sites display the Reel.com logo. It's part of our plan to brand ourselves in a race against critical mass."

Reel.com's clientele is a focused group with almost 70% of their traffic accountable from people directly typing the Reel.com Web address into their browser, rather than finding the service via links from search engines, advertising, and editorial mentions. The fact that these customers are probably looking for specific titles can also be proved by looking at their top-selling videos. You won't find *Star Wars, E.T.,* or Disney animated classics on Reel.com's all-time bestseller list (although the Disney studio orders from Reel.com frequently). Their top five include *The Princess Bride, Koyaanisquatsi, The Evil Dead* (horror film), and *Better Off Dead* (John Cusack), with their biggest seller being *Embrace of the Vampire,* an unrated erotic fright film starring Alyssa Milano, best known as Tony Danza's daughter on the television sitcom *Who's the Boss.* The common denomination of these best sellers is that they are out of print and/or have a cult following. And when people find what they want, they buy a lot, as evidenced by Reel.com's biggest order of 81 tapes, totaling $1,235.

Of the 16,000 visitors to Reel.com each day, about 500, approximately 3%, make a purchase. While there is no minimum order, the average new tape purchase is $26.00 (2.5 movies), with used tape purchases averaging $16.50 (2.75 movies) and the standard rental at $7.50 (2 movies). Generally their profit margin on sales is 25%.

Overall Reel.com's biggest selling category is erotic thrillers because they are the closest category they offer to x-rated tapes. "Let's say they are helpful in people's eternal quest to see attractive men and women naked," says Skorman. (Reel.com will not sell to anyone under 18 to protect against shipping inappropriate content.) Foreign films are also a significant seller because they are less available in general video markets. Nonetheless, selling American films to foreigners is not quite as popular due to technological issues.

About 18% of Reel.com's orders are shipped outside the United States with the most popular countries being Japan, England, South Korea, and Germany. These orders are strictly sales and not rentals, which would take too long in the round-trip mail. Besides, the NTSC-standard format tapes would not work in PAL video playback machines standard outside the United States.

In addition to an incomparable inventory, Skorman places a high value on fulfillment speed. Rentals, international orders, and some hard-to-find product are shipped from Reel.com, but the balance, approximately two-thirds of their orders, is drop shipped from one of their wholesalers in New York or Chicago. While order requests are moved electronically, actual physical fulfillment can take from two hours to two days, depending largely on the amount of activity at the wholesalers. While this drop shipping arrangement lets Reel.com carry their extensive inventory virtually, occasionally the electronic fulfillment system with these outside vendors causes difficulties. "Sometimes there are problems with numbers and letters," Skorman explains. "Humans usually catch the errors, but nobody seemed to notice when we sent 31 copies of a film to one customer. Fortunately, the customer alerted us and even sent the copies back."

Reel.com didn't have any of these problems when they first launched in January 1997, because initially they were strictly a content site with the commerce engine officially debuting over three months later on April 15. Within the first three weeks they shipped their one-thousandth order. Skorman considers this launch approach his biggest risk and it was done strictly as a marketing move. "We prematurely launched our virtual store before it was ready so we could stake out our position before someone else ... and it worked," says Skorman.

At this time Skorman had advance knowledge that a well branded, online entertainment-oriented retailer was going to start selling video. This fueled Skorman's sense of urgency to get Reel.com up and its sales mechanism in place. The launch came not a nanosecond too soon. "We just made it by the skin of our teeth," he says. "Fortunately they were distracted by their core business and couldn't pay that much attention to video. By the time they could, we essentially owned the category."

Less than a year after this launch showdown, Reel.com had filled more than 38,000 orders in which they sold 91,000 tapes and rented 4,500 videos. In terms of revenues, December 1997 showed receipts totaling more than $300,000 for the month. And each subsequent month just gets better, with an average growth rate of 30%.

While this part of his plan worked flawlessly, it was one of the few factors that did. For example, Skorman budgeted $400,000 for his launch but it ended up costing him $1.4 million. "The overruns came from three sources: technical, technical, and technical. Every aspect was mishandled, from the design to the programming to the implementation."

Another one of his unexpected expenses was for his domain, reel.com, which cost $20,000. "Reel.com was owned by a semiconductor company and was named after the owners," explains Skorman.

Actually the company spent three months in creative meetings to decide on a name. Choices included MovieMap.com and EarthquakeVideo.com (because they are San Francisco–based). "I wanted a name that could go in different directions, that could be malleable as a content site, transaction site, or other movie direction. We knew we'd do both but we didn't know which was going to be our image. This domain worked for both."

In addition to budget overruns, there were some nearly devastating technical issues. Now that he is on the other side of these problems, Skorman gets to contrast his current typical day, during which he "spends 14 hours on phone meetings and putting out fires," to his early launch when he was "in a constant panic over continual site crashes."

Reflecting on Reel.com's infancy, Skorman makes it abundantly clear that he considers himself a merchant and not a technologist. "I really blew it. My biggest mistake was not taking the technology seriously," he admits. "I thought I could just farm it out. Unfortunately, fraudulent and incompetent people told me what I wanted to hear and then would blow it. It horrifies me how we did everything else right and how much this initially held us back."

Unfortunately the technical difficulties were not limited to pockets of bad code but literally affected every aspect of the site. In short, the programming in the initial stages was so deplorable Skorman describes it as a "foundation of sand," riddled with bugs so bad the site would be down for days.

Another example relates to their server logs, which provide vital marketing information such as the number of people visiting, where the site's visitors originated from, and the click-through rates on banners. While Skorman naturally assumed they were getting data from all four of the company's servers, he learned a month later that he was getting information from only one server, thus providing him with inaccurate information.

Now that Reel.com's technology is humming along, Skorman can focus on his next goal, an IPO by the end of 1998. "As a public company we can practically print money, which means that we can be the eaters rather than being eaten," he notes. Considering the business muscle behind Reel.com, an IPO seems inevitable. The combination of an illustrious board, which includes two former Blockbuster Video chairmen (Tom

Byrne and Scott Beck, the latter now the CEO of Boston Chicken), with Skorman's dedication and experience makes the online video retailer destined for NASDAQ.

For Stuart Skorman, 49, Reel.com was a natural offshoot of the last 20 years of his life, all of which have been spent in retail. The last nine of those years he spent in video as the founder and CEO of the Empire Video Superstore chain located in the Northeast, which he sold to Blockbuster Entertainment Group in 1994. After the sale he consulted for the video giant, helping to develop a touch-screen kiosk system of his Movie Matches content, a database that originally began during his Empire Video days. During his work for Blockbuster, specifically working with kiosks, Skorman realized "electronic information-based retailing was the future" and the Reel.com concept began to germinate.

Despite the fact that videos are his business, we must not overlook Skorman's genuine love of movies, as evidenced by the extraordinary and useful content available at Reel.com. Skorman estimates that he has watched at least 7,000 films, a figure boosted significantly when he was running Empire Video and was watching at least one video a day for nine years. (His favorite films are *Blade Runner, Twelve Angry Men, The Man Who Would Be King,* and *Apocalypse Now.*)

Because he and his staff know their products so well, it lets them truly provide incomparable customer service, which brings joy to their customers' lives.

"When we first opened, we had an e-mail from a woman who was looking for a certain movie she wanted to watch with her gravely ill husband," Skorman relates. "They both recalled seeing it separately years ago, but could only describe certain scenes. Based on that, we were able to determine that the movie was *The Fighting Sullivans.* We searched several vendors, found a copy and sent it to the woman. She returned her rental with a heartfelt message about how viewing the movie with her husband had been one of the sweetest moments they had shared after months of illness and hardship."

Reel.com's combination of product knowledge and personal attention can easily be traced back to Skorman's tenure with Empire Video, where the combination was not only appreciated by customers but reciprocated in record-breaking profits. During the company's last three years, Empire Video had the highest rental volumes per store of any chain in the country. Skorman has applied lessons learned from Empire to his Web enterprise.

Skorman reveals that he believes that giving customers great product information is the key to information age retailing. "During the nine years I spent at Empire and Blockbuster, I focused on information-intensive retailing, which makes Reel.com uniquely well positioned to succeed. Besides, I love great adventures into the unknown," he adds.

Moving into a digital realm from Empire is actually a natural progression for Skorman because it perfectly positions him for the next era of film consumption. In essence, Reel.com is not about selling tapes or renting them, but preparing for the future.

By the year 2000 Skorman intends for Reel.com to remain "the Web's biggest and most respected virtual video store." But his plans move well beyond the turn of the century. By 2005 Skorman sees Reel.com as a major player in the slowly emerging video-on-demand business, essentially using the Reel.com of today as a mechanism to establish relationships he can carry forward.

"I like to say that we're the first video store of the future because we are electronically merchandising the movies," says Skorman. "For the moment we are just using these old technologies called U.S. mail and VHS to get them to you. But as soon it can be zapped to you electronically, we intend to be the first ones to do the zapping."

---

*For up-to-date information about the
success of*
Reel.com
visit
www.StrikingItRich.com

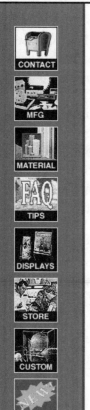

If It's Plastics, Call Us First!

San Diego's Award Winning Plastics Company
Plastic for Industry * Office * Home

1-800-4-RIDOUT　　•　　PlasticWiz@aol.com

Manufacturing for Industry
Acrylics and engineering plastics.

Materials for Industry
High Temp, Cryogenics & more

Expert Tips
FAQ's about plastics from the
plastic wizards.

Brochure Holders
High quality holders and display
frames.

Showroom Store
Open 6 days a week.

Custom Fabrication for Small
Business & Individuals
Your imagination is the only limit!

What's New
What can new plastics do for you?

Skateboards
Check out our flexdex¨
skateboards!

About Ridout Plastics
Find out more about San Diego's
Award Winning Plastics Company!

5535 Ruffin Road
San Diego, CA 92123

Phone: (619) 560-1551

ELLIOTT RABIN

RIDOUT PLASTICS

www.ridoutplastics.com

Elliott Rabin's $8,000 Website paid for itself with its first customer.

"This client wanted to move his company to San Diego where we are located," says Rabin. "So he went to a search engine, punched in 'San Diego and plastics' and our name came back at the top of the list. After seeing the manufacturing pages on our Website, he called me up and—boom—a $100,000-a-year account. Thank you."

While Rabin knew instinctively he should establish a site for his company, Ridout Plastics, it was October 1995, and success stories from other business-to-business Websites were nonexistent. Sure Rabin had heard all about Amazon.com, CDnow, and other emerging, successful *consumer* entities, but they were no indication as to how his enterprise specializing in custom-designed plastic components could fare. Even though Ridout had been in business for over 82 years (Ridout is the name of one of the original owners), Rabin couldn't reconcile a fit between his custom fabrication services for individuals and small business and the emerging digital frontier.

Amazingly, the inspiration for Ridout Plastic's Website occurred while Rabin was navigating Coca-Cola's homepage. While perusing the soft drink king's site—examining its layout, design, and navigation—Rabin said he realized then and there that the Web could present a brochure to the world. Determined to understand how he could sell plastic on the Internet, the Coke site helped him make the link.

"Here I was looking at Coke, something one would never buy online, and yet here was all this information about the product. That made me realize that all we have to do is show people information about what we can do and have done, and they will make a connection. Ultimately if it makes sense to them, they will contact us."

Rabin is quick to note that there was "a ton of hype" about the Web in late 1995 and that nobody really understood its potential as it related to a specific business such as plastics. "Our main product is capability," he explains. "The capability to solve problems with plastics. It was only through experiencing how I could interact with the Web that I realized we could post a virtual brochure." Doing so may not seem like a lofty business proposition, but the goal of Rabin's site is simple: produce an inquiry via phone, fax, or e-mail. At that time he wasn't interested in online ordering.

Even though Rabin could sell some of his inventory on the Web, he prefers not to, since it contradicts his mission statement of "Achieving Innovative Solutions Through People and Plastics™." According to Rabin, since Ridout carries over 7,000 products, in addition to thousands of special order items, the only way to credibly produce these "innovative solutions" is through one-to-one interaction.

"Plastics require a fair amount of training. So we want our customers to call. We never get complaints that we don't offer ordering online probably because these days most people are so happy to deal with a human."

Ridout offers a form on their site that captures all the information the company needs to respond quickly. Of the 12 completed forms they receive in a day, phone or fax numbers are included 99% of the time, to which Ridout replies within 24 hours. Rabin says that people who need immediate answers call their 800-number, which is clearly posted in the site.

Because they use a specific 800-number tagged exclusively to their Website, Ridout can instantly identify orders generated from cyberspace. In a typical day they receive about 13 calls, of which 70% eventually buy. The order size ranges from a low of $50 to a high of $40,000 with an average of $500–750.

While Rabin and his customers prefer the phone process, a few holdouts bother him. "Our most frustrating customers are the ones that have some very specific questions and use e-mail only, refusing to call our 800-number or give us their fax or phone number," he laments. "In our business, we usually ask the customer more questions than they ask us, to help solve the problem of what plastic to use, and so on. In these cases, it takes forever to squeeze information out of this customer, and because it takes so long, they often get irritated. If they would just trust that we are not used-car salesmen, they would get an immediate answer."

Despite his preference for analog communications, Rabin is considering offering his brochure holders via interactive ordering, one of the few items he offers that he feels could be sold online directly without disturbing his sensibility. Their brochure holders are Ridout's biggest sellers from Web inquiries and their highest profit item. Because of the straightforward nature of the product, Rabin feels this is one Ridout item where human intervention may not be necessary. The same holds true for their forthcoming posting of two product lines online: Lucite Beanie Baby cases and high-end skateboards.

Rabin's willingness to integrate some Web-based ordering is indicative of his understanding of the flexibility necessary to be successful on the Internet. For instance, although his prelaunch plan included a blank check, he balanced it with the motto "dive in, head first, eyes open."

This proved to be a winning combination. Though he has a strong computer background, Rabin did only the initial design himself in a word processor, opting to have a professional do the design and coding. The result is a site that is fast-loading and informative, something appreciated by Ridout's 600 visitors a day who constantly compliment the company on its simplicity. The company itself has won several prestigious awards, including the U.S. Small Business Administration San Diego's Family Owned Small Business of the Year and Best Small Business Website in San Diego.

"I think we got it right the first time, to just keep it simple," Rabin advises. "We stayed away from frames and Java since many users did not have the latest browsers. Understand what drives a customer to your site, and what you're going to do for them when they get there. If they need information, make it painless. If they need entertainment, then entertain them."

While their site is straightforward, Ridout's initial Web hosting arrangement was a bit kooky. Instead of signing up with an Internet service provider and paying a monthly fee, Ridout took advantage of a deal from a local business newspaper who offered free Website hosting space for anyone who bought a minimum amount of advertising with the paper. For $500 a month, Ridout got the print ads, the Website, plus unlimited but reasonable changes, hosting, and CGI scripting.

Due to slow servers and a decline in customer service, Ridout moved on about two years later. Meanwhile, the arrangement initially was a good one for Rabin, who viewed the deal a bit differently than the newspaper did. "In my mind we were paying $500 a month for hosting and getting the print ads for free." Since he liked having a presence in the local paper it was the ideal arrangement—almost.

The only service not included in the newspaper's buy-print-ads-get-free-Web-space proposition was an e-mail address. So Rabin had to settle with America Online for the company's e-mail.

"AOL worked fine for us before we went crazy with sales because we could get on from anywhere," Rabin remarks. "While it's bad for attachments, overall it was still convenient for us because we could install the software on any computer to centralize the mail. We used AOL for simplicity."

Perhaps because of this vital connection to the service, Rabin accepted an advertising opportunity on AOL, an opportunity that turned out to be his biggest marketing flop.

It was the summer of 1997 and Rabin was anxious to get Ridout Plastic's new signature model Flexdex skateboard in front of the public. He bought a banner ad, which led to a microsite on AOL's Digital City San Diego (San Diego being his hometown with a significant skate boarding population). The deal was $2,000 plus 20% of the gross sales for a six-month run. To entice visitors and to track interest in the product, Rabin offered a free sticker to anyone who requested it. Two months later, not one request. Rabin knew that technically the ad worked because he would periodically click on it and fill out the form. Of the experience he concludes, "It was the classic case of what if I post a Web page and nobody comes?"

Because of the nature of Ridout's business, less than 5% of their customers come from AOL. This can be attributed to their clientele of small and medium-sized businesses and an increasing percentage of international customers. While 15% of Ridout's business is non-U.S., this percentage is growing. "I was surprised at how much business we were getting from Canada. Canadians seemed to be hooked into the Net earlier than other countries."

In terms of dollar volume, Chile is their most active foreign country, with orders from one client alone averaging $25,000. If they decide to translate their pages, Rabin says that Spanish would be his first choice. (They have two Spanish-speaking staff members in the sales office, and about 30% company-wide.)

This foreign element is one of the few aspects of their business that is limited by their need to communicate by phone with their clients. It is also a motivating factor behind designing a query system on the Web that could get to the root of a potential client's needs. Rabin figures the antidote for foreign sales is to post as much information on the Website as possible to convince these potential non-U.S. customers that Ridout can deliver before they invest in overseas phone calls.

With the exception of his AOL experience, Rabin has not done online advertising. Therefore these non-U.S. visitors are getting to Ridout without the benefit of any preconditioning or branding. Ninety-five percent of Ridout's traffic comes from the search engines, which Rabin finds are much better at directing customers. While Lycos and AOL's Netfind contribute perceptibly to their traffic, Yahoo is responsible for delivering over 50% of their visitors.

Type in "plastic" as a Yahoo search query and you'll find the company in not one but two categories: "Business and Economy: Companies: Manufacturing: Plastics: Fabrication" and "Regional: U.S. States: California: Cities: San Diego: Business:

Industrial Supplies." This fortunate double listing, likely the result of having registered so early in the search engine game, coupled with Rabin's winning description ("For industry & individuals, cut to size acrylic, polycarbonate, frp, custom fabrication, brochure holders, pop displays, cases, awards") remains his best promotional vehicle.

Nonetheless, Rabin also knew he could drive traffic with strategic links from companies germane to his business but not competitive with them. For example, he e-mailed General Electric and suggested that they point people to Ridout for those who needed products made out of Lexan®, an unbreakable clear plastic sheet made by General Electric used for glazing windows and machine guards, among many other uses. Same for Rohm and Haas, which manufactures Plexiglass® and for whom Ridout is one of their distributors.

Partly because Rabin wasn't doing any online advertising and his links and search engine listings were so successful, it wasn't until the beginning of 1998, two and a half years after he launched, that he moved Ridout to a vanity domain. Until then his customers found him at http://www.sddt.com/~plastics instead of the conventional http://www.companyname.com. "It wasn't offered by the newspaper hosting our site and we didn't feel a need for it because everyone was finding us through search engines who link and don't show an address." Rabin notes. "Also we don't think of ourselves as a brand."

Clearly having a less-than-simple URL has not hurt Ridout's business. Even with first-year revenues from their Web presence in 1995 of a respectable $150,000, Rabin could not have imagined that 1998 could exceed $1.1 million. Furthermore, 15% of his company's new business originates online.

These figures will only continue to grow. While a number of small and large plastics companies are on the Net, Ridout continues to have the best conceived site. Even one of his competitors, who happens to be in San Diego, doesn't concern Rabin a bit. "Their site is a bit insulting to more educated users who are looking for content, not entertainment. They do not have our depth of knowledge or our inventory."

One of Rabin's biggest revelations since launching Ridout Plastic's site is the quality of customers he has attracted from his Web presence. "We spend four times more on *Yellow Pages* advertising, about $25,000, than we spend on our Internet presence. And to think that for all this we are essentially advertising around the world and getting all this corporate business. We never dreamed we would pick up so many quality accounts from Fortune 500 companies."

Perhaps because he launched with such modest expectations Rabin is constantly impressed with what his Net presence has done to grow his company's revenues and stature. "Every day I am totally blown away that people out there find us and want to do business with us."

For up-to-date information about the success of
Ridout Plastics
visit
www.StrikingItRich.com

Tradeshop Incorporated

Toll Free 800-224-8066 * Fax 503-916-8687

The company built for, and by, real people!
[Chris] [Gary] [Duane] [Ray] [Jan] [Brian] [Wendy] [Lucky]

Celebrating fine jewelry and diamonds, from the bench perspective, I've served the Jewelry Industry for thirty years, owning Oregon's largest union wholesale service center, but now we work for you, on the web! ...elegantly at your schedule.

Loose Gems?

We got 'em :)

Knowledge is Power!

Explore the possibilities when you and the experienced master craftsperson work directly together, *without the salesbabble*. Certified Diamonds, at internationally competitive dealer prices, and world class custom on-line to show you what we can do...

client comments	1	2	3	4	5	6	7	8	9	10	11
Each a project	12	13	14	15	16	17	18	19	20	21	22
Dream come true!	23	24	25	26	27	28	29	30	31	32	33

I built this business by putting my customers interests first, that won't change as we grow to serve you even better. Your satisfaction is our main objective, Imagine that!

Products
* Diamond Search Engine ★★★★★
* Loose Diamond Specials
* Celtic Wedding Bands ★★★★★
* Jewelry & GemStone Specials
* Wedding Rings Platinum & Gold
* Current Projects On-Line ★★★★★
* Gold, Silver, Platinum Bullion HOT!
* Hand Engraved Ornate Rings

Our New Web Domains
* CelticRings.com
* IdealDiamonds.com
* AffordableDiamonds.com
* DiamondValue.com

Neat Stuff
* Digital Imaging ★★★★★
* Web Site News & Web Plans

Information
* Web Client's References
* Business Credentials ★★★★★
* Professional Business History
* Whimsical History Tour :)
* Killer Platinum Custom
* Diamond Grading 4-C's Info
* Lost Wax Casting Refresher
* Web Site Over-View
* Special Order Web Policies
* Order & Wire Transfer Info
* Web Awards ★★★★★
* Gemology Pages ★★★★★
* Magraw Hill Book! ★★★★★
* Cool Links

RAY ELSEY
TRADESHOP
www.tradeshop.com

If you believe Web retailing makes sense only for commodity items such as CDs and books, products that are identical no matter where you buy them, and that consumers will likely never spend thousands of dollars online, Tradeshop is your wake-up call. Tradeshop breaks all the rules, with an average order running $7,000. And that's for one item: jewelry—with the exception of furniture and clothing, perhaps the most touchy-feely purchase possible.

Given the paradigms of online retailing, we could hope that if we follow the golden thread that has made Tradeshop such a success and apply that to a commoditized business, the enterprise should flourish. It's a fair hypothesis until you realize that the core of Tradeshop cannot be replicated. It's Ray Elsey, 48, its founder, whose heart is behind Tradeshop's dazzling success as the Web source for custom jewelry, certified diamonds, and factory fine jewelry.

Ray Elsey is a man with a mission. "I want people to understand the bloated nature of traditional jewelry marketing, where the store has to pay 8% of their gross to the mall, along with an overhead that mandates 300% markups," he says.

"The average person who finds me is generally a young professional, business owner who works on the Internet. I see an across-the-board mix of Web-savvy people and I'm still amazed that there is such a wide variety of professionals and individuals represented in my customer files."

Elsey's clientele may redefine the word "variety" as it ranges from Fortune 100 executives to struggling students.

"We built a very fine platinum mounting for a very fine diamond for FedEx owner David Werner," Elsey recalls. "It was really funny too. When the FedEx courier was keying in the shipment he looked up and said of the recipient, "Hey, I know that guy!"

Other business luminaries in the Tradeshop files include Sean Forbes (who purchased a three-carat diamond for $21,000 which was later conservatively appraised at $45,000), a slew of Dun & Bradstreet executives, the project manager for the Cassini Space probe, the heads of quality control for NASA and Saturn motor cars, along with countless orders from employees at Microsoft.

"We've done some special engraving for Bill Gates and sold quite a few items in the five-figure range to their 'everyday' employees," says Elsey. "I don't think we are in the executive newsletter or anything."

While Elsey enjoys selling to business executives, perhaps he gets more satisfaction from selling to ordinary people. He especially loves taking care of those in need of an item for a special occasion but whose budgets have been heckled at their local jewelry stores.

"I offer small band rings and other inexpensive items costing less than $100," he explains. "We try not to just cater to the large ticket items here. My favorite sale was to Christopher McCoy, a graduate student tired of being led away from the diamond rings toward the tasteless band rings while being told he could never get a diamond with only $350 to spend," says Elsey. "We set him up with a finely crafted solitaire with a lovely 1/3-carat diamond. His expression of thanks is what echoes in my mind in the late nights when I'm working. He personifies why I'm doing this."

Christopher McCoy can attest to Tradeshop's slogan: "Dream big. You can afford to be here." With an average markup on custom jewelry of only 25% and certified diamonds at 12% maximum (versus 300% or more), Elsey clearly stands by his motto. Despite these fractional profits, in 1998 Tradeshop will net $1.1 million on gross revenues of $4.5 million.

Despite Tradeshop's competitive prices, their products are still major purchases, costing up to tens of thousands of dollars. And while these extraordinary values may attract potential customers to Tradeshop, Elsey wins their business with pages that focus on education and establishing credibility. On this latter point, Elsey doesn't tell future customers to trust him. He shows them.

Since most purchases are handled via wire transfers, Elsey insists you check Tradeshop's banking references. He makes this easy by supplying the necessary contact names and phone numbers along with a scanned letter from the bank discussing Tradeshop's corporate account profile.

Since Tradeshop was born from a union outfit in Portland, Oregon where there is virtually no organized labor, Elsey offers the phone number for the International Service Worker's Jeweler's Union, local 41, in addition to another scanned letter discussing how Elsey has always used professional craftsmen exclusively. The craftsmen are paid top wages, despite the fact "that they are competing against a much lower-paid workforce."

The offline credibility inventory continues with information to contact Oregon's Better Business Bureau and the Portland Chamber of Commerce, to both of which Tradeshop belongs.

Having established professional trustworthiness, Elsey brings his proposition home with customer referral pages gushing with joy over their purchases, most of which are linked to several photos of each of the pieces ordered.

Between unsolicited customer praise and bullet-proof credentials, you can't help but notice that your internal dialogue shifts from *if* you will buy from Tradeshop to *when* you will buy from Tradeshop.

"Regardless of what you bring to the Web, make sure you take the time to explain fully what qualifies you to be considered for a purchase," Elsey advises. "You must still prove yourself. It's not much different than the other world."

With over 50% of his visitors who call the 800-number making a purchase, Elsey has nailed one of the most important precursors to Web success: making it easy to buy. If the primary objection for a potential Tradeshop customer is trust, Elsey completely overcomes this hurdle by offering prospective clients all the information necessary to establish trust. If it's about quality, Elsey shows hundreds of photos of his custom work to demonstrate his company's creativity and expertise.

After examining Tradeshop's Webpages you begin to understand that while its tiny markups and extraordinary quality initially attract customers, the only marketing initiative Elsey really cares about is customer service.

"I see my desire to be effective as the core of my marketing effort," he says. "We have a strong referral business of very happy customers. Since the quantity and quality of referrals are so amazing, I bet I rely less on the search engines than perhaps anyone you are going to meet in business on the Web."

One must also consider that the name and domain Tradeshop are not particularly intuitive or memorable, hence not a noteworthy marketing move, but Elsey loves it.

"I'm an old tradeshopper and began in my teens when I would do filing casting for my father to make my allowance," he explains. "Since I always want to be the 'shop,' the name seems logical and very descriptive. I'm of the bench and the process. Marketing is something that I'm writing my own rules on now."

Other marketing tracks Elsey does not participate in include trading links with other pages (although a couple hundred voluntarily link to him), promotional mailings, and online advertising. He runs one ad in an offline national AT&T business-to-business directory annually for $18,000. "This is not perhaps the most logical place but I like the publication and I use it as a resource, so it made sense for me."

Elsey has ignored traditional marketing in favor of word of mouth because he considers his growth from such to be more sincere. "I consider referrals to be what I base my future on. Since I earn that, I think it's the most genuine way to go." Furthermore, Elsey feels if he were to advertise he would be making the same mistakes other retailers do since inevitably the costs inflate a business's overhead—costs that are eventually passed on to the customer.

In addition to referrals, Tradeshop sees a repeat customer rate that is equally as enviable. "Last year I sold a woman a 3-carat diamond and she returned to buy a 3.79-carat. Right before this order I shipped a three-quarter carat to a customer who purchased a 2-carat E-VS1 for $22,000." The list is endless.

When people come to www.tradeshop.com, they spend most of their time in the diamond search engine ferreting out the perfect stone. Updated five times a day with a database of over tens of thousands of entries, Tradeshop offers only major lab–certified diamonds complete with reports. "We've sold a $63,000 diamond the likes of which few in the industry ever see," boast Elsey. "A D-flawless 2.31 carat. Not just pretty, but laboratory report perfect." According to Elsey, on the street this rock would have cost over $100,000. His profit on the sale: $2,000. This is where people save the most money. It should be no surprise, then, that sales of parcels of diamonds between $100,000 and $150,000 are common.

Certified diamonds are by far Tradeshop's biggest seller, and the reason is clear. Tradeshop shows clients all the information relating to the diamond including the grading, explaining the implications of each, carefully guiding them to the best stone for what they want.

"Prices for certified diamonds are routinely bloated, often twice what we offer them for," claims Elsey. "Once a potential customer is educated through our pages, sees our diamond list and the prices, along with our credentials, history and reference pages, they can't help but purchase here."

After the diamond search engine, the next most popular spot is the Current Projects page, where special orders and custom designs are tracked for all to review. "We like the fact that we feature the ability to build anything and that makes for some very interesting projects."

Tradeshop's open-mindedness is truly appreciated by his customers, one of whom wrote Elsey with this tale:

> I have to admit, when I thought up this idea for Celtic wedding rings I was frustrated because no one locally would undertake this project. The design was too complicated and finely detailed. As a last hope, I went to the Internet where I found you. You were the only person who embraced the idea instead of telling me how it couldn't be done.

Since undertaking this project, Tradeshop has been swamped with orders for Celtic design band rings. They start at $400 in gold and go up to $900 in platinum and account for 22% of his custom sales.

"I've been honored at the response here and I name the customer's patterns and rings after them for all time. For example, many people have ordered the 'Demas Ring Design,' made for Peter Demas, a wonderful Internet surfer that I met and really enjoy."

One order, however, initially intimidated Elsey, but it has since become one of his favorites. A customer contacted him saying that he always wanted to create the ring from the JRR Tolkien book *Lord of the Rings*, the ring of Babbahar. The client wanted this ring in pure gold and platinum. Realizing the complexity of the job, Elsey asked the customer to illustrate what he wanted. "He showed me drawings and a clay mockup and I just couldn't refuse the job," says Elsey. "It remains the most interesting job I've done on the Web and I often point to this to show folks that we can build anything."

The nature of the Web allows Elsey to do custom work quickly and cost-effectively. Via his site, the drawings are rendered and finalized and the waxes are approved, allowing the customer to become an active participant in the process, and actually designing and building the project with him.

"We had an engineer at Boeing design his wife's wedding ring who was still living in BellaRuss [formerly in the Soviet Union]. Everyone on both continents got to watch this world-class project being born," says Elsey. "Or the couple being able to announce their wedding plans by sending all their friends the URL for the rings we'd just finished. ... Or the mom from California calling in tears after seeing the ring we'd just built for her daughter in Washington, D.C. ... Where to start, where to end. If there is magic in the world, the Web is it."

Custom work is by definition dangerous because the stakes are high and the margin for error wide. Elsey gets around this using the Web to gain approvals and be sure he is on track with his customers 100%. The result: a 100% satisfaction rate. "It amazes me how the Web does so many things so well. A cost-effective presence, instantaneous communication with the clients that includes pictures of waxes, et cetera. Does it get any better?"

Today's scenario was a fantasy to Elsey in 1974 when as a master jeweler and diamond setter he started Oregon's largest professional union tradeshop called Associate Jewelers. But he knew he was destined for the Web from the moment he first saw it in 1995. By the middle of that year, he had established an online presence.

"My pages started as a way to show other jewelers what I could do and rapidly turned into a sales engine beyond my expectations," he reminisces. As the Website flourished, Elsey knew he had to break away from Associates. He sold his half in August 1997 and devoted himself full-time to Tradeshop.com. He considers this the biggest risk he has ever taken.

"I owned all the computer gear myself when we started, and we've purchased and paid cash for everything from office fixtures to vaults. So we have neither long-term debt nor any need of a line of credit," says Elsey. "I like simplistic models and I wanted to model this after a Kool-Aid stand, although I'm still working on processing forty bizzillion gallons of Kool-Aid."

Though he had $40,000 earmarked to launch, he needed to devote only $20,000. "I never had to touch the last half and the first $20,000 was repaid in the first months of business."

"At times it's been so successful it's a bit scary," says Elsey who admits that one of the most important pieces of equipment he installed upon opening was a fold-out couch. "The activity is so much stronger than I thought possible in the initial phases of our business plan. In the first four months we even grew out of the office I thought would last us for years."

In that same four months, Tradeshop grossed $1 million, the total of what Associate Jewelers did in one full year. "My first amusing memory was 'will I make the rent and not go backward in life?,' which is really laughable now." Laughable to say the least, when in December 1997 alone, Elsey netted over $78,000 on sales of $500,000 plus. With a staff of seven, which includes his son, daughter, and wife, his low monthly expenses help keep the business superprofitable.

"I'd normally not be quite so forthcoming in sharing quite sensitive business information," Elsey admits. "But honestly, I think that if one small business person becomes inspired to create a Website and winds up in a place like where I am now, then I have done a very good thing."

More important to Elsey is that his enterprise was never strictly about numbers, but about being effective on his own terms. "I'd have to say that in reality this is totally unreal, almost like a Star Trek episode where someone is just minding their own business and is beamed up to some fantastic technological world, where what was impossible seems rather ordinary."

Ironically, the success of Tradeshop might not be evident looking at their pages, which are far from slick and best described as informal. Designed and programmed by Elsey, the site is clearly homespun right down to the spelling, which is so bad and so ubiquitous that after the fifteenth error it stops being annoying and actually becomes entertaining.

"I have promised myself to start using a spell checker or something. When I update the site, I'm in a hurry most of the time and I have a lot to say."

In addition to pointing out spelling errors, Tradeshop shoppers give Elsey lots of feedback on the site. Elsey feels that customers and visitors should dictate the evolution of his pages rather than trying to make assumptions based only on sales of particular categories.

"Once I heard from a guy in New York who said, 'You're not half as smart as you think you are. Oregon is one of only two states that does not have sales tax. Do you realize how much that is going to save me on this 5-carat diamond? I'd advise that you mention that instantly,' and instantly my pages were graced with this idea."

No sales tax is just another one of many of Elsey's competitive advantages. While the assumption would be that Tradeshop's biggest competition is highly branded jewelry stores such as Zales, Elsey considers keeping up with his own business his greatest challenge.

A fraction the size of Zales, Tradeshop fulfilled over 4,000 orders for fiscal year 1998. Given his growth trend, he looks to an IPO one day. "I hope to take my company public, to complete the circle. It somehow seems fitting that the company I founded on the principle of 'treating the people good' might eventually be owned 'by the people.'"

Another of Elsey's future plans is an expanded worldwide customer base. About 5% of current sales are non-U.S. to countries such as Canada and Ireland, along with faraway destinations such as Japan, Jakarta, and Indonesia.

Despite his international clientele, page translations are not in the future. "Actually with the way I spell, I should consider having them first translated into English," Elsey jokes. "However, it seems as if English is destined to be the language of the Internet by default. We don't feel any pressure to become multilingual."

While Tradeshop may stick to one language, Elsey will expand into several different sites, each of which will further niche the best aspects of his business.

First up is IdealDiamonds.com, "where math is the rule and the diamonds represent that most lovely of cuts," as Elsey describes it. "This will be a place where one can find the finest of platinum and gold products at exceptionally low prices."

Next to follow is AffordableDiamonds.com, "the common sense stone store." This site is intended for folks with uncompromising budgets who want jewelry that is far superior to the average diamond available locally. Profit margins on this site will run 25–50% of the industry average, which means that a couple could get a quality wedding set for under $200.

Elsey has high hopes for these Website siblings to his flagship site, but he won't articulate them because he's usually happily wrong. "Every projection I've made thus far has fallen far short of the mark," he says. "Each time I saw an inch, the reality was a foot and I realized later that I had no frame of reference in the first place."

"I have learned that I can dream bigger than I dared imagine," he continues. "I feel like Willie Wonka in a magic world making magical things, in a magical way."

For up-to-date information about the success of
Tradeshop
visit
www.StrikingItRich.com

U.S. WINGS™
Made in the U.S.A.

U.S. Wings is a manufacturer and distributing dealer for:
Avirex – Flying Tigers – Alpha – Cooper – Schott– Cockpit
U.S. Wings carries a full line of:
Authentic Leather Bomber Jackets – Aviation Jackets
Flight Jackets – Warbirds T-Shirts – Military Memorabilia
Aviation Art – Caps – Military Khaki Outerwear – and more!
U.S. Wings is the exclusive distributor of:
Authentic Cooper Horsehide Leather A-2 Flight Jackets
and carries Licensed Authentic Flying Tigers products

Cooper Horsehide A-2
exclusively from U.S. WINGS

exclusively from U.S. WINGS
NEW! Sterling Silver
WWII Pilot Wings

Aviation Gift Ideas

☐

World Wide Toll Free Order Line:
1-800-650-0659 (English Orders Only!)

Sidebar navigation:
- Products
- Cooper Jackets
- History
- Bomber Jackets
- Flying Tigers
- AVIREX Jackets
- Hand-Painted Jackets
- The A-2 Jackets
- Schott Jackets
- Aviation Art
- Corporate Jackets
- Order
- Return Policy
- Links

U.S. WINGS

www.uswings.com

Imagine the frustration of having a cyber clientele that includes heads of state and the highest-ranking government officials—including someone who lives in a big White House—and not being able to talk about it.

Fortunately for Sergeant David Hack, a career military man, keeping information classified is one of his hallmarks. In fact, it is just part of the job as the CEO of U.S. Wings, the premier destination for authentic, government-issue aviation bomber jackets and military khaki outerwear.

While he can't discuss politically affiliated customers, he can disclose other luminaries such as the heads of every major airline in the world, along with Federal Express founder Fred Smith and Nevada attraction Congo Jack, who not only adorns himself with an official U.S. Wings jacket, but their 100% silk aviation scarf, khaki pants, shirt, and logo cap.

So why all the devotion to a staple garment available at any high-end clothing store? According to their customers, U.S. Wings has the finest jackets at the best prices anywhere in the world. Furthermore they are the only official licensee for Flying Tigers–branded apparel. Since they've launched in April 1996 they have filled 12,000 orders, many of which are not for one or two jackets but up to 100.

"For Christmas a corporate officer for an aviation manufacturing company wanted to give his friends something special," Hack recalls. "The order was for 100 authentic A-2 jackets, 25 to be shipped to Europe, 75 shipped domestically. This order ran over $25,000, all charged to his American Express card. At first, we were concerned that the card wouldn't clear, but it did."

These A-2 jackets, the foundation of the U.S. Wings inventory, are by far their biggest seller. "You see them everywhere these days, not just wrapped around the pilots at the local airfield," says Hack. "The A-2 jacket is as much a part of America as Harley Davidson motorcycles, Corvette sports cars, or Cessna airplanes."

According to Hack, even though this 50-year-old fashion staple is still associated with a reckless, daring image, the person wearing them today varies considerably, from accountants to doctors to high school girls. In fact, 50% of U.S. Wings purchases are made by women. Because of the appeal of flight jackets, U.S. Wings' primary audience is not just professional aviators, but everyone.

Given the breadth of their clientele, one might think that such a large customer base would be easy to market. While Hack has found a marketing mix that works, he had two challenges to overcome: (1) selling products that cost between $100 and 700 and (2) selling clothing, something most people would want to try on first, if not to judge quality then at least to determine fit.

Hack knew from the beginning that one of the best ways to establish trust and credibility was through Webpage design that was not only pretty to look at but functional as well. His vision was realized. U.S. Wings has won many design awards, including Best of the Planet for design, layout, and content.

Hack's mandate to his designers has never changed. He insists that they build pages that load quickly despite their graphic intensity, to which he adds plenty of copy to accurately characterize the fine craftsmanship of his inventory.

For example, there isn't one photo of their signature 100% silk aviation scarf, there are three: a close-up, along with a view of it wrapped around the front of a jacket, and a view from the rear of a jacket. To this he adds a description of the quality of Tibetan workmanship and history of this aviation fashion accessory.

With over 40 pages, U.S. Wings' Website requires anywhere from 4 to 16 hours a week in updating. Hack has also learned to keep archives of old pages as well, even when the need for them seems remote.

"There was a situation where a whole product line was discontinued and we had to take the entire line off our Webpages," says Hack. "Then the product was actually 'recontinued' after a few months and we had to put the whole product line back. Because we saved copies of our old files, including the photos of the products, we were able to get the pages back up in less than 5 minutes."

Keeping copies of everything and having control over his Website was a lesson David Hack learned hard. While it's not unusual for a Website owner to have problems with an Internet Service Provider, (ISP), usually a lack of service or slow servers are the core issues. In David Hack's case, his site was literally held hostage.

When the U.S. Wings domains were first registered, the ISP responsible listed themselves as the administrative and billing contact in addition to being the technical contact, the latter being standard. When Hack wanted to change providers, the current ISP wouldn't release the domains or the files.

"We learned that your ISP doesn't own your files. Many think they are like a landlord, that if you don't pay your rent they can hold your furniture as collateral. That's illegal. You own your files. You paid for them. A landlord cannot keep your furniture. Your host cannot keep your files."

Although Hack is happy with his current ISP, he still advises that, if your designer is also your host, you keep copies of all your files off site, including the HTML coding, graphics (down to divider bars), and photos. "Always ask for the original artwork back," he advises. "Tell them you need it for print ads if you have to."

Because of an unscrupulous ISP, Hack's original $10,000 budget swelled to $50,000. "There should be some guidelines as to what people should be able to charge," says Hack. "For example, they charged us a $150 service fee to register each domain in addition to the $100 Internic charges. Most companies charge only $50. Then they charged us $500 to list our URL with three search engines."

Needless to say, Hack has since learned what the norm is for such services, but not until these less-than-ethical folks soaked tens of thousands of dollars from him. "I called the Ohio Attorney General's Office and asked what could I do and they told me, 'We are sorry, but there are no laws on the books to protect consumers against Internet fraud."

Hack looks forward to the day when there are laws. To him it is a crime like any other. "It's the same thing as a guy walking up to me with a gun and saying 'give me your money.'"

Now that Hack has aligned with a reputable ISP/design company, he has found that combining the two has worked well. While his wife Lani (U.S. Wings' President) did the initial design of the site, an in-house graphic designer at their ISP took over. Considering the amount of tinkering Hack likes to do, having the host, designer, and occasional programming done in one place has helped keep his business efficient. He pays an average of $100 per hour for their services.

Not having to deal with page design internally means that Hack can pay more attention to his customer service initiative, which includes incorporating customer feedback into his site immediately. "If I get an e-mail from a customer who is confused about how to order or any of our policies, I know I have to rewrite the Website text immediately," says Hack. "I have to act fast because that's the nature of doing business on the Internet."

The Sergeant has also learned that even when he thinks he has an element nailed, there is still someone who is confused. "New people to the Web don't realize to click on the side bars to navigate our site," he remarks. "I was tempted to put 'To go into our site, click on the buttons on the left side of the screen' on the main page because I got phone calls from people new to the Web."

For these reasons and more, David Hack never turns off his computer during waking hours, as a way to monitor both his customers and his ISP. Because of his experience and need for top care by his hosting company, Hack feels his biggest business risk to date was selecting his ISP since all his business relies entirely on whether or not his site is up. No active Website, no revenue. This is a frightening reality when you consider that your entire enterprise can be shut down in a mouse click, from hundreds of miles away. "The moment you sense your ISP is bad, move on," says Hack. "Your company comes first."

Even though they are a cyber success, U.S. Wings began as a paper catalog in 1986. Six months after launching the Website he dumped the catalog , which was Hack's primary goal in going digital in the first place.

As a catalog, Hack was spending $90,000 annually in printing and postage to send his catalog to 50,000 people. "I thought I would be able to jettison the catalog immediately," he says. "I thought like everyone that the Net would be an instant success." While it would eventually lead him to grosses exceeding $3.7 million in 1998, he didn't even get his first order online until three weeks after he launched. Today he receives an average of 25 orders a day.

Perhaps most notable is the fact that Hack has grown U.S. Wings with virtually no advertising, instead opting for a heap of strategic marketing.

While he spent $15,000 on print advertising in *Trade-A-Plane Magazine*, *Flying Magazine*, and *Cowlas Magazine* (a military/aviation publication), Hack says "it got me nowhere." He adds that, in retrospect, advertising is the only area in the launch of his business on which he would have spent less.

In 1997 Hack decided to try online advertising with America Online, but they didn't call back. Even banner ads he didn't pay for were a disappointment. For three months through the Banner Ad Exchange, Hack found not only that the arrangement didn't pull visitors, but also that a banner for someone who "stole his site" was displayed. Although theft is rare, U.S. Wings was a victim of an entire Webfront steal, where another company mounted Hack's entire Website on a different server with a different name but all other elements intact.

"They saw how successful I was," says Hack. "I was able to catch them doing it, though. All our material is copyrighted and we will prosecute those who steal our files."

The site is now gone. So this is a case that U.S. Wings will not be prosecuting. However, another of what Hack refers to as a "knock-off" site called War Surplus based in Pittsburgh has cyber-heisted U.S. Wings' photographs. "We had these photographs taken specifically for us. We have the negatives. We know they are ours." What irks Hack even more is that they are using images of one product as representing another. For example, War Surplus is using a U.S. Wings photo of an Averix jacket next to a description of a Cooper brand garment, which, according to Hack, are very dissimilar.

While the Banner Exchange led Hack to discover the underbelly of the Net, on the flip side Hack has also had the opportunity to associate himself with brands he feels reflect the professionalism of his company and the quality of his products. For example, he was one of the first 20 retailers invited to join MasterCard's Shop Smart Program. This association allows Hack to display the MasterCard Shop Smart logo as well as be linked off the MasterCard Shop Smart guide. In exchange Hack gives away a free cap when customers use MasterCard to purchase a product. Since then, the Director of MasterCard International has even purchased a flight jacket, a Flying Tiger T-shirt, and a silk scarf.

Perhaps Hack's most effective marketing has been customer service. In fact he goes so far to describe his storefront as his "customer's site." "We give our customers exactly what they want," he reveals. "They wanted to order online with a secure server. We make sure all of the information is secure and confidential. They wanted to call in an order. We give them an 800-number to call us. They wanted to fax us their orders. We included a fax order form right on the site."

Since word of mouth is so strong on his products, Hack astutely figured that his customers could be his best billboards. To that end, he began offering two complimentary gifts with the purchase of any U.S. Wings flight jacket: their 100% white silk aviation scarf and their signature U.S. Wings baseball-style cap. It should be noted that this hat is not your standard issue polyester advertising premium. To the contrary, the U.S. Wings cap is top of the line, complete with leather bill and a hand-stitched logo.

"They get the cap for free and they inevitably call back and buy two more because their wife, neighbor, boss, whoever wants one too." For this reason U.S. Wings sells over 100 of these $12.95 caps a week. The same holds true for the silk scarves. Together these two items are the U.S. Wings' second and third biggest sellers behind flight jackets.

It's important to note that the wholesale costs of the cap and scarf are $9 and $12, respectively, and that the profit margin on their $229 jacket is 35%, or $80. Hack is giving away 26% of his profit margin on the jacket as a premium, despite the fact that he sells the jackets for $50 less than just about anywhere else. Now note how he is getting this back in immediate resales, with over 50% of his customers ordering more caps or scarves within one week of receiving their jackets, the average reorder being two caps. Essentially Hack has created a time-delayed upsell and his strategy has worked beautifully. "We've sold up to a dozen silk scarves to one customer," he notes. "You give a little to get a lot. I feel like the Fuller Brush man who ingratiated himself to his customers by giving them a brush first ... and they always got to keep the brush."

Although Hack is a gracious retailer, he has unfortunately had more than his share of fraud, an issue for which he finally feels he has won the battle.

The core of the issue is black market credit card rings, where, according to Hack, "the scam artists back each other up." For example, one order came from Russia. The credit card was rejected. The same customer returns the next day with a new number, which MasterCard approved. Hack fulfilled the order for four jackets totaling $1,700.

"Forty-five days later my bank debits my account," he relates. "And why? The credit card holder says that he didn't place the order. And they get away with this because there are no Russian credit card fraud laws."

While this example is typical, it is not the worst U.S. Wings has suffered. In November 1997 the company had over 20 instances of fraud totaling $17,000—all international orders to Eastern bloc countries. "We still fulfill but it takes 90 days before we ship overseas. So there is plenty of time for chargebacks," Hack explains. "We require a wire transfer or a signed letter if they want faster fulfillment."

In addition to their new overseas shipping policy, the U.S. Wings Website constantly reminds future customers that they "will prosecute credit card fraud," a warning, Hack says, that has been working since he posted it. They also require that all jackets are signed for with a photo ID.

With the exception of international orders, 75% of U.S. Wings' customers use the company's 800-number instead of on-line ordering. Even though it costs Hack an average of $3 per call, he doesn't feel a need to emphasize Web ordering just to save money. "People want to know that there are people at the other end of a Website," he advises. "They need to feel comfort-able ordering from you. We are more than happy to answer any questions by our 800-number. We consider that well worth it."

If Hack were to encourage a specific ordering method, it would be by fax, which now only accounts for 3%. "I wish it were more because it is so much easier and it is signed. You don't have to worry about international."

In a smart marketing move, Hack also uses the phone more than most Web retailers since he personally confirms about 10% of the U.S. Wings orders.

For Hack it is a way to spot check customer service. "A good manager is a good checker," he says. "If you are going to learn a business, you should be the heartbeat. Go back to customers and find out what motivated them to shop online and pick the product they bought."

Hack admits that he is essentially interviewing them, a technique that he asserts has sharpened the site. Typically he asks them how they found the site, what they thought about it, and how he can improve it. Via these calls, Hack learned that the loading time was an issue and immediately adjusted it. And despite the common belief that people prefer e-mail confirma-tions, Hack says that not one customer has ever complained about getting a call. "I am the one receiving electronic mes-sages," Hack boasts. "They e-mail me thanking me for the call."

E-mail is Hack's primary communication tool. Retired from the U.S. Army (an Army Ranger, 101st Airborne Division, Life Member #3100; his personal Jeep is on permanent display at the 101 ABN Division Museum), the 58-year-old Hack is totally disabled due to combat wounds and relies on the digital domain to interact with the world.

A highly decorated veteran, Hack is a true military man and as such is devoted to military authenticity, which is just part of the reason film companies have come to depend on U.S. Wings for their costuming needs, most notably the HBO film, *The Tuskegee Airmen.*

The producer of the film felt that the jackets they used had to be authentic, not replicas. He has since publicly stated that they found the best-quality A-2 jackets in the world at U.S. Wings. "They bought 50 jackets for the film and sewed the appropriate patches on," Hack says. While the film may have been about fighter pilots in World War II, the production company secured these jackets in the most modern of ways: They ordered online.

Anecdotes such as these are a constant reminder to Hack that the future of the commerce is on the Internet, advice first relayed to him as early as 1989 by one of his brothers. Shortly thereafter, another brother and his attorney reiterated the same prediction and Hack was convinced. "I knew I had to act," he says. "Even though I had no idea what to expect."

For up-to-date information about the success of
U.S. Wings
visit
www.StrikingItRich.com

America's
Largest
Producer of
Tin-Mill Products
WEIRTON STEEL

Research and Development

Commercial Products

On-line Product Sales

International Capabilities

Order Status Reports

Monthly Feature

Site Directory

Help

P A T R I C K   S T E W A R T
R I C H A R D   R E I D E R E R
C H R I S T O P H E R   P E T E R S

WEIRTON STEEL

www.weirton.com

Question: What happens when you hold Web-based auctions featuring remnant steel? Answer: You get gross revenues of $48 million a year. That is, if your company name is Weirton and you have the courage to challenge tradition. "The success Weirton has had may be indicative that if the Web can work for steel, it can work for anything," notes Chris Peters, Weirton's full-time Internet consultant.

If opposites attract, then Weirton Steel's Website is a heaven-made marriage since it unites one of the oldest industries with one of the newest. When you factor in their October 1996 launch, you realize this wasn't a "me too" proposition, but a desire to do something radical in an industry associated with conservatism.

Weirton Steel is the country's eighth-largest integrated steel producer and the largest producer of tin mill products. The major market sectors supplied by Weirton include food and beverage cans, piping and construction and shipping containers. Their annual raw steel production exceeds 3 million tons in sheet and strip form sold as hot-rolled, cold-rolled, and coated products. Weirton is also regarded as a leader in tin mill research, which in part accounts for their innovative thinking.

"In December 1995, Pat Stewart and I presented an Internet overview to the executive committee, which includes most of the officers in the company," Peters remembers.

"In that presentation, we discussed the rapid growth of the Web and how other businesses were beginning to benefit from this technology. Our suggestion was that Weirton Steel create a Website to publish general sales information and to help us learn more about the effect it could have on how we conduct business.

"During that presentation, our President and CEO, Richard Riederer asked why we couldn't sell product online. Unable to provide a sound answer, he gave us the charter to tackle that objective and suggested that we put it on a very fast track. Seven months later we were online, thanks to his unconditional support."

Actually the proposition was far more visionary. More than just "being online" the company chose to reposition their excess and nonprime steel products for sale by auction, a concept that, while wildly popular on the Internet today, was innovative at that time.

"Because each of our products is a unique item, we recognized that they each carried a unique value," say Peters. "Our method of selling at the time was to determine a fixed price and fax the information to our buyers. This did not allow for unique valuation, rather it represented *our* estimate of the average value."

The auction format allows each buyer to value the product independently. For instance, a rejected coil that has "wavy edges" will have more value to Buyer A who can efficiently remove those edges than to Buyer B who can't. Therefore, Buyer A can place a greater value on that product, which can result in a higher bid price. The difference in valuation can be significant, based on the core competencies and needs of the bidders.

While Weirton is refreshingly candid about the monetary figures related to their Web venture, the only number the publicly held company will not divulge is their profit margin on the auction items. However, they have said that they are now making notably more profit on this category than they were when they were faxing bulletins.

Weirton's foray is also a prime example of the Web making it much easier for their customers to buy. For example, the database sorts bids based on criteria that make the most sense to the bidder, a tremendous time savings from poring over faxes.

Secondly, the Web opens Weirton to global markets. Since launching, Weirton's site attracts visitors from 40 to 50 countries each month, accounting for 7–10% of their total visitors. Most of this traffic originates from the United Kingdom, Japan, Russia, Canada, Australia, France, and Spain. But Peters points out that it varies from month to month. "We find our foreign traffic is influenced by domestic turmoil. When Russia started exporting more steel, we saw a surge and when we did our assumption was competitive intelligence."

Even though Weirton attracts an accountable amount of international traffic, none of their online sales has been made to foreign countries yet. This is due to the nature of their product; single coils of secondary steel weigh an average of 15,000 pounds. Since they are so heavy, it is uneconomical to ship them more than 300–400 miles from the mill.

Even though the Website is theoretically limited to a geographically suitable range of customers, not all of them were happy about the launch. "Some of our customers were upset, feeling that they were going to be excluded from buying our product since they either weren't online or didn't want to compete against others in an auction format," Peters explains. "But many of those buyers have since decided to use the online system. In fact, several of them are now our most enthusiastic users."

While most buyers visit the site between 8:00 A.M. and 4:00 P.M., more than a few log in throughout the night, until 2:00 A.M. One such buyer is so appreciative he told Weirton that he could now focus on his plant's operations during the day, have dinner with the family, put the kids to bed, and then review and bid on available products late at night. This was a newfound freedom he never could have imagined.

At the time Weirton launched, they knew about 75% of their customers were online. While this majority noted that they had access from the office, Weirton felt they needed to help provide connectivity options for the remaining 25%. Their solution was to provide a "signup disk" from a reputable Internet Service Provider (ISP) for anyone who asked. After talking to five different providers, they selected America Online. To alert their customers, they sent out 4,000 direct mail pieces with a tear-off card, which, when returned to Weirton Steel, would result in an America Online disk with instructions for getting connected. One hundred and twenty-five people responded, about 3%. This figure is congruous with the their current 2% of visitors coming to the site through AOL.

This attention to detail can be seen in every aspect of Weirton's launch. To say they were thorough may be an understatement. For example, they commissioned not one, but four surveys.

The first survey focused on their percentage of customers who were using the Net and the ways in which they were using it. According to Peters the results were surprising. This is how Weirton learned that 75% of their customers had access, a number much greater than they had anticipated. What also surprised them were the types of companies that were more likely to have access. "Our original thought was that the large companies probably had access and the smaller ones didn't," relates Peters. "Just the reverse was true. The smaller companies were far more dynamic. Many of them saw the Web as an advantage and quickly adopted it for use at work."

Next Weirton conducted a series of in-person interviews with a number of existing Weirton Steel customers. Peters explained that the goal was not to focus on technology or any certain process. "We wanted to hear anything that they felt was important. So we simply opened with the question, 'What can we do to make your life easier?'"

He says that what most amazed them was the consistency of these customers' answers. Their first response was that they needed timely and accurate information, when they wanted it, "without playing phone tag or waiting for a fax." The information they wanted most was on pricing, availability, and order status. While these customers loved the idea of the Internet, they had one important caveat before they were open to using it: The data had to be secure so that no one else could monitor their information.

The results of the third survey told Weirton what their customers' most commonly read publications were and what information is required to do their job.

Some of the most valuable information, however, came from their fourth survey, which focused on their buying processes and preferences. "We asked them questions about how often they buy materials, what tools they use to help them locate and purchase product, and how their internal processes impacted their purchasing," Peters explains. This data determined the context of the Weirton site.

Although this $1.4-billion company could have sunk hundreds of thousands of dollars into their site, they launched it with a relatively modest $200,000 budget. They spent $75,000 on external development, $50,000 for internal development, and $75,000 for advertising and public relations.

Weirton Steel's external development costs were spent with Internet Services Corporation, who built their site. Weirton carefully selected ISC for their combination of technology expertise and understanding of business communications, an unusual and robust pairing perfectly suited to Weirton's needs.

The $50,000 in internal development costs were allocated primarily for Weirton staff's time to collect, filter, and review the content information. "This is one area where our prelaunch plan was off the mark," reveals Peters. "We underestimated the amount of time necessary to pull together the content, such as the background and product information. We wanted to make the most of this technology, and to us that meant that we didn't want to take copy that had been written for brochures."

The remaining $75,000 was spent on advertising and public relations. Peters and the team knew that attracting visitors was important and that it wouldn't be accomplished simply by registering with the search engines. "Our advertising and PR plan called for a very visible campaign through traditional media to let our audience know that the Weirton Steel site was available," notes Peters.

Knowing that they were the first steel producer in the world to sell steel online was naturally an attention-getting story and was featured in numerous trade publications as well as the London *Financial Times* and *Information Week*.

In addition to PR via print, Weirton got the word out through their people, most notably their sales force. "We taught the sales staff exactly what was in the Weirton Steel site and helped them to understand the benefits." What gave this training more impact was installing a static version of the site on every salesperson's laptop and training them on how to demonstrate it to Weirton customers.

This strategy had a huge payoff. First, it showed the sales staff how the Weirton site could help them sell by providing information that typically required time on the phone. Second, it demonstrated Weirton's commitment to the technology to their customers in a way that better serviced them. The customers immediately recognized the potential and instantly began requesting changes and enhancements.

From the beginning Weirton's site was very ambitious, with over 250 pages of content on their launch. To maintain simplicity, they designed it in a modular format with a brochure component and an auction component.

While there are many goals of the brochure-like area, the chief one is to generate sales. To achieve this they post information that helps visitors better understand their capabilities, their products, and what differentiates them from their competition. "Through the information presented we hope to generate enough interest that the visitor will initiate communications with our sales staff," says Peters.

While the audience for Weirton Steel's Website is primarily existing and prospective customers, they also target a variety of job functions among those customers, including buyers, specifiers, engineers, accountants, operations staff, and executives.

The Website was also designed to attract a secondary audience of prospective joint venture partners, investors, current and prospective employees, journalists, and even students. For this reason they insist on having a content-rich presence, which has paid off. In addition to auction traffic, as of the first quarter of 1998, Weirton attracts 3,000 visitors and 27,000 pageviews monthly—respectable numbers for such a niche entity.

"We are educating the general public about the steel-making process," declares Peters. "We find that this part of the site is visited by everyone from students to investors to our employees' spouses. While it has the least quantifiable payback, we believe the benefits it brings to those who use it and the steel industry as a whole make the effort well worthwhile."

Given the goals of the content area, the auction component is the antithesis of the brochure section. It doesn't provide any narrative on the product. It is simply an inventory of the products available, of which 50–100 new items are posted daily. Peters says that what drives sales to the auction area is that both registered and unregistered visitors can view the catalog, although only registered buyers can bid. Because of the nature of their variable product, there is no average winning bid dollar amount, but if you average the winning bids the figure is about $3,200. The greatest dollar value for a single coil was $7,645. About 60 products are awarded each day. Generally they quickly sell all product they post.

While Weirton was the first steel producer worldwide to sell steel online, other producers are ramping up. "There are other sites, not sponsored by steel producers," explains Chris Peters, "but they are serving primarily as 'dating services,' matching up buyers and sellers but stopping short there."

Eclipsing Weirton's success would be difficult considering they have fulfilled over 6,000 orders since their launch and have average monthly sales in the $3.5–4.4 million range bought by their 158 registered users.

Ironically, as long as they are selling remnant product, the only limit to their Web success is their own efficiency. "Our online product offering currently is limited to excess and secondary products," Peters reminds us. "Naturally, the objective of our operations staff is to strive for as little excess and secondary as possible."

In time Weirton plans to enable ordering of all their products, not just excess. Meanwhile their biggest challenge is not direct competition but the industry itself. Most buyers are not looking for new suppliers. They are geographically limited to mills within an economical shipping radius and have probably connected with the mills that are best for them. The market isn't that big and the industry doesn't change dramatically, so researching new sources isn't much of an option.

The steel industry is also one of the most closely watched and thoroughly analyzed industries in the country, as steel production and consumption are important economic indicators. As such, a wealth of information is available about the market, including mill capacities, limitations, quality, and on-time delivery. Buyers looking to purchase from another mill have easy access to much of the necessary sourcing information offline.

While the financial upside is greatly appreciated, another benefit to Weirton is that they have learned to take a more introspective approach to commerce. "This experience has taught us to cast off our traditional business methods," says Peters. "The MIS and marketing departments recognized the Web's potential as a communications tool. Our CEO saw it as a means to change the way we do business."

Since both viewpoints were correct for Weirton, Peters says the bottom line for them now is to "question everything and rule out nothing."

For up-to-date information about the success of
Weirton Steel
visit
www.StrikingItRich.com

INDEX

Ad banner, defined, xxv
Adult content, xvi
Amazon.com:
  convenience offered by, ix-x
  and Discount Games, 114
  expenses of, x
  and FragranceNet, 55
  and Ken Crane's Laserdiscs, 136
  and KoreaLink, 136
  and The Mountain Zone, 163
  prices, ix-x
  and Reel.com, 200
  and Ridout Plastics, 207
  rules at, ix
  selection at, ix-x
Alta Vista:
  compared to Yahoo, 28
  and FragranceNet, 60
  and HorseNet, 85
  and KoreaLink, 136-138
  and Long Island Hot Tubs, 146-148
America Online:
  and FragranceNet, 61
  and Gamesville™, 74
  and HorseNet, 86
  importance of, xvii
  and International Golf Outlet, 93
  and iPrint, 108
  and Ken Crane's Laserdiscs, 110
  and KoreaLink, 138
  and Long Island Hot Tubs, 148
  and Practical Online Weightloss Clinic,
    180, 182
  and Ridout Plastics, 210
  and The Knot, 121-22, 126, 128
  and U.S. Wings, 229
  and Weirton Steel, 238
Animated banner, defined, xxv

Apfel, Jason, 55-64
  See also FragranceNet homepage
Ask The Builder homepage, 1-11
  advertising prices, 2, 7
  Ask The Builder newspaper column, 3
  banner ads, 1-2, 7
  bid sheets, 6
  Builder Bulletins, 4
  click-throughs, 7
  company history of, 1-3
  competition, 9
  content, 4
  CPM, 6-7
  design, 9
  Heartland Building Products advertising,
    2
  mission, 9-10
  newsletter, 6
  Pella advertising, 1
  personalized attention to e-mail, 5
  reciprocal linking, 4
  sales, 1-2
  Saver Systems Synthetic Wood Sealant
    banner ads, 8
  site building processing, 8-9
  site launch, 8
  Tim's General Store, 8
  Tim's Tips, 6
  traffic reports, 4-5
  URL mentions, 34
  welcome screen, 8
  "What's New" section, 4
Auditing, defined, xxv
Autoresponder, defined, xxv

Banner ad, defined, xxvii
Banner and exchange programs, xxv
Bezos, Jeff, x

Cache, xxv
Carter, Tim, 1-11
  See also Ask The Builder homepage
CASIE, defined, xxviii
Cassette House homepage, 12-21
  average order size, 19
  banner ads, 16
  company history, 13
  content, 15
  credit card fraud, 20
  customers, 15-16
  design, 14, 20
  domain name, 21
  e-announcements, 17-18
  international sales, 19-20
  inventory, 17
  links, 16
  order-taking service, hiring of, 18-19
  paper catalog, 13
  phone orders, 18
  prices, 14
  tape traders, 14-15
  TapeTrading.com banner advertising, 16-17
Cheon, Joe, 133-141
  See also KoreaLink homepage
Click rate, defined, xxvi
Click-throughs:
  Ask The Builder homepage, 7
  defined, xxviii
Coastal Tool & Supply homepage, 22-33
  advertising buys, 28-29
  Best of Category Tool List, 24
  competition, 32
  Create-a-Tool-Box option, 24
  credit card fraud, 27
  customer service, 25-26
  deep discounts, 23
  demands of e-mail, 26-27
  design, 24
  Gift Central area, 24
  integration of physical store/catalog items, 31
  international sales, 23
  inventory, 23
  launch, 25
  mission, 29-30
  online security, 27
  paper catalog, 31-32
  purchase process, 24-25
  service center database, 26
  shopping cart technology, 27-28

  site building process, 30
  site-wide search feature, 30-31
  subscribers, 29
  WoodWorkers.com link, 28
Content, defined, xxviii
Content sites, defined, xviii
Cost-per-click (CPC), xxviii
Cost-per-lead (CPL), xxviii
CPM, defined, xxvi
Crane, Ken, 111-119
  See also Ken Crane's Laserdisc homepage

Directory, defined, xxvi
Discount Games homepage, 34-43
  average order, 37
  checkout page, 42
  competition, 42
  credit card fraud, 36
  cross-linking, 40
  customer service, 41
  design, 37-38
  discounts, 39
  electronic catalog, 39
  e-mail, 42
  expenses, 39-40
  international sales, 37
  inventory, 35
  links, 40
  post-sale response of, 41
  prison inmates and credit risk, 36-37
  revenues, 40
  sales, 37
  shopping cart system, 38
  source of success, 42
  welcome screen, 38-39
DogToys.com homepage, 186-195
  advertising, 190-191
  auctions, 193
  "Biscotti Conditioning Theorem," 192
  by breed section, 188
  competition, 195
  customer acquisition, 193-194
  Fundraising Is Fun, 192
  growth, 194-195
  inventory, 187
  nonprofit organizations, 192-193
  "Power Lunch," 190
  price-sensitivity of customers, 191
  promotion, 191
  retailing, 194
  RetailPets.com, 194

by size section, 188
by squeak, 189
wow factor, 187
Yahoo! Store, 189-190
Durham, Joe, 38

Elsey, Ray, 215-23
 See also Tradeshop homepage
Expert Marketplace homepage, 44-53
 advertising buys, 52
 banner ads, 52
 commission tracking, 51-52
 consulting contract leads generated by, 48
 customer service, 50
 database, 47
 Dun & Bradstreet relationship, 49-50
 Gold Package, 47
 growth rates, 52-53
 guarantee, 47
 launch, 49
 objective of, 46
 online ordering, 50-51
 Performance Appraisal, 48-49
 Premier ExpertNet (PEN) Group Affiliate,
  47-49
 revenues, 53
 service performed by, 45
 subscriptions, 46

Farros, Royal P., 103-109
 See also iPrint homepage
Fassino, Rob, 121-31
 See also Knot, The, homepage
FragranceNet homepage, 54-64
 advertising buys, 60
 average orders, 56-57
 biggest selling day, 62
 budgeting, 59
 click-throughs, 60-61
 customer service, 55, 59-60
 daily specials, 61
 discounts, 56
 formula for success, 63
 growth rate, 59
 international sales, 58
 inventory, 57
 launch, 58-59
 Partners Program, 61
 planning, 58-59
 prices, 56

sales, 56, 62
search engine advertising, 61
site budget, 58-59
visitors, 56, 61
Frames, defined, xxviii
Franklin, Skip, 165-75
 See also Mountain Zone homepage
Furse, John, 65-75
 See also Gamesville™ homepage

Gamesville™ homepage, 64-75
 advertising, 66-67, 69
 advertising buys, 69-70
 Bingo Zone, 66, 72
 competition, 75
 database, 68
 demographics, 74
 description of, 65
 e-mails, 70
 geographic parsing, 68-69
 growth rate, 74
 international sales, 69
 interns, 70
 job offers made through, 73-74
 links, 70
 marketing campaign, 70-71
 Mr. Bean banner, 67
 odds of winning, 71
 Picturama, 66, 72-73
 prize fulfillment, 71-72
 prizes, 71
 returned check rate, 67-68
 search-engine advertising, 70
 time-based advertising, 68
 "virtuous circle," 71
 visitors, 66, 72-73
 winnings, payment of, 71-72
Gizzio, Jill, 187-195
 See also DogToys.com homepage
Gold, David, 45-53
 See also Expert Marketplace homepage

Hack, David, 225-33
 See also U.S. Wings homepage
Harrison, Daniel, 143-51
 See also Long Island Hot Tub homepage
Hits, defined, xxv
HorseNet homepage, 76-87
 advertising, 79-81
 America Online, and site design, 86
 business model, 78

HorseNet homepage *(cont.)*
chat services, 80
content, 78, 80
copromotion deals, 83-84
domain name, 83
EquiVid microsite, 81-82
Video Grab Bag clearance area, 82
free classifieds, 78-79
"hoofprints in sand" background, 78
HorseNet e-mail addresses, 80
inbound links, 77-78
international sales, 85
links to competition, 77
phone orders, 82
publicity, 84
sales, 81, 85-86
search engine advertising, 84-85
site building, 79
visitors, 78-79
HTML, defined, xxvii
HTML e-mail, defined, xxvii
Humble, David, 177-84
See also Practical Online Weightloss
Clinic homepage
Hyperlink, defined, xxvii

iCats, 189
Impression, defined, xxvii
"Incredibly successful," defined, xvii
International Golf Outlet homepage, 88-101
advertising, 94
advertising budget, 94-95
and America Online (AOL), 93
banner ad, 94
business plan, 90, 92
catalog, 96-97
competition, 100
and CompuServe, 92
concept, 90
content, 95-96
customer relations, 100
custom golf club fitting, 95-96
database, 97
design, 99
discounts, 91
domain name, 89
drop shipments, 98
duty-free merchandise, 91
e-mail, 97
first order, 100-11
foreign language pages, 90-91

international sales, 90-92
inventory, 98
keyword purchases, 94
launch, 90
links, 92-93
"New Visitors Click Here" button, 100
online order tracking system, 99
orders, 99-100
sales, 98-99
strategic partnerships, 92-93
visitors, 95
Internet Advertising Bureau (IAB), defined,
xxvii
iPrint homepage, 102-109
advertising, 105-106
banner ads, 105-106
customer relations, 107
custom work offered by, 104-105
description of, 103-104
first order, 107
growth rate, 109
launch, 106-107
mission, 109
order tracking, 108
pricing, 104
strategic partnerships, 106-107
visitors, 106
I-Sales electronic discussion mailing list, 32

Kane, Steven, 65-75
See also Gamesville™ homepage
Ken Crane's Laserdisc homepage, 110-119
advertising, 118
average order, 113-14
discounts, 113-14
DVD store, 117-18
electronic mailing list, 116
history of, 111
in-store customers vs. online customers,
114
inventory, 115-16
links, 117
ordering difficulties, 115
reciprocal linking, 117
revenues, 111, 114·
search engines, 117
Keywords, defined, xxvii
Knot, The, homepage, 120-31
ad revenue, 123-24
advertising, 123-24
advertising buys, 130

audience, 122, 125-26
average visitor, 125
business plan, 121
chat, 125
community features, 122, 126
content, 122, 124-25
cross-links, 129
customer feedback, 126-27
description of, 121
etiquette, 126
history of, 122-23
name, selection of, 122
newsletter, 125
promotional relationships, 128-29
strategic relationships, 129
success of, 121-22
travel sales, 127-28
wedding gown catalog bundles, 127
Wedding Singer, The tie-in, 130-31
KoreaLink homepage, 132-41
advertising, 136-37
banner ads, 140
click-throughs, 137
demographics, 134
description of, 133
guests, benefits/access offered to, 135
interactivity as core of, 134
inventory, 136
KoreaLink.net, 139
links, 138
membership, 134-35
personal ads, 134
revenues, 137
sponsors, 136
traffic, 133-34, 138
visitors, 134

Lasater, Richard and Sally, 77-87
See also HorseNet homepage
Link, defined, xxvii
Liu, David, 121-131
See also Knot, The, homepage
Long Island Hot Tub homepage, 142-51
and Alta Vista, 147-48
and America Online, 148-49
awards received by, 149
catalog on disc, 150-51
chats, 150-51
content, 143
e-mail, 146-47
international sales, 150

inventory, 144
launch, 143, 149
Link Exchange banners, 148
message boards, 150-51
newsletter, 145
orders, 146
and PostMaster submission service, 147
pricing, 144
sales, 145-6
search engines, 147-48
seasonal spikes in business, 144-45

Meta tags, defined, xxix
Mogren, Todd, 23-33
See also Coastal Tool & Supply homepage
Moss, Chuck, 35-43
See also Discount Games homepage
Mountain Zone homepage, 164-75
advertising, 172-73
awards received by, 166
banner ads, 171-72
book fulfillment, 169
commerce offerings, 165-66
competition, 174-75
content, 165-67
contests, 173-74
customer service, 170-71
800 number, 170-71
e-mail, 174
launch, 167-68
Mountain Mailing, 174
niche stores, 169
Official American Mount Everest site,
    166-67
product categories, 168-69
soft dollar sponsorship deals, 172-73
strategic partnerships, 172
The Zone Network (TZN), 175
TV advertising, 173
visitors, 166
Munson, Art, 13-21
See Cassette House homepage

Online ad, defined, xxvii

Page impression, defined, xxvii
Page request, defined, xxvii
Pageviews, defined, xxviii
Pay-per-click, xxviii

Pay-per-lead, defined, xxviii
Peters, Christopher, 235-41
    See also Weirton Steel homepage
Peters, Tom, 187
Practical Online Weightloss Clinic home-
    page, 176-84
    advertising, 180-81
    advertising tracking, 182-83
    and America Online, 180-82
    banner ads, 181-83
    client feedback, 184
    and DietCity.com, 183
    employee opposition to, 177-78
    instructions/personal shopping list, 179
    international sales, 183-84
    Jenny Craig compared to, 179
    keyword purchases, 182
    launch, 178
    original concept of, 177-78
    pricing, 184
    search engines, 182
    signup/monthly fees, 179
    site design, 184
    subscription, 178-79
    traffic, 178
    ultimate goal of, 185
    value proposition, 179-80
    visitors, conversion to subscribers, 180
    Weight Watchers compared to, 179
Prequalifying voice interview, xvi
Prosl, Greg, 165-75
    See also Mountain Zone homepage

Rabin, Elliott, 207-13
    See also Ridout Plastics homepage
Reciprocal links, defined, xxviii
Reel.com homepage, 196-205
    advertising, 199-200
    affiliates program, 200
    average order, 201
    biggest selling category, 201
    clientele, 200
    concept of, 197
    customer loyalty, 197-98
    customer service, 204-205
    depth of selection, 198
    domain name, 202
    early technical difficulties, 203
    expenses, 202
    future of, 203-205

international sales, 201
inventory, 201
launch, 202
Movie Guide, 197-98
Movie Anatomy section, 198-99
Movie Matches system, 198-99
search engines, 199
strategic partnerships, 199
TV Guide arrangement, 199
Reiderer, Richard, 235-42
    See also Weirton Steel homepage
Ridout Plastics homepage, 207-13
    advertising, 211-12
    and America Online, 210-11
    average order, 208
    banner ad, 210-11
    brochure holders, 209
    design, 209-10
    domain name, 212
    forms, 208
    inspiration of, 208-209
    international sales, 211
    launch, 213
    links, 212
    mission, 208
    quality of customers, 213
    Web hosting arrangement, 210
    Yahoo listings, 211-12
Roney, Carely, 121-31
    See also Knot, The, homepage
Roseman, Stuart, 65-75
    See also Gamesville™ homepage
Run-of-site (ROS), xviii

Schofman, David, 89-101
    See also International Golf Outlet
        homepage
Search engines, defined, xxviii
Secure server, defined, xxviii
Session, defined, xxviii
Shopping on the Internet and Beyond, xiii
Skorman, Stuart, 197-205
    See also Reel.com homepage
Spam, defined, xxix
Stewart, Patrick, 235-42
    See also Weirton Steel homepage
Sticky/stickiness, defined, xxxi
Success characteristics, xix
Success stories, shared Webpreneur quality,
    xix

Tibbetts, Todd, 165-75
  See also Mountain Zone homepage
Tradeshop homepage, 214-23
  AffordableDiamonds.com site, 223
  Celtic design band rings sold on, 219-20
  certified diamonds sold on, 219
  clientele, 215
  concept of, 215-16
  craftsmen used by, 217
  cross-linking, 218
  custom work, 220
  domain name, 218
  future of, 222-23
  history of, 220-21
  IdealDiamonds.com site, 223
  inventory, 218-19
  launch, 221
  links, 218
  mission, 215
  orders, 222
  phone purchases, 217
  pricing, 216-7
  referrals, 218
  repeat customer rate, 218
  revenue, 221
  sales tax references, 222
  wire-transfer purchases, 217
  Transaction sites, defined, xvi

Unique session, defined, xxix
Unique visitors, defined, xxix
URL, defined, xxix
U.S. Wings homepage, 224-233
  advertising, 229
  and America Online, 229
  biggest business risk to date, 228-29
  credit card fraud, 231
  customers as billboards, 230-31
  customers/clientele, 225
  customer service, 230, 232
  design, 226, 228
  early ISP, 227-28
  e-mail, 232-33
  and Flying Tigers-branded apparel, 225

international sales, 231-32
"knock-off" sites, 229-30
paper catalog, 229
updates to, 226-27

Visitor, defined, xxxi

Webcrawler, 40
Weirton Steel homepage, 234-41
  advertising, 239-40
  auction format, 236
  audience, 240-41
  competition, 241
  content, 240
  description of, 235
  external development costs, 239
  future of, 242
  and global markets, 237
  goals of, 240-41
  internal development costs, 239
  launch, 238
  public relations, 239-40
  and sales force, 240
  surveys, 238-39
  traffic, 237
Wolfson, Michael, 121-31
  See also Knot, The, homepage
Wow factor, 187

Yahoo:
  and Cassette House, 16
  compared to Alta Vista, 28
  defined, xxxi
  and Discount Games, 40
  and FragranceNet, 61
  and KoreaLink, 138
  and Motorcycle Online, 156
  and Practical Online Weightloss Clinic,
    181, 182
  and Reel.com, 199
  and Ridout Plastics, 211
  and The Knot, 129

About the Author

Jaclyn Easton has been reporting on Internet commerce since the beat began in 1994. As a columnist for *The Los Angeles Times*, an Emmy winner for her work on CBS News, Los Angeles, and the host of the nationally syndicated radio show "Log On U.S.A.," Easton has established a stellar reputation as The Resource for e-commerce information and analysis. She can be reached at *easton@easton.com* or through this book's Website at *www.StrikingItRich.com*.